THE
ROMAN
CATHOLIC
CONTROVERSY

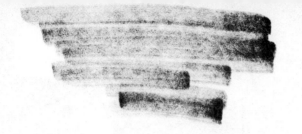

BHP Books by James R. White

Grieving: Our Path Back to Peace
The King James Only Controversy
The Roman Catholic Controversy

THE
ROMAN
CATHOLIC
CONTROVERSY

JAMES R. WHITE

BETHANY HOUSE PUBLISHERS
MINNEAPOLIS, MINNESOTA 55438

Published by Bethany House Publishers
A Ministry of Bethany Fellowship, Inc.
11300 Hampshire Avenue South
Minneapolis, Minnesota 55438

Printed in the United States of America.

Library of Congress Cataloging-in-Publication Data

White, James R., 1962–
    The Roman Catholic controversy / James R. White.
       p. cm.
    Includes bibliographical references and index.
    ISBN 1-55661-819-0
    1. Justification. 2. Catholic Church—Controversial literature.
3. Catholic Church—Doctrines. 4. Evangelicalism—Doctrines. 5. Catholic
Church—Relations—Evangelicalsim. 6. Evangelicalism—Relations—Catholic
Church. I. Title.
BT764.2.W45   1996
280' 042—dc20   96–25280
                                         CIP

God gives few greater blessings to a local church and its people than a dedicated, godly, hard-working pastor. The Phoenix Reformed Baptist Church, and my family in particular, has been blessed of God with such a pastor. Content with God's call upon his life, dedicated to the care of the sheep entrusted to him, my pastor embodies the biblical ideal of the godly elder.

I dedicate this work in Christian thankfulness to

Pastor Don Fry.

JAMES WHITE is Scholar in Residence in the College of Christian Studies, Grand Canyon University. He also teaches for the Arizona Campus of the Golden Gate Baptist Theological Seminary, and is Director of Alpha and Omega Ministries, a Christian apologetics organization based in Phoenix, Arizona. He is the author of *Letters to a Mormon Elder* and *The King James Only Controversy*.

CONTENTS

FOREWORD

Reformation is needed more than ever among Christians in the West. A tidal wave of modernity has swept across us, changing much that was presupposed for centuries. Now a new tidal wave, called by the scholars *post*modernity, is sweeping across Western thought, undermining the very idea of absolute truth. What should be the reponse of the Christian church in the face of these waves of philosophical attack?

Many Christians suggest that a new alliance is needed between Roman Catholics and evangelicals to face these modern errors—an alliance that will lift us in the spirit of unity above our remaining doctrinal differences. It is argued that such an alliance should seek to build upon our common and historic Christian beliefs so that we can stand *together* against the present secular assault. Some evangelicals insist such an effort will bring more converts to saving faith in Christ. Others are more cautious in their claims and seek to delineate the limitations of such a relationship. It seems *all* agree that a modern reformation is needed among those who confess His name.

Reformation in our time? Yes, most certainly. May it please God to grant us grace for the living of these days and power to set about reforming the church. But I believe with James White that this must be a reformation that begins with a renewal of confidence in the Word of God as the *supreme authority* in all matters of Christian faith and practice, a movement rooted again in the gospel of grace *alone*, received by faith *alone*.

Historian J. H. Merle d'Aubigne wisely wrote many years ago:

"The only true reformation is that which emanates from the Word of God." As modern evangelicals wring their hands, hoping to preserve Western culture and its values, they are in grave danger of losing the very truths that profoundly shaped their culture—namely, the sufficiency and authority of the Word of God and the gospel of grace.

Evangelicalism arose historically because sixteenth-century believers rediscovered the *evangel* (i.e., "Good News"). Out of this recovery a movement of people and churches spread across Europe that forever altered the ecclesial and social landscape. This movement was awakened and renewed throughout the centuries as the Spirit gave new life. Could we in our generation be in danger of losing the central emphases of this great recovery? James White thinks so, and so do I, but not for the reasons often cited in debates with modern secularists. Rather, we are in danger of losing our place in ministry precisely because we are losing our grip on the essential truths of the Bible regained in the time of the Reformation. This is why the Roman Catholic controversy with evangelical Protestantism will not simply go away under the cover of goodwill.

White plainly demonstrates that the modern Roman Catholic Church, through her current teachings, has not changed nearly so much as many assume. He shows that modern Catholic doctrinal formulations (e.g., *The Catholic Catechism*, 1994) still significantly conflict with the plain teaching of God's Word. He is painstakingly clear and precise in his exegesis of the critical texts of Holy Scripture. He has learned well, from frequently debating popular Catholic apologists, how to frame the right questions and how to provide substantive and logically clear answers.

Furthermore, White treats other important doctrinal differences under the umbrella of the Gospel itself. By this I mean that he shows how the Mass, Purgatory, and prayer to Mary and the saints are all doctrines that actually undermine the grace of God in the Gospel. Popular evangelical critics of Roman Catholicism have all too frequently attacked these practices with little knowledge of what is actually taught and what these beliefs mean for the centrality of Christ in the Gospel. White does not fall into this trap because he understands both Roman Catholic teaching and the Scripture. He takes the time to properly delineate both and then shows why Catholicism fails to measure up to the Gospel revealed in Scripture. The reader will have a better grasp of what is at the heart of modern evangelical faith after reading James White.

I believe that the careful reader will find in *The Roman Catholic Controversy* one of the clearest presentations available on the foundational doctrine of *sola scriptura*. Catholic apologists universally begin their attack upon evangelicalism by undermining this truth, which is called the formal principle of the Reformation. Here they seek to display evangelical weakness, thus defending Rome as the true and only church. Evangelicals have all to often done a very poor job of presenting this doctrine, thus lending certain credence to Catholic attack. James White points us in the right direction on this vital matter.

If you wish to discover or intelligently reaffirm the two essential evangelical truths that are critical for a reforming church in our time, read this book. The tone is irenic, charitable, and fair. The content is substantial without being pedantic or massive. Both the serious reader and the person coming to these issues for the first time will benefit from this book.

In the past five years several dozen books have been published on this subject. James White has surely given us one of the very best. Those interested in seeing what is at the core of the present evangelical and Roman Catholic controversy should read this excellent book.

John H. Armstrong
Editor, *Roman Catholicism:*
Evangelical Protestants Analyze
What Unites & Divides Us
Author, *A View of Rome*

PREFACE

The Apostle Paul must have asked himself the question more than once. "Why me? Why am I the one lying out here under the harsh Asian sun, having just been stoned by an angry mob?" (Acts 14:19). Or "Why am I the one God expects to write this harsh letter to the churches in Galatia? Why am I the one who has to struggle with false teachers, false brethren, and every other kind of stress and strain?" For anyone who thinks the Christian life is a bed of roses, Paul's life is a call back to reality.

It strikes me that it would have been much easier for Paul to follow a road of compromise. Many would identify his stance as narrow, unloving, and quite doctrinaire. Were the differences between him and the Judaizers in Galatia *really* all that important? Weren't there real believers on both sides of this issue, as we so often hear today? Surely no one today would have faulted him for allowing differing opinions to coexist. Paul must have hurt a lot of feelings with his strong letter to the Galatians. He may have even alienated some people! So why did he do it?

Paul's standard, and the standard I pray God will help me to maintain both in my personal life and in my life as a minister and teacher, begins and ends with the all-powerful God. God defines all existence, and God's existence demands that we be concerned about truth—objective, universal, knowable truth, not the wishy-washy "your truth versus my truth" concept that has not only infected Western culture but has infiltrated the Church as well. The clash between those who seek to live out a biblical worldview and those who allow contemporary culture to determine their form of theology, beliefs, and practice comes in large part from the thoroughly different views we have of truth and whether we *really* believe God has revealed truth in a clear, knowable way.

Paul took the stance he did because he believed God is glorified when His truth is made known. God is not glorified, then, when His truth is denied, redefined, or compromised. In the same way, since God has revealed the Gospel of Jesus Christ and has deemed it proper to save men and women *only* through that Gospel, the purity of that Gospel—its truthfulness—must be safeguarded at all costs. *The Christian's highest standards must be formed in light of God's glory and God's truth in the Gospel of Christ.* Anything less does not even qualify as "mere Christianity."

My Approach

This book arises out of a sincere attempt to follow in the Apostles' footsteps with reference to the glory of God and the truth of the Gospel. My motivations are transparent. I love God and I love the Gospel He has revealed in Jesus Christ. I truly believe the Gospel to be the power of God unto salvation. When I consider what God has done in Christ—the grace He has shown in giving His own Son as the atoning sacrifice for God's people—the love He has shown in granting to us this grace in Christ Jesus "before the beginning of time" (2 Timothy 1:9, NIV)—I am overwhelmed at the depth of the wisdom and glory of God. I desire to serve Him with a whole heart.

To believe in the God who has revealed himself in Christ is to be a lover of truth. How can we claim to follow the One who called himself "the way, the truth, and the life," if we do not take such a claim seriously? And if we believe in truth, we must be diligent in making use of the means God has given us to know and apply His truth. This requires that we be students of His Word, the Bible, constantly seeking to learn more about its teachings and to bring our own beliefs into line with it. It is also imperative that we think as clearly and logically as we can. God is not honored by muddled thinking.

Once I have established God's glory and truth as my priorities, then I must act in accordance with those standards. I must govern all of my life by this commitment. No matter how unpopular or radical such a stance may seem in my particular culture and time, God calls me to live a life that goes beyond mere cultural or traditional standards.

What does any of this have to do with a work that seeks to examine the central issues that separate Roman Catholics and Protestants? I firmly believe that in our modern context, there are many on *both sides* of this issue who are, perhaps unwittingly, sacrificing absolute truth on the altar of compromise and expediency. They no longer see the truth of the Gospel as an important element in their Christian life. They have been deeply influenced by the popular culture that scoffs at the idea of absolute truth and are offended by the antics of "conservatives" who claim to know truth yet demonstrate a deep disregard for it by their cavalier attitude and sloppy thinking. Instead of a pillar, the truth of the Gospel has become an add-on; maybe something for the theologians to argue about, but surely not something that should keep us from joining hands with everyone everywhere in a wonderful show of unity. For many today, there simply are more important things than guarding the truth.

But for the person who wishes to get beyond all the smoke and confusion and approach the Roman Catholic/Protestant issue from a biblical perspective, the issue of *truth* becomes central. When one focuses upon the definitive issues of the Christian faith, it becomes quickly evident that Roman Catholics and Protestants disagree on the Gospel itself. It is not just a matter of slight disagreement over side issues but disagreement of a fundamental nature. Nothing is accomplished by downplaying this fundamental difference. *Everything* is risked by ignoring it.

Would it be easier to ignore this issue and focus upon other things? Most definitely. Despite the accusations of others, I do not relish controversy or confrontation.[1] I doubt the Apostle Paul liked it either, but he couldn't seem to avoid it. Why? Those who believe the truth is worth fighting for will almost always find themselves in the minority. Those committed to the reality and importance of God's truth cannot ignore issues as fundamental as "what is the Gospel?"

Why *Me*?

What do I bring to this topic that might be useful to you? I am not a former Roman Catholic. I'm a Baptist of the Reformed stripe.

So why am I addressing this topic? Why should my particular invitation to dialogue on this most important subject interest you?

Over the past five years the Lord has given me the opportunity to engage in eighteen public, moderated debates against the leading Roman Catholic apologists in the United States. I am not referring to the rather common radio debates, which are more often radio arguments, but to scholarly, moderated, controlled debates where a particular subject is addressed by both sides with equal amounts of time to speak and reason on the topic. The topics have been wide-ranging, from *sola scriptura* (the ultimate authority of Scripture) and the Papacy to the Mass and justification by faith. These debates have taken place in Roman Catholic high school auditoriums, Roman Catholic churches, and on the campus of Boston College. Almost all have been taped and the recordings distributed widely. Some have been televised. It is my hope that in all of them, the Lord has been honored.

My interaction with the leading Roman Catholic apologists has given me insight into the best Rome has to offer to defend her own beliefs and to counter Protestant beliefs. I have read widely in Roman Catholic sources in preparation for these debates, and that reading and study form the background of this book. Hence, this work is not written in the ivory tower of an academic setting, far removed from the living-out of the issues involved. While scholarship is brought to this topic, I also bring a living faith to it. I speak quite plainly from my heart, for it is my desire that you walk through this topic with me from start to finish, joining together in a journey that will be challenging as well as vitally important.

This is not an exhaustive work. I have purposely avoided many worthwhile areas of discussion to instead focus our attention on the *central* issues. A great deal of material has been placed in the end-notes to keep the discussion moving, and I hope those who desire more information will mine the nuggets provided there. Still, there is much more that could be said on each topic. It is my hope and prayer that the reader who desires more will use this work as a starting point and then go on to more in-depth expositions.

Come Let Us Reason

The relationship between Roman Catholics and Protestants is an emotionally charged issue. Feelings run high on both sides. Therefore, I ask that from the start we make a commitment to hear out both sides, to think clearly, and to keep God's truth at the forefront. I have done my best to avoid offense,[2] but I know some will be offended nonetheless. I ask that you remember one thing: Christian love cannot be separated from Christian truth. True love rejoices with the truth, and true love *tells* the truth. I am convinced that it is an act of love to speak the truth to someone, especially when it will cost you to do so.

1

I Can't Believe He Did That

It's happening more today than it has in quite some time. You might be reminiscing with some friends about the past, and a name comes up that you haven't heard in a long time. "Oh yes—Tom. I remember him from our old Bible study class way back. What ever happened to him?" The answer amazes you. "I heard he became a Roman Catholic." Or a letter arrives in the mail from an old friend. After the typical "How are the kids, mine are fine" comes the news, "I have something important to share with you. I was recently received into the Roman Catholic Church."

For many decades evangelical Protestants in the United States have pretty much assumed that if conversions take place, they only go in one direction: from being Roman Catholic to joining a "Bible-believing, Gospel-preaching church." Most conservative Protestants honestly do not believe Rome has a lot to offer, since so many of them came *from* the Roman communion into evangelical churches. How such things as the liturgy or creeds could be *attractive* to someone is often lost on fundamentalists and evangelical conservatives. It has been felt by some that those very creeds, seemingly dry and lifeless, and the ornate liturgy, apparently without meaning, were what drove them from Rome to begin with. Understanding why a biblically grounded fellow evangelical would make the decision to go *into* the Roman communion can be hard to grasp.

For most Protestants the first question that comes to mind when they hear of such a conversion is, "How could you do that? Rome teaches so many things that aren't in the Bible—or even directly contradict it!" Many assume that Roman Catholics have no biblical defense for their beliefs. It is easy to understand why this assumption is made; a high percentage of Roman Catholics *don't* have such a defense. This is due to the fact that many of them have rarely opened a Bible let alone seriously studied it, making Protestants believe there must not be any way of defending Roman ideas from the Bible.

Roman Catholic apologists are quick to admit the problem. One noted speaker often begins his talks by saying, "Now, you can tell who is a Protestant and who is a Catholic just by looking at them. Look at the person sitting next to you. Do they have a Bible? They're not Catholic." The joke speaks to a real truth. However, just because the large majority of Roman Catholics are not as likely to be as biblically literate as their conservative Protestant counterparts does not mean that Rome cannot defend her beliefs from the Bible. It is a critical mistake to think otherwise.

Because most Protestants have never been challenged on the fundamental issues that separate Roman Catholics and Protestants, they are usually ill equipped to engage in serious dialogue with a knowledgeable Roman Catholic. In conservative evangelical churches, we rarely hear sermons or Bible studies on the issues that come up in such a dialogue. Preaching on the importance of *sola scriptura* or justification by faith *alone* without human merit will not get nearly the response that a rousing sermon on salvation or some current social evil can garner. And why should we be concerned about such heavy theological topics, anyway? It is rather common to hear modern preachers decrying "stuffy theology" from the pulpit. "People want something practical!" they say.

But any Protestant who has seriously tried to intervene in the life of a fellow believer who is traveling down the road to Rome knows very well how nice it would have been to have heard just a few more sermons on justification, a few more Bible studies on the ultimate authority of Scripture. Just like the Christian who is utterly confused and humbled at the hands of a Jehovah's Witness when discussing the Trinity or the deity of Christ, those Protestants who care enough to engage the topic (many do not think the issues important enough to discuss—an attitude decried by conservatives on *both* sides of the Protestant/Catholic divide) often come away humbled and confused as well.

Take Bill, for example. Bill grew up in a conservative Christian home. He attended Sunday school in a Baptist church from as far back as he can remember. He was active in youth choir, went on missions trips during the summers, and even attended a Bible college for a couple of years before going into business. He is active in his local Baptist church, working with the youth soccer program and teaching a Sunday school class of fifth graders. At the mall, Bill has just run into Scott, an old friend from his teenage years. He and Scott both sang in youth choir; they even passed out tracts together near the downtown mission. Bill is in for a surprise.

Bill: Remember the choir director at church, Scott? We had some great times with him, especially when we kept bugging him to sing "Love Is the Flag Flown High."

Scott: (suddenly feeling a bit uneasy): Yes, I remember him well.

Bill: So, where are you attending church these days?

Scott: Well, Bill, I've been thinking about getting back in touch with you about that. I've had a change in direction, you might say.

Bill: Oh? Last I had heard you were over at Southside.

Scott: Yes, I was there for quite some time. But a few years back—well, I was received into the Roman Catholic Church. I've been there for a couple of years now. Bill, I'm really happy there.

Bill: You've become a Roman Catholic? I can't believe it! How could you do that? You know a lot of what they teach isn't in the Bible at all. Worse, some of it is *contrary* to the Bible. I remember when we talked about things like Purgatory and the Pope and worshiping Mary and all that—remember? You even said once, "Yeah, Purgatory. You'll find that in your Bible dictionary—right next to venial sins!"

Scott: I do remember saying that. But, Bill, I've got to tell you, we were both wrong. There's so much more to it than we ever thought. And the Bible *does* teach about venial sins, and Purgatory, and the Pope, and we *don't* worship Mary. . . .

Bill: Wait a minute, Scott. I'm still in shock here. You're actually telling me that you are a member of the Roman Catholic Church? That you believe the teachings of that church—that the Pope is the Vicar of Christ on earth, that Mary is the Mother of God, and that you have to work your way to heaven?

Scott: I believe everything the Church teaches, though you aren't very accurate in your understanding of what the Church *does* teach—neither was I, I can assure you! Look, Bill, I had all the same ideas you have now. But I looked into what Rome *really* teaches. I discovered that not only did I have a lot of misconceptions about the theology of the Roman Catholic Church, but I found out they had a tremendous foundation for their own beliefs in the Bible! And what really clinched it, Bill, was that I couldn't defend what *I* had always believed against the objections raised by the Apostolic Church.

Bill: Like what?

Scott: Well, like believing the doctrine of *sola scriptura*, that everything has to be spelled out in the Bible or it's not to be believed. Where does the Bible teach *sola scriptura*, Bill? You and I had always *assumed* the Bible was our sole rule of faith, but where does the *Bible* teach that? If you can't support that from the Bible, then you have a self-refuting belief, don't you?

Bill: Well, in the book of Matthew, Jesus said that we should reject traditions. I think it's in the fifteenth chapter or so, isn't it?

Scott: Yes, that's correct. But if you look at the passage carefully, Jesus said to reject *human* traditions, not divine traditions. He himself held men accountable to extrabiblical traditions. For example, in Matthew 23:2, He told people that they needed to obey the person who sat in the "seat of Moses." Now where in the Old Testament do you find the teaching about "Moses' seat"?

Bill: Well, I'd have to look it up. I can't think of any place.

Scott: I looked. It isn't there. And what of Paul's command to the Thessalonians, "Hold fast to the traditions we passed on to you, whether by word of mouth or by epistle"? I never heard any discussion of holding fast to traditions that had been passed on orally in any Bible study you and I ever attended, did you?

Bill: Again, I'd have to look that one up. But I can't believe you are really convinced of all the unscriptural doctrines Rome teaches. Like, what about the Gospel itself, Scott? Do you really think you can work your way to heaven?

Scott: No, of course not, and neither does any informed Roman Catholic. The Catholic Church doesn't teach that you can work your way to heaven, Bill. That's a Protestant myth. In fact, one of the turning points in my journey to Rome was when I discovered that the Council of Trent had *condemned* anyone who said you could work your way to heaven! The very first canon on justification from Trent says, "If anyone says that man can be justified before God by his own works, whether done by his own natural powers or through the teaching of the law, without divine grace through Jesus Christ, let him be anathema."

Bill: But what about the Mass, and confession to priests, and all that?

Scott: I've discovered a lot about the history of the Church over the past few years, Bill, and I'll tell you that the early Christians believed in all those things, just like the Church teaches today. And there is solid basis in the Bible for the Mass as a propitiatory sacrifice, for the office of the priest, for confession, absolution, the Sacraments—all of it.

Bill: You aren't going to tell me you can find biblical support for worshiping Mary, are you, Scott?

Scott: No, I'm not, because I don't worship Mary.

Bill: Scott, you and I have both watched Roman Catholics lighting candles to Mary, saying the Rosary, all of that. How can you not call that worship?

Scott: Believe me, Bill, the teachings about Mary were the toughest. I just couldn't understand them at first. But slowly, over time, I realized that most of my problems had to do with Protestant myths, like the idea of *worshiping* Mary rather than *venerating* her. I also came to understand how *biblical* the devotion to the Mother of all Christians is. I'd love to explain this all to you, I really would. . . .

Bill: And the Pope? Do you really call him "Holy Father"?

Scott: Yes, Bill, I do. He is the successor of Peter, the one on whom Christ built His church, as Matthew 16:18–19 teaches. He's the modern fulfillment of Christ's prayer for Peter that his faith would not fail.

Bill: I can't believe this. You really *are* convinced of all this, aren't you?

Scott: Yes, Bill. And you've got to admit, I have the advantage right now. I've been where you are, and I know what you believe.

You haven't been where I am. You can't honestly say you've given Rome a fair chance, can you? Instead, you've accepted what *others* have said at face value. Most of the time when we were young we heard from former Roman Catholics. Now, tell me, Bill, would you want your church judged solely on the word of *former* members?

Bill: Well, no, probably not.

Scott: I'd really like to talk to you some more about this, Bill. Let me just tell you that I haven't abandoned anything. I've simply found the *fullness* of what Christ gave us in His Church. I've found the Apostolic Church, the historic church, the one Christ founded and promised never to abandon. I believe and love the Bible as much as I ever did. I simply have learned that it doesn't teach what Martin Luther thought it did.

What would you do if you were Bill? After the shock wore off, you might realize that there are a lot of things you've taken for granted, a lot of things you need to study and ponder. You might realize that your life as a Protestant has been one of unchallenged assumptions, and in this you would not be alone.

Does It Really Matter?

That is the question being asked today. Does it really matter? Should we care about what *separates* us? Or should we focus solely on what *unites* us? Are we fighting against the unity Jesus prayed we would have (John 17), or are we rightly standing for the truth of the Gospel itself (Galatians 1–2)? What is the foundation of Christian unity? Can the bare confession "Jesus is Lord," *without any reference to what that means*, function as a solid basis for unity? Or do we have to go beyond that to ask questions about *who* Jesus is, *what* He did, and *how* we come to know Him?

If merely saying "Jesus is Lord" is enough, doesn't that mean that we have "unity" with groups such as the Church of Jesus Christ of Latter-day Saints (the Mormons), who likewise can make this confession, though with a fundamentally different meaning and intent? Jehovah's Witnesses say "Jesus is Lord," but they also believe Jesus is Michael the Archangel and they deny He rose physically from the dead. Christians have historically insisted that belief in the deity of Christ and in the Resurrection is central to what it means to be a Christian and have denied fellowship to those who say "Jesus is Lord" yet deny these beliefs. If unity in *doctrine* on the *person* of Christ is necessary for meaningful unity, is unity on the *doctrine* of the *Gospel itself* also just as necessary?

"All who accept Christ as Lord and Savior are brothers and sisters in Christ. Evangelicals and Catholics are brothers and sisters in Christ."[1] So says the widely read and distributed accord *Evangelicals and Catholics Together* (ECT). Many Christian leaders accept this statement as true. Yet, leaders on *both* sides question the ease with which such a statement is made. What does it mean? How far can we probe such a statement before encountering unresolvable differences? And should we even try to test such a statement? Shouldn't we just rejoice together and leave all the rest for the "theologians"? Many think so.

Those who support the *ECT* accord and other such statements insist that we have a common evangelistic mission, and we must not dishonor the Lord by quibbling over nonessentials. The question that must be asked, however, is this: Does not a common evangelistic mission assume a common *evangel*? If we are to share in preaching the Gospel, shouldn't we first be in agreement on what the Gospel is? And are the differences between Roman Catholics and Protestants such that an honest inquirer must conclude that we do not, in fact, believe in the same Gospel?

The phrase "a different gospel" has, unfortunately, been trivialized of late. Some people use the phrase to vilify anyone who disagrees with them, no matter how insignificant the difference might be. I have personally been accused of teaching "another gospel" by adherents of the "King James Only" movement because I wrote a book refuting their claims.[2] Those who have made such a charge have rarely examined what I believe about the Gospel itself. They simply find it useful to say that since I disagree with them on the matter of Bible translation, I must preach a "different gospel" and fall under the condemnation of Scripture.

It seems clear that any claim regarding the preaching of a different gospel must be examined with incredible care. Paul insisted that the Gospel is the very power of God onto salvation (Romans 1:16), so we are dealing with eternal truths of the utmost importance. Saying that *any* church is preaching a different gospel is a most serious matter, and we should be very slow to make such a charge, recognizing the tremendous responsibility to be truthful and accurate about such things. At the same time, once we have determined on the basis of diligent and honest examination that a church or group is preaching a gospel that is contradictory to that taught by the Apostles of the Lord, we should not—indeed, we *cannot*—avoid openly identifying this teaching as a dangerous error that is to be avoided at peril of spiritual loss.

All of this assumes, of course, that God has been sufficiently clear in His revelation of truth to us that we can tell the true from the false. Even that assumption is under constant attack in our world today. Theological relativism is just as prevalent, and dangerous, as moral relativism.

Does it matter? My answer is an unequivocal *yes*. I believe the differences that separate Roman Catholics and Protestants on the matter of the Gospel itself are fundamental.[3] I know many Roman Catholics who agree with me in that evaluation, I hasten to add. We do not share a common *evangel*, a common Gospel, and therefore cannot, logically, share a common evangelistic mission, a common evangelistic goal. We do not have a common message. Yes, we both say, "Jesus is Lord," but the Apostles went beyond those three words to explain *what* that means. And when Roman Catholics and Protestants go beyond the bare confession, the hoped-for unity disappears in the particulars of what the Gospel is and how people are made right before God. The gulf is too wide to be bridged by good intentions. Ultimately there is an impasse on the nature of the Gospel itself.

I am *not* saying that there are no professing Roman Catholics who are truly saved, or that there are no Roman Catholic leaders who embrace God's grace in a saving manner. When I speak of Rome's "teachings," I refer to the official teachings of Rome, enshrined in her creeds, encyclicals, and conciliar documents. It is plain to all who will look that there is as wide a diversity of understandings of those teachings among Catholics as there are differing perspectives among Protestants on similar issues. It is vital to differentiate between the official teachings of Rome and the individual understandings of those teachings.[4]

Many conservative Protestants, convinced that the Roman Catholic system has departed—*fatally*—from the true path, struggle to admit that there are still those within Roman Catholicism that are heirs of eternal life. It should be remembered, however, that Protestants have always acknowledged the wideness of God's grace and mercy in this way. We look back upon believers like Wycliffe and Hus and recognize that they found the truth of the Gospel even while they were within the confines of the Roman communion. Luther surely understood what it was to be justified by faith while a Roman Catholic monk. Are we really to assume he was the first, or even the last? Surely not.

I will approach the discussion of Roman Catholicism from the perspective that the Gospel message itself is an issue upon which compromise is impossible. No unity can exist where the Gospel is no longer central to the teaching of the Church. Along with the great truths of the Trinity, the deity of Christ, His physical Resurrection, and the Second Coming, the fact that God justifies us freely by His grace through faith in Jesus Christ *alone* must, I believe, be included in the most basic, fundamental definition of the Christian faith. It will be incumbent upon me to demonstrate honestly and clearly that the Roman Catholic position on the topic of the Gospel—a position defined not by selective citation of obscure sources, but by fair citation of mainstream, official sources—falls outside the realm of biblical truth, not just in minor, secondary issues but with reference to the very heart of the Gospel itself.

Before we can focus upon the primary and central issues, we need to "clear the air," so to speak. The debate between Roman Catholics and Protestants has been clouded by those on both sides who focus on nonessentials, engage in less-than-honest argumentation, and generally seek to stir up the emotions rather than the mind. I insist that the central issue is the Gospel itself. To demonstrate this, we must briefly look at examples of nonessentials that are often made the centerpiece of the debate. This should help both sides to bring their attention to bear on the issues that *really* matter.

2

CUTTING THROUGH THE FOG

Politicians use it to their own benefit all the time. Lawyers value it as one of the most powerful weapons in their arsenal. What is it? The technical term is "obfuscation," defined as the process of confusing, making unclear, and darkening. The more common term is "the fog." Everyone has experienced it. Sometimes it is unavoidable. Some topics are so complex, so convoluted, that we can't avoid being in a fog about them. But many times the fog is man-made. When someone doesn't want his or her audience to see the facts of the case clearly, the "fog" is extremely useful. By throwing out all sorts of irrelevant facts, inconsequential arguments, and pious platitudes, the skilled speaker can misdirect the attention of his audience and obscure the fact that he is in the wrong and his position is lost.

One of the greatest failures of modern education is that it produces people who can't evaluate arguments. It is an art to be able to think logically, to examine the statements of both sides of an issue, and come to a reasonable conclusion. For thousands of years this skill was taught from childhood. As recently as the last century it was common for all students of higher learning to engage in debate, to observe disputations, and to be tested on their ability not only to form meaningful arguments but to see through bad argumentation and debate.[1] It is a lost art that is terribly missed.

Nowhere is the skill of navigating through the fog of argument more needed, and more lacking, than in the arena of Roman Catholic/Protestant debate. While there are certain difficulties inherent in the subject itself, the simple fact is that we have to cut through centuries of man-made fog to get to the real issues. This fog billows from some of the strongest emotional attachments and traditions known to humankind. A quick glance at the history of Northern Ireland will verify that observation. Many Roman Catholics hold traditional beliefs about Protestants that have nothing to do with the real issues, just as a large portion of Protestants believe things about Roman Catholicism that likewise have little bearing on what is important. And many ministers and leaders on both sides have done little to dispel the fog, choosing instead to utilize emotional arguments. Unfortunately, they only perpetuate the fog that shrouds the whole topic.

As we work through the central issues, we will have the opportunity to examine a number of the myths believed by Roman Catholics about Protestant doctrine and practice. For now, I wish to address primarily my fellow evangelicals, calling us to look carefully at what is important and what is *not* important.

Double Standards

Hypocrisy offends everyone; though if we are honest, we would admit we all engage in it at times. Nevertheless, it seems the more concerned we are about being fair and honest in our thinking, the more likely we are to recognize our own hypocrisy. And at the same time, those who are the most blind to their own use of double standards seem to be the very ones willing to accuse others of the practice.

Our Lord is not honored when we contradict ourselves, argue in ways contrary to the truth, or otherwise bring shame upon He who called himself "the truth." Living lives committed to His truth should be our first priority as believers. Yet when faced with shortcomings in our own traditions, our own beliefs, we often disparage the other side's views rather than reckon honestly with our own.

Before Protestants criticize Roman Catholicism, they should think through their criticisms. What if these criticisms were applied to their own beliefs and practices? What then? How would they fare if tested by the standards applied to others? Many a good argument goes by the wayside if we hold ourselves to the highest standards of fairness, equity, and honesty. And despite the strong feelings that accompany a discussion of important doctrinal matters, truth is never served by using an unequal set of balances.

We also need honesty and integrity in how we represent the beliefs of others, even when we are critical of those beliefs. Nothing is more troubling than to be misrepresented. I am understandably bothered when someone says, "He teaches such and so," when in fact, I teach just the opposite! Our intense dislike of misrepresentation should make us sensitive to our need to portray the beliefs of others accurately. If we want to refute distortions of our own beliefs, we must be careful not to actively misrepresent the beliefs of others.

I heard a good example of this recently while listening to a local radio program. I noticed that the teacher consistently misrepresented the Roman Catholic doctrine of Purgatory. Rather than honestly presenting the concept as Rome has officially defined it, this staunchly conservative Protestant repeatedly made statements that demonstrated either a complete lack of understanding of the real Roman Catholic position, or an utter lack of concern that his statements were false and misleading. In either case, any knowledgeable Roman Catholic who might have stumbled upon the program would have dismissed this person's comments out-of-hand. And who could blame him? Don't we just as quickly dismiss criticisms of our faith that are based upon obvious ignorance or lack of study?

There are many times in my ministry when I have been tempted to use arguments that are less than accurate. I have often encountered individuals involved in false religious systems who were obviously unprepared to answer my criticisms of their position. In those situations it would be easy to use sensationalistic arguments that appeal directly to the emotions. In fact, I know *many* who do that very thing and get away with it ninety-nine percent of the time! They end up looking good because they get the easy "conversions." Yet I have asked the Lord to protect me from slipping into that mindset. Why? Because Christ is not honored by sensationalistic arguments, nor by "conversions" garnered by the sacrifice of truth and honesty. Do we really think lasting conversions are born from falsehoods and emotionalism? Surely not. Hence we must hold to the highest standards, even when talking with a person who cannot hold us to those standards himself. The one we seek to serve is the Lord, and His honor and glory calls us to pursue excellence in our presentation of the truth.

Some Roman Catholics may disagree with my representations of

Roman Catholic theology in this work. Given the wide spectrum of beliefs found under the banner "Roman Catholic" in the United States today, such would hardly be a surprise. I will, however, not only cite the official documents from which I take my definitions and understandings, but I will present the best defenses of these positions that I have encountered over the years in working among Roman Catholics.

What Are Nonessentials?

When the arguments in a debate focus on side issues, the cause of truth is not served. Every moment spent talking about topics that do not matter is a moment no longer available to discuss *important* issues. We may invest great energy in presenting our position on a hundred things, but if we do not address the central issues, the defining topics, we have wasted the time of everyone involved. This is not to say that a nonessential topic is always unimportant. It is just to insist that nonessentials never take the place of the defining issues.

The essential topic in the Roman Catholic/Protestant debate is the Gospel of Jesus Christ. A number of issues are closely related to the Gospel that, by virtue of that relationship, need to be classified as "essentials." For example, the issue of authority—Scripture, the Church, tradition—must be addressed as an essential, since it defines the terms used in the discussion of the Gospel itself. And though the connection may not immediately be obvious at this point, the topic of the Virgin Mary, too, ends up being intimately connected with the discussion of the Gospel and Roman Catholicism.

Other topics can have great importance as well. Issues such as the canon of Scripture, the Apocrypha, and certain historic events all have relevance in the current controversy. But all of these must be viewed in the context of their relationship to the core issue—the Gospel itself.

So what do I mean when I speak of nonessentials? Primarily those topics that may have some importance, some value for discussion, but more often than not tend to sidetrack rather than enhance. I refer to traditions, practices, and beliefs of Roman Catholicism that do not impact the essential doctrines of the Gospel. A few examples might help.

Lord, Bless These Chips

I flew to San Antonio to visit two men that I knew well—but had never met. It was a meeting born out of our modern electronic world. I had undertaken extensive correspondence with both men through e-mail. While we had spent many hours discussing spiritual things, we had done so without ever seeing one another's faces. We met at the airport, and since it was around lunchtime, we stopped at a nice Mexican restaurant.

My friends were from a tradition that is much more liturgical than my own Baptist background. One was Episcopalian. The other had spent many years in the Roman Catholic Church and was in the process of leaving that church. When the tortilla chips arrived, we stopped to bless the food. As soon as the final "amen" was said, I looked up and noticed both of my friends crossing themselves. And, of course, they noticed me—not doing much of anything, other than looking at them. We chuckled a bit at the awkwardness of the moment and went on from there.

I have often reflected upon that second in time. My religious background had taught me—not so much *directly* but by *attitude*— that crossing yourself was, well, pagan. It just wasn't to be done. *That's what the Catholics do*, I thought. The unspoken rule told me it was wrong. Of course, it's *not* just what Roman Catholics do—lots of Protestant groups do it, too.

It reminds me of something that happened during a baptismal service at a large Baptist church I attended years ago. The woman who was about to be baptized crossed herself in front of the entire congregation, just before she went under the water. The pastor was preoccupied with the baptism and didn't seem to notice. There was an audible gasp, followed by my immediate thought and probably that of many others: *Well, there's one who just doesn't understand.* But upon reflection, I have to wonder who didn't really understand.

When you think about it, crossing yourself has nothing to do with the Gospel. It is a nonessential. Godly men have crossed themselves, and godly men have refused to cross themselves. Ungodly men have crossed themselves, and ungodly men have refused to cross themselves. It is not an issue that impacts the Gospel. Yet, for many, it is an immediate "red flag" and may cause a person to go into attack mode for all the wrong reasons.

Now, before my conservative brothers and sisters get too upset, I should point out that crossing yourself *can* be wrong—that is, when a person turns the gesture into an act of superstition, believing that it somehow guarantees safety, or earns merit, or in any other way becomes something *other than* an outward identification with the cross of Christ. Then it becomes an issue worth addressing. But done by Christian people with pure motives, it is a nonessential, a matter of freedom.

What Did They Do With Jesus?

"What did they do with Jesus?" was the comment a friend of mine made the first time he entered a Protestant church. Having been raised a Roman Catholic, and having recently heard and embraced the Gospel, my friend was attending a large Baptist church for the first time. As he looked toward the front of the auditorium he saw a large wooden cross above the baptistry. And, as such crosses commonly are in Protestant churches, it was empty. "What did they do with Jesus?"

Surely there is merit in the objection that is often raised regarding the crucifix (a depiction of Jesus still on the cross), in light of the Roman Catholic doctrine of the Mass and the plainly biblical teaching of the *completed* work of Christ on the cross. Christ is risen and seated on the right hand of God the Father in glory. The cross stands as a constant reminder of the means by which God reconciled us to himself. The danger comes when the image of Christ hanging on the cross becomes a focal point of devotion that leads one away from the truth of the Gospel. In that sense it can become a stumbling block.

Some Protestants go beyond this and object to all crosses, vacant or not. I happen to enjoy wearing a cross, whether on a chain, as a pin on my lapel, or on a ring. There are many reasons for this, but one comes from my experiences witnessing to Mormons. Many of them have pointed to my cross and objected to my wearing it, and that has opened up many opportunities for me to witness, beginning with Paul's words in Galatians 6:14: "But may it never be that I would boast, except in the cross of our Lord Jesus Christ." It is a constant reminder of what Christ did for me. And it has more than once recalled to my mind the spiritual realities that are truly important—a reminder I often need in the course of the day.

Bayberry or Vanilla?

I also love candles, especially bayberry-scented ones—in crystal containers—when it is cold and blustery and close to Christmas. Around the holiday season my office is all lit with candles. Because I live in the desert, it's one of the few times I can enjoy candles burning without having to turn on the air conditioner!

Roman Catholics light a lot of candles in their worship services. It is a nonessential. But when candles are burned as a symbol of prayers for the dead, it becomes an improper act for a Christian. Simply lighting candles in a religious setting or celebration such as a wedding is a matter of solemnity and decoration. Many churches use candles as part of their regular worship. Again, it is a nonessential. It is not an evil thing, nor does it tell you anything about the person who lights candles, religiously or otherwise. Look past the action and examine the motives.

What About Liturgy?

For many conservative Protestants, the very term "liturgy" seems connected with Roman concepts. Priests in long robes, dark churches, stained-glass windows, processions, standing, kneeling—everything and anything associated with "high" worship as found in the Roman liturgy, in the thinking of many, is tainted with the stain of Rome. Lutherans, Anglicans, and some Presbyterians have various elements of formal liturgy in their services as well, but for some reason most people don't think of those denominations in the same way they think of Roman Catholicism.

It is interesting to note, however, that *every* service has liturgy, even if it is plain and simple rather than formal and complex. The service itself is a form of liturgy. Whether we stand and sing or sit and sing, how we have the Lord's Supper, how we baptize, or whatever we regularly do in a religious service is a form of liturgy. Godly men have worshiped in ornate forms of liturgy. Godly men have worshiped in simple forms of liturgy. It is not the complexity or form but the intent of the heart that is the key. For some, Roman liturgy is merely a religious ceremony with little meaning. Many have told me: "I attended Mass every Sunday, but it never meant anything to me. It was just so much religiosity." Many have said they never once heard the Gospel of Christ explained clearly and plainly, despite having attended hundreds of services in the Roman Catholic Church. We can see the danger that arises when liturgy, no matter how ancient or well-intended, takes over to such an extent that the preaching and exposition of the Scriptures are minimized or completely done away with.

But we must also remember that there are many who sit in the pews of conservative Protestant churches for whom the service has little meaning as well. For them it is just a religious exercise, differing in form from the Roman Catholic service, but a ritual nonetheless. All such gatherings have little meaning for those who have not sensed the move of God's Spirit and responded to His grace and mercy.

Great men of God have lived their lives engaging in high forms of liturgy. I think of Bishop Ryle, an Anglican, and a great man of God, who wrote such classic works as *Holiness* and *Practical Religion*. Many Baptists would not feel comfortable in a service led by the bishop because of the high liturgy, but dare we determine a man's spiritual maturity on the basis of the complexity of the liturgy he attends? As long as the traditions that give form to the liturgy are subservient to the Scriptures (and *every* form of liturgy is impacted greatly by traditional understandings), we must be slow to judge, especially when we lack understanding as to *why* others believe and worship as they do.

A Jesuit Behind Every Bush

Conspiracies sell. No matter what the topic, if you link it to some great worldwide conspiracy, there is a ready market for your ideas. Entire books have been written against the Roman Catholic system that were based on little more than a handful of facts and a bucketful of conspiracies. The most fanciful flights of imagination have been put forward as "gospel truth" by those who see Rome as the greatest evil imaginable. Any incident, no matter how innocuous, is filled with the most ominous meaning by those who find the Pope a convenient foil for their political and religious theories.

What is most troubling about such works—whether they be books, magazines, comic books, or whatever—is not just the double standards they utilize in their attacks upon the Roman system, but more importantly the fact that their constant drumbeat of conspiratorial thinking distracts any honest investigator from the *real* issues of the Gospel of Christ.

When Christians encounter falsehoods in *any* arena, their first obligation is to present the Gospel of Christ in a clear, convincing manner. There are times when other issues must be addressed in order to facilitate that clear presentation, but such preparatory topics should be handled as quickly and efficiently as possible. They should not obscure the primary reason the Christian is engaging in dialogue with the person who is trapped in a false system. Anyone who goes into such a situation seeking only to win an argument is already on the wrong basis. And tearing down someone else's beliefs without providing a positive presentation of the truth is likely to produce a disenchanted agnostic who rejects *all* religion, or a surface-level "convert" who withers and dies in time (see Matthew 13). A Christian who shares with those who have a preexisting faith system should always seek to use the highest standards of honesty in bringing such a person to a knowledge of the truth.

Converts who come from one religious system into another often see their former faith in the worst possible light, which is understandable. Many former Mormons, for example, see Mormonism as the "worst" enemy of the Gospel; former Jehovah's Witnesses have similar feelings toward the Watchtower Society, and many former Roman Catholics see in Rome the very essence of Babylon. Such feelings often arise as a result of years spent in service to a religious system without the benefit of the truth of the Gospel. It is not any *one* system of belief that is *the* enemy of the Gospel of Christ. Overreaction to one gives credence to another. Balance is the key, and that balance is found in a deep and steady commitment to biblical standards.

Didn't the Reformers see Rome in similar terms in their day? Yes, and the feeling was mutual. Rome saw the Reformers in just as negative a light as the Reformers saw Rome, and the fact of religious persecution on both sides of the issue is a matter of historical record.[2] The persecution that characterized both sides makes it easier to comprehend the rancor of those days and the resultant willingness to accuse the opposition of the worst possible motives. When you could, quite easily, die if you fell into the hands of the opposition, such a reality tended to raise the emotional level. And because the vast majority of Reformers came *out of* what most admit was a very corrupt Roman Catholic Church—which made up almost the entirety of the opposition they faced—the reason why they used the terminology they did is easily understood. In the same manner, the Roman Catholic apologists of the day saw the Reformers as servants of Satan—rending the church and leading millions astray. Mix in stakes, fire, and the sword, and you have a highly explosive situation. Despite the tremendous persecution, the Reformers directly, accurately, and forcefully addressed the issue of the Gospel. They realized then what we must realize now: the gulf that separates us is real. It has to do with the very message we proclaim to the world.

Thankfully, most conversation today can take place without fear of death or punishment for being on the wrong side of the issue. Yes, there are current incidents of religious persecution and intolerance. There are evidences of evangelicals being beaten and persecuted in Mexico, Brazil, and other countries that might be identified as "culturally Catholic." But in most situations in the United States this debate can be undertaken in a somewhat less emotionally charged context.

Keep Your Eye on the Ball

Before we move on to the central topics, I pause to reiterate a most important point. We must major on the majors, and minor on the minors. If someone's objection to Rome is based on nonessentials and not on major issues, something is wrong. If we fail to see the central issue—how people are made right with God—we will generate a great deal of heat—but little light—in our debates. Our thinking must be clear and unshakable: What is the Gospel? What does the Bible teach about the Gospel? What does Rome teach about the Gospel? If there is a difference, what is it? Where does it come from? Everything else pales into insignificance.

3

THE ESSENTIAL ISSUE: THE GOSPEL OF PEACE

The "gospel of peace." That's what Paul called it (Ephesians 6:15). It is not the most popular means of describing the Gospel today, but it is biblical. And it makes sense because it finds its origination in the God who is described over and over again as the "God of peace" (Romans 15:33, 16:20; 2 Corinthians 13:11; Philippians 4:9; 1 Thessalonians 5:23; Hebrews 13:20). The Gospel makes peace—peace between God and man. It ends the enmity that exists because of sin. God *makes* peace through the blood of the cross of Christ (Colossians 1:20).

Lest we lose our focus, let me remind you of the issue at stake: peace with God. People on both sides of the Roman Catholic/Protestant debate who are honest realize that these arguments have to do with nothing less than people's eternity destiny. If you take nothing more from this book than the content of this chapter, I will have accomplished what a Christian author desires to do: communicate the core truths of the Gospel of Jesus Christ.

We cannot discuss the Gospel without discussing peace. A gospel that does not bring peace is not a Gospel at all, for surely anything that is described as "good news" (what the word "gospel" means) must speak of true and lasting peace. A message of works-righteousness, for example, that calls someone to strive to obtain peace with God through various ceremonies or duties, could not logically be called a gospel, for such would not qualify as good news. Such a message would bring about not peace but turmoil to the hearts of those who struggle to meet the impossible standards built into such systems.

When we link "the gospel" and "peace," we are using the word "peace" in a particular way. The Bible speaks of peace among nations and peace between individuals, but here we are limiting ourselves to a specific use of the term: the healing of the relationship that exists between God and man. For in reality, nothing else matters. If we do not have peace with the Creator, all else is meaningless. Peace with other people is a triviality when we are at war with God. And as long as the sin issue is unresolved, men and women are at war with God.

The nature and the effect of the Gospel is vitally important as we seek to focus on the central issues that separate Roman Catholics and Protestants. Because the Bible speaks often of the Gospel and plainly teaches that the Gospel brings about peace, we must ask: Does the Gospel taught by Rome bring about the peace described in Scripture?

Christians are a people marked by peace. The Lord Jesus spoke words of comfort to His disciples the night before His death:

> Peace I leave with you; My peace I give to you; not as the world gives do I give to you. Do not let your heart be troubled, nor let it be fearful (John 14:27).

The peace Christians have is of supernatural origin. It comes from Christ and differs fundamentally from the peace of this world. It is *Christ's* peace that we hold as a precious possession, and it is *His* peace that we proclaim to the world:

> The word which He sent to the sons of Israel, preaching peace through Jesus Christ (He is Lord of all) . . . (Acts 10:36).

Christians preach peace through Jesus Christ. Not the mere *possibility* of peace, but a real, established, God-ordained peace that has already been brought about and completed in the work of Jesus Christ. We do not merely invite people to *try to make peace*. Instead we say, "Come, enjoy the peace God has already provided for in Jesus Christ!" We do not ask people to bring anything in their hands in attempt to buy peace, for "He Himself is our peace" (Ephesians 2:14). Everything focuses on Christ. His Father is the maker of our peace, His work the ground of our peace, His Spirit the testifier of our peace, His person our peace itself. All is found in Christ: we add nothing to His perfect work.

The perfection of our Savior establishes the basis for our peace with God. His work on the Cross is the means by which we who are sinful can be at peace with our holy God. Nothing else avails to bring us into right relationship with Him. We are incapable of making peace ourselves—all sides agree to that. But beyond this, we are incapable of *maintaining* peace with God if, in fact, our relationship with Him is based on anything other than the firm foundation of the Just One who died for the unjust, the Savior who gave His life as a ransom for many, the Shepherd who gave His life for the sheep. Christ's death as the foundation of this peace is laid out clearly in Scripture:

> Being justified as a gift by His grace through the redemption which is in Christ Jesus; whom God displayed publicly as a propitiation in His blood through faith. This was to demonstrate His righteousness, because in the forbearance of God He passed over the sins previously committed; for the demonstration, I say, of His righteousness at the present time, so that He would be just and the justifier of the one who has faith in Jesus (Romans 3:24–26).

We will discuss justification in some depth later. Right now let's examine the work of Christ in making redemption, and the fact that God, by His grace, justifies men *freely, as a gift*, without cost. God then is described as the "justifier of the one who has faith in Jesus."[1] God justifies, God makes righteous, on the basis of the works of another—Jesus Christ. People do not justify themselves. Then are all justified? No, for not all have faith. Paul goes on to describe the means of justification—it is by faith, and faith alone. He writes,

> For we maintain that a man is justified by faith apart from works of the Law (Romans 3:28).

And then,

> Now to the one who works, his wage is not credited as a favor, but as what is due. But to the one who does not work, but believes in Him who justifies the ungodly, his faith is credited as righteousness (Romans 4:4–5).

Those who have faith in Jesus Christ appropriate His righteousness. His perfect righteousness is "imputed" (credited) to the believer on the basis of faith. It is not credited to those who work to gain it (Romans 9:30–10:4), but only to those who trust in the all-sufficient Savior *alone*. And why does God make the passive act of faith the means of justification? The Scriptures have a ready answer:

> For this reason it is by faith, in order that it may be in accordance with grace, so that the promise will be guaranteed to all the descendants, not only to those who are of the Law, but also to those who are of the faith of Abraham, who is the father of us all (Romans 4:16).

Justification is by faith because it is in harmony with grace. Grace—the free and unmerited favor of God—cannot be earned, purchased, or merited. By nature it is free. Faith has no merit in and of itself. It performs no meritorious work so as to *gain grace or favor*. It trusts in the Giver of grace and is the only basis by which God declares a sinner, in light of the work of Christ, "righteous."

This takes us back to the issue of peace, for having laid out the means of justification, Scripture proclaims,

> Therefore, having been justified by faith, we have peace with God through our Lord Jesus Christ (Romans 5:1).

Peace with God. That is, and always will be, the issue. How do we have peace with God? The passage is plain: "having been justified by faith." Being justified by faith comes *before* having peace.[2] Here is the point: Those who are not justified by faith cannot claim peace with God. Those who are justified by faith are assured of that peace. We have[3] peace with God. The deepest need of our heart can be obtained in only one way: through the justifying work of God in Jesus Christ, by which He justifies sinners who have faith in Jesus. Does it sound too simple? For many it is (see 1 Corinthians 1:18ff.). But the very "foolishness" of the preaching of the Cross displays the wisdom of God.

I have an abiding certainty of acceptance by God. Do you? Not a temporary state where things are all right. I am talking about real peace, the kind of peace the Bible describes. Peace with God! Most of us have heard the Jewish term *shalom* and know it means "peace." But *shalom* means much more than that. *Shalom* is a full, rich term that speaks of wellness, health, a rightness of relationships. It does not mean merely the lack of conflict—it goes far beyond that. *Shalom*, for example, would never describe a cease-fire in wartime. In a cease-fire, shooting might break out at any moment. The uneasy calm would not qualify as *shalom*. In the same way, if our relationship with God is such that it might break down in the next instant, resulting in enmity between us and God once again, we do not have biblical peace.

The peace I have with God is not of my own making. In fact, its steadfastness depends totally on the work of another, the perfect Peacemaker, the Savior, Jesus Christ. It is abiding and secure because it is solely His work. If it were based on my actions, my contributions, it would be anything but secure, anything but lasting. But it is true peace, lasting peace, blessed peace because it is based on His perfect and completed work on the Cross, given to me by God's free and eternal grace (2 Timothy 1:9–10). This peace will not break down tomorrow, making me at enmity with God again. It is a perfect peace. It cannot be disturbed by a higher power or authority, since the Creator himself has vouchsafed it to me! Peace with God. Certain peace. Mine through Jesus Christ and Him alone.

Do you have this kind of peace? Or do the following words better describe the state of your heart?

> The reason for the uncertainty of the state of grace lies in this, that without a special revelation nobody can with certainty of faith know whether or not he has fulfilled all the conditions that are necessary for achieving justification.[4]

These are the fundamental, important issues that separate Roman Catholics and Protestants, and nothing less than peace with God himself is at stake. Do we "fulfill" conditions so as to "achieve" justification? Or has Christ fulfilled all those conditions for His people, so that He can be described as the one who "will save His people from their sins"? (Matthew 1:21). Do we merit for ourselves the grace needed for our sanctification, for the increase of grace and charity, and for the attainment of eternal life,[5] or has Christ merited all of these for us, so that we can be certain of the continuation of the peace we have with God?

This book is about the Gospel. But before we can discuss the Gospel, we must answer the question, *"Who defines the Gospel?"* Is the Bible sufficient to tell us what the Gospel is? What is the final authority for defining the Gospel? Ironically, we will have to spend more time discussing the sufficiency of Scripture than we will to determine what the Bible actually teaches about the Gospel! Such is the nature of this conflict.

So before delving further into the Gospel, we must first address the issue of authority. Who defines the Gospel? How can we know what the Bible really teaches?

Rome claims that individual Christians have no right to go to the biblical text and draw any conclusions that are not in line with what Rome teaches. In light of such claims, we must look very closely at the issue of authority before we can "nail down" the Gospel and quiet the controversy that rages concerning what it really means. To these issues we now turn.

4

WHO DEFINES THE GOSPEL?

The fact that I am focusing on the Gospel as the central issue at stake between Roman Catholics and Protestants doesn't mean it is the only important difference that exists. In fact, there is an even more primary difference, one that defines the categories of any other discussion that takes place between the two sides: *authority*. Often the ramifications of this topic are lost on those who enter into conversation, resulting in a lot of miscommunication and confusion.

It is easy to see why authority is so foundational. The viewpoint that best defends its claim to authority rules the day. Note the words of the Council of Trent (1546):

> Furthermore, to check unbridled spirits, it decrees that no one relying on his own judgment shall, in matters of faith and morals pertaining to the edification of Christian doctrine, distorting the Holy Scriptures in accordance with his own conceptions, presume to interpret them contrary to that sense which holy mother Church, to whom it belongs to judge of their true sense and interpretation, has held and holds, or even contrary to the unanimous teaching of the Fathers, even though such interpretations should never at any time be published. Those who act contrary to this shall be made known by the ordinaries and punished in accordance with the penalties prescribed by the law.[1]

The Roman Catholic Church claims the ultimate authority to interpret of Scripture. She maintains that only she can properly interpret the Scriptures, and that those who ignore or reject her teachings think and act contrary to the very will of Christ. Four hundred years after Trent, the Second Vatican reiterated this claim in the document *Dei Verbum:*

> But the task of authentically interpreting the Word of God, whether written or handed on, has been entrusted exclusively to the living teaching office of the Church, whose authority is exercised in the name of Jesus Christ. This teaching office is not above the Word of God, but serves it, teaching only what has been handed on, listening to it devoutly, guarding it scrupulously and explaining it faithfully in accord with a divine commission and with the help of the Holy Spirit; it draws from this one deposit of faith everything that it presents for belief as divinely revealed.
>
> It is clear, therefore, that Sacred Tradition, Sacred Scripture, and the teaching authority of the Church, in accord with God's most wise design, are so linked and joined together that one cannot stand without the others, and that all together and each in its own way under the action of the one Holy Spirit contribute effectively to the salvation of souls.[2]

It is very important to understand these assertions of authority and power. Many are not aware of how far-reaching Rome's claims are. To illustrate, note the words of Karl Keating, one of today's leading Catholic apologists, as he explains how a Roman Catholic knows that Scripture is inspired:

> But the basis for one's belief in its inspiration directly affects how one goes about interpreting the Bible. The Catholic believes in inspiration because the Church tells him so—that is putting it bluntly—and that same Church has the authority to interpret the inspired text. Fundamentalists believe in inspiration, although on weak grounds, but they have no interpreting authority other than themselves.[3]

Keating is correct: the basis for our belief in the inspiration of the Bible does directly impact how we go about interpreting the Bible. If we believe the Bible is inspired on the basis of accepting the claims of authority made by the Roman Catholic Church, then we will obviously interpret the Bible in light of the teachings of Rome. From the very start, an external authority exists outside of Scripture that will determine what we "find" in Scripture. Rome's authority, then, becomes the foundation upon which all else rests.

Immediately we note circular reasoning: Roman Catholicism claims the final say in interpreting the Bible, yet it also points to Bible passages as the basis of its authority.[4] The result of this circular reasoning causes great confusion when Protestants and Roman Catholics come together to discuss such things as the Gospel. No matter how deeply we delve into the exegesis of Scripture, eventually the issue of authority will arise. As Protestants we will be told that our interpretation is not possible because it goes against "the unanimous consent of the Fathers" (i.e., it goes against the traditional interpretation of a passage as found in the writings of the early church leaders like Irenaeus or Tertullian or Augustine), or that we are in error because we lack the insight provided by the "oral tradition" that is in the possession of the "Teaching Magisterium"[5] of the Roman Catholic Church. In either case the issue will not be *what the actual text of Scripture says*, but what the Roman Catholic Church, claiming Christ's special empowerment, *says* it says.

This was brought home to me a few years ago when I debated Roman Catholic apologist Gerald Matatics before an audience at Boston College. The subject was the canonicity of the Apocrypha. The Roman Catholic Church maintains that the Apocrypha should be included as a part of the Old Testament. The debate thesis was "The Roman Catholic canon of the Old Testament is correct." Mr. Matatics was affirming, and I was denying. As the debate moved on, it became quite clear that my opponent intended to pursue a course that led me to summarize his position as follows: "The Roman Catholic canon of the Old Testament is correct because Rome says it is. Period. End of discussion." Mr. Matatics spoke of the fact that the Church had the authority to proclaim the canon, and that the Church, being founded by Christ, was the only infallible source of knowledge regarding the canon. While I focused upon the testimony offered by history itself, my opponent based his argument upon the overriding claim of authority made by Rome.

When we came to our closing remarks, I stood before the audience and proclaimed, "The Book of Mormon is the Word of God!" I paused long enough to make sure everyone heard what I was saying. I then proceeded to explain that such claims are made by Mormon missionaries every day, and when asked *why* they believe this, we eventually hear something about how "the Prophet says so." But this mere assertion does not make the Book of Mormon the Word of God. Nor can we say, "The Roman Catholic canon of the Old Testament is correct because Rome says so." Yet, given the claims of ultimate authority made by Rome, how can it be otherwise? Ultimate authorities cannot be examined by a higher standard because by definition none could possibly exist. Therefore, once one accepts the claims of Rome regarding her authority, everything else falls into place, and all testing of those claims must be suspended. Rome may condescend to offer a proof here or a supporting text there, but in reality, how can she offer any kind of evidence when she says that in the final analysis only she can properly interpret that evidence? If you find the offered evidence unconvincing, you are told it is only because you do not submit to her authority. When you ask why you should submit to her authority, she offers you the same evidence once again. It is a vicious circle that traps many an unwary person.

But Look at the Mess *You* Are In!

Rarely are we allowed to see the boldness of the Roman Catholic claim at the start of a discussion. Instead, the argument normally appears in the context of solving the seemingly endless disputations found among those who do not have some "higher authority" by which to solve their disagreements. The modern picture of Protestantism is ripe for such argument, of course. It is hardly humorous to note that if you put ten Protestants in a room and ask them a theological question, they will arrive at a minimum of a dozen different answers. Shall we baptize infants? Lutherans, Anglicans, and Presbyterians say yes, though for different reasons! Is baptism necessary for salvation? Most Church of Christ denominations say yes. Baptists say no; it is a sign of one's obedience to Christ, but not a means of salvation. Presbyterians see it as a sign of the covenant, Lutherans as the means of regeneration through "infantile faith." What about tongues, prophecies, end-times events? You name it, and you'll find differences of opinion about it. The confident Roman Catholic looks at this situation and concludes that such ought not to be.[6] Christ surely did not intend such confusion on important matters of faith for His church, so we must conclude that the Roman way is the proper way. An external authority that is invested with divine authority to interpret the Bible produces the desired result: assurance and confidence.

Or does it? While many today think they have solved the problem of "chaos in the ranks" by submitting to the magisterial authority[7] of Rome, have they really accomplished their goal? Can we escape the uncertainty of differences of opinion regarding the meaning of biblical passages by submitting ourselves to a church that claims to be the ancient, Apostolic voice of Christ?[8] Surely there is an emotional warmth in the thought that the ancient church, wrapped in the mists of time, has stood firm through all those centuries. Many find such a portrayal sufficient reason for conversion to Rome, and Roman Catholic apologists are quick to evoke such images in contrast to the comparative transience of Protestant denominationalism. Over the past years I've encountered many people whose journey to Rome was sparked by the desire for what I call the "infallible fuzzies," that comforting feeling of being "in" with the ancient, unchanging, all-powerful, and infallible church.[9]

The powerful attraction of this concept should not be underestimated. Rome offers certainty on the basis of her alleged infallibility. Do you want to avoid questions about the canon of Scripture? Trust Rome. So you want to know the Bible is inspired? Trust Rome. Do you want to know exactly how the Gospel works? Trust Rome. Are you troubled by the claims of Jehovah's Witnesses and others regarding the Trinity or the deity of Christ? Trust Rome.[10] Does it bother you that you can't find evidence of Papal Infallibility or the Bodily Assumption of Mary in the Bible (or in the early history of the church for that matter)? Trust Rome! And how could it be otherwise, since she claims the final and ultimate authority in all things religious? For our purposes it is vital to realize that the same answer is put forth in the face of the overwhelming evidence of Paul's epistles to the Romans and Galatians regarding the free gift of God's justifying grace in Jesus Christ. Trust Rome.

The picture of certainty based upon the ancient and unchanging Roman Church is, however, an illusion. At every point it breaks down. First, the modern Roman Church is not the historical Roman Church. Rome as she exists today is a very different institution than she was in the eleventh, eighth, or third centuries.[11] The early bishops of Rome would have great trouble recognizing the modern Roman Catholic Church as being the same church over which they once presided.

Yet the argument breaks down most fundamentally at its very beginning. We are told that Protestants cannot have any kind of certainty because we only have ourselves to trust. Since we reject Rome's authority, we are left with the Bible, the Spirit, and ourselves, and look at what that results in: disputes—with all sides saying they base their beliefs upon the Bible and are guided by the Spirit. That first step of trust, we are told, is misplaced. In fact, the very idea of making such a private, personal decision is derided as being contrary to Scripture, for we are told this amounts to "private interpretation."[12]

The Roman Catholic has no more certainty than the Protestant at this point. The Roman Catholic makes a decision to follow a particular guide. That decision is fallible. He could make other decisions. *Many* religious groups offer to act as religious guides today, all claiming divine authority for their mission. The Mormon Prophet in Salt Lake City claims divine authority, replete with clarifying Scriptures, a restored priesthood, and accompanying miracles and signs. A mere century and a half after the founding of the Mormon Church, nearly ten million people follow that prophet's authority. So, too, the Governing Body of Jehovah's Witnesses in Brooklyn, New York, functions as a divinely appointed and attested guide in religious life for millions of Witnesses around the globe. A Roman Catholic born into the faith may not have consciously chosen among these options. But the person contemplating conversion to Rome with the goal of finding infallible certainty outside of personal responsibility before God cannot avoid the simple fact that the first step along that path is an obviously fallible step. Rome's voice is just one among many, and it is up to the individual to choose to follow it or not. Therefore, the offer of certainty is illusory: you have to make a fallible decision to buy into the plan, and any certainty offered thereafter rests solely on the first—fallible—choice that was made.[13]

The Great Scandal

The issue of certainty strikes at the heart of the Protestant system. For some reason, people think that unless you have absolute, total, and infallible certainty about all things, you have no certainty about anything. If you don't claim to know *all* truth—exhaustively, in every detail—you don't know *any* truth at all. The more you think about it, the more absurd the idea becomes: "If you don't know calculus, you can't add or subtract." I can be quite certain that $2+2=4$ even if I don't know the first thing about derivations or logarithms or any such thing. It is possible to know something *truly* without knowing something *exhaustively*. I can have a certainty borne of true knowledge without having an absolute certainty based upon exhaustive knowledge.

For example, I know the basics of why the fluorescent bulb over my desk provides light for me right now as I work. I have a rudimentary knowledge of electron flow, the interaction with the gases in the bulb, and the emission of electromagnetic radiation. In fact, having been a science major in college, I probably know *more* about how the light works than someone without a science background. But I cannot explain the specifics, cannot provide the mathematical formulae, and cannot answer a myriad of questions that could be asked about the process as a whole. I have *true* but *limited* knowledge of how that light works. But my limitations do not mean that I cannot know the light is on and that it is providing me with what I need to be able to see.

In the realm of faith, I have *true* but *limited* knowledge of God. In fact, no one outside of the Trinity itself has *exhaustive* and *complete* knowledge of God. I do not believe that we as finite creatures will ever possess such knowledge. But since I do not have *exhaustive* knowledge of God, does this mean I have *no* knowledge of Him at all? Of course not. To take it a step further, I do not have *exhaustive* knowledge of everything the Bible says about God. While for years I have studied the Bible extensively, learned its languages, studied its backgrounds, I still do not know everything the Bible teaches about God. And I would daresay that no man, no matter how intelligent or diligent, can mine or ever has mined all the golden nuggets of truth about God from the Scriptures. Does this mean I have *no* knowledge of God at all? No, I have a true knowledge of God based on the Scriptures, but my knowledge is limited.

Which brings us to the scandal. My knowledge is limited. And what is more, it is fallible. The very fact that what I know is limited means I may be in error about a conclusion I have embraced simply because I don't have all the facts and have come to that conclusion prematurely. The instant we admit our fallibility the cry goes up, "Aha! See? You need an infallible authority!" Well, before we all line up to join one of the many groups claiming such authority, let's stop and consider a few things for a moment. Did God create us as limited creatures? Yes, He did. Did God entrust His Word to such creatures? Yes, He did. Do you really think God is shocked that human beings end up disagreeing over what His Scriptures teach? No, not for a moment.

The "great scandal" to which I have referred is the idea, popularized during the Reformation and strongly rejected at the time by Rome, that each and every person—man or woman, rich or poor, learned or unlearned—is responsible as a priest before God for what he or she believes. "The individual priesthood of the believer" is one of the many phrases that have been used to describe this revolutionary idea. Luther and the other Reformers encouraged the plowman, the merchant, and the peasant woman to open the Word of God and read—for themselves. And what a scandal it was! Reading the Bible without the interpretation of the Church, without the oversight of the priest? How could this be? But the idea went to the heart of the problem: God holds us individually responsible for what we believe and why we believe it. "The Pope told me so" won't cut it in the end. Nor, may I add, will "My pastor told me so." Every limited, finite, fallible person is called to "search the Scriptures" and "examine everything carefully; hold fast to that which is good" (1 Thessalonians 5:21).

Roman Catholics say this doctrine results in chaos, and they point to the doctrinal chaos among Protestant denominations today as strong evidence. To a point, there is truth in this claim. Obviously, if we don't have a centralized Church enforcing one particular viewpoint, a broader range of opinions will arise. But the charge of chaos is something else. That allegation is built upon a misrepresentation of the Protestant concept of the priesthood of all believers—a misrepresentation embraced by Roman Catholics *and* Protestants alike.

The individual priesthood of the believer does not mean there is no Church. It does not mean there are no pastors and teachers. It does not mean we are not to learn from one another, learn from the great Christians of the past, or "start from scratch" with every new generation. The doctrine does not do away with the biblically based authority of elders to teach and train and rebuke, nor does it give license to anybody and everybody to go out and start some new movement based on their own "take" on things. While this may happen, it is an *abuse* of the doctrine, not an *application* of it.

As we shall note later when discussing the idea of the "development of doctrine," the Scriptures provide the boundaries within which we are to live out the priesthood of the believer. The Bible itself speaks of submission to elders, of holding firm to the Apostles' doctrines, and of testing everything by the ultimate authority of the Scriptures themselves.

What the doctrine *does* do, however, is insist that we are to be personally responsible before God for what we believe. We cannot pass this responsibility off to someone else. We can learn from others, seek the advice and teaching of others, but in the final analysis, we cannot blame anyone but ourselves for the outcome. This idea has many ramifications, but I will only note two: first, we need not seek, nor expect to find, absolute certainty on all things pertaining to God in this life; second, the Scriptures are a sufficient source of our knowledge of the faith.

With reference to the first idea, we should see now that the search for the "infallible fuzzies" is a search destined to failure. Because we are fallible creatures our understanding will be fallible as long as we live on the earth. God does not call us to exhaustive knowledge of everything. He calls us to be serious students of His Word who diligently apply what we have learned to our lives. The certainty we have is not exhaustive, absolute, beyond human expectation. It is solid, expectant, full of hope, which comes from repeated exposure to God's truth and the repeated experience of His faithfulness. To ask for more is to ask for something God has never promised and common sense tells us we will not have in this life. What is more, the certainty offered by obedience to an external authority (such as the Magisterium of Rome) does not fulfill the longing of those looking for a release from personal responsibility in things religious. The choice of what infallible guide to follow is not only a personal one (and hence fallible), but is simply moving the responsibility down the line a step. It does not release us from the possibility of error. If anything, it increases the possibility, for there are no checks and balances to keep such ultimate authorities from wandering off the path of truth and simply instructing those following to "trust" in their leadership—a situation well documented in history and remedied, at least in part, by the Reformation.

All of this brings us to the second concept: the sufficiency of the Scriptures to function as the *regula fidei*, the "rule of faith," for the Christian Church. It is here that we find, as we would expect, a great divide between Protestants and Roman Catholics. The Protestant belief in the sufficiency of Scripture is historically known as the doctrine of *sola scriptura*, "Scripture alone." Most Protestants do not understand the doctrine; they merely assume it. Most Roman Catholics misunderstand it, and in my experience debating some of the leading Roman Catholic apologists, I have discovered that most of them purposefully misrepresent it. Since it directly impacts our discussion of the Gospel of grace, we must now turn to a consideration of why Protestants believe in *sola scriptura* and why Roman Catholics consider it the formula for doctrinal chaos.

5

SOLA SCRIPTURA: GOD SPEAKS CLEARLY

When Basil of Caesarea (c. 330–379) encountered opponents who claimed authority for their own custom and tradition (over against that which prevailed in Basil's experience), he responded in these words:

> If custom is to be taken in proof of what is right, then it is certainly competent for me to put forward on my side the custom which obtains here. If they reject this, we are clearly not bound to follow them. Therefore, let God-inspired Scripture decide between us; and on whichever side be found doctrines in harmony with the word of God, in favor of that side will be cast the vote of truth.[1]

Disputes about what Christians should believe have existed since the days of the Apostles. We do not have apostles today, but we have the testimony they have left us in "God-inspired Scripture." Basil was content to allow that divine document to stand as judge between him and his opponents. He admitted the fact that just as he and his followers had customs, his opponents had their own customs as well. But he did not bow to the weight of these, nor did he insist they had to follow his own. Instead, he referred to that which was binding on all Christians in all places at all times: the Scriptures.[2]

At the time of the Reformation two great cries were heard in the land, and as was common in the day, they were both in Latin! The "material" principle of the Reformation, the concept that dominated the majority of the preaching and proclamation of the Reformers, was *sola fide*, salvation by grace through "faith alone." This was the great message of the free gift of God's grace and the fact that He makes men right with himself through Christ's atoning work. But the "formal" principle of the Reformation, that which gave rise to the rest, was *sola scriptura*, "Scripture alone." The Reformers boldly taught that dogmas and beliefs defined on a basis other than the Scriptures were not binding on the Christian conscience. This does not mean they rejected everything that every Christian in earlier ages had said: indeed, they often cited the early Christians as supporters of their own positions. However, they recognized that those earlier believers were not inspired, were not inerrant, and, in fact, quite often made errors in their judgments and beliefs—just as people do today. The only *infallible* rule of faith, they argued, is found in the pages of Holy Writ.

Few Protestants today can define *sola scriptura* briefly, succinctly, or even accurately. And it is my experience that this same problem plagues Roman Catholics as well. It is particularly pernicious in its impact among the defenders of the Roman Catholic system. Even though a tremendous amount of discussion takes place about *sola scriptura*, very few actually touch upon the central issues, and most of the time they spend their time attacking (or defending) straw men.

Let me warn the reader: We will go into some depth in our discussion of *sola scriptura*. This is necessary, even in light of my previous emphasis on keeping the Gospel as the central issue, because the position we take on *this* issue will determine to a large measure the outcome of the discussion on the Gospel. I have observed that many of those who have moved into Roman Catholicism from evangelical churches have done so because they could not defend *sola scriptura*. I will begin by dispelling many of the common myths about what *sola scriptura* does and does not teach, and then move on to a positive presentation of the doctrine.

What *Sola Scriptura* Is Not

1. *First and foremost, sola scriptura is not a claim that the Bible contains all knowledge.* The Bible is not a science textbook, a manual on governmental procedures, or a catalog of automobile engine parts. It does not claim to give us every bit of knowledge that we could ever obtain. It is not a leather-bound encyclopedia of human knowledge and wisdom. Those who point out that there are truths

found outside the Bible are not objecting to *sola scriptura*.

2. *Sola scriptura is not a claim that the Bible is an exhaustive catalog of all* religious *knowledge*. The Bible itself asserts that it is not exhaustive in detail. When John commented on the wide range of the Lord Jesus' ministry he wrote,

> And there are also many other things which Jesus did, which if they were written in detail, I suppose that even the world itself would not contain the books that would be written (John 21:25).

This passage is cited by Roman Catholic apologist Karl Keating in these words:

> The Bible actually denies that it is the complete rule of faith. John tells us that not everything concerning Christ's work is in Scripture (John 21:25), and Paul says that much Christian teaching is to be found in the tradition that is handed down by word of mouth (2 Timothy 2:2).[3]

Notice that Keating equates John's statement that the Bible does not record *everything Jesus did* with a denial that the Bible is the *complete rule of faith*. We again encounter the common misconception that unless something is *exhaustive* in detail it cannot be *sufficient* as a source of truth. We are not told why it is we must have an *exhaustive* accounting of everything Christ ever did or said to have a complete and sufficient rule of faith in the Scriptures. Do we need to know the color of Bartholomew's hair for the Bible to be a sufficient source of divine truth? Do we need to know the daily menu of the Apostolic meals? Do we need descriptions of the clothing worn by Judas Iscariot? Certainly not![4] It is obvious that the Bible does not need to be *exhaustive* to be *sufficient* as our source of divine truth. Instead, the Bible must provide to us *what God intends for us to have* to function in the manner described by the doctrine of *sola scriptura*.

3. *Sola scriptura is not a denial of the authority of the Church to teach God's truth.* Quite often a dichotomy is presented: one has *either* the Bible, *or* the Church, but not *both*. Many Protestants, reacting against what they see as an overemphasis on the Church in Roman Catholic theology, end up going too far in the other direction, and downplay the vital (and biblical) role the Church is given by the Lord Jesus Christ in the Scriptures. For some reason, some Protestants are

troubled by such passages as 1 Timothy 3:15, which says,

> But in case I am delayed, I write so that you will know how one ought to conduct himself in the household of God, which is the church of the living God, the pillar and support of the truth.

The description of the Church as the "pillar and support of the truth" is thoroughly biblical and proper. There is, of course, a vast difference between recognizing and confessing the Church as the pillar and support of the truth, and confessing the Church to be the final arbiter of truth itself. A pillar holds something else up, and in this case, it is the truth of God. The Church, as the body of Christ, presents and upholds the truth, *but she remains subservient to it.* The Church remains the bride of Christ, and as such, she listens obediently and intently to the words of her Lord Jesus Christ, and those words are found in Scripture itself.[5]

While Rome has gone far beyond the biblical parameters regarding the roles and functions of the Church, many Protestants have not gone nearly far enough in recognizing the divine order laid out in the New Testament. The Apostles established local churches. They chose elders and deacons, and entrusted to these the task of teaching and preaching the Gospel of Jesus Christ. Those chosen of God to minister the Word to the congregation are worthy of double honor (1 Timothy 5:17). There is no warrant for the "Lone Ranger Christian Syndrome" so popular in Protestant circles these days.

4. *Sola scriptura is not a denial that the Word of God has, at times, been spoken.* Rather, it refers to the Scriptures as serving the Church as God's final and full revelation. There is nothing in the doctrine that denies the simple reality that at times in the past God's Word was spoken (through the preaching of prophets or Apostles) as well as written.[6] It is vitally important that the reader recognize that the Protestant position insists that all God intends for us to have that is infallible, binding, and authoritative today, He has already provided in the certain, clear, understandable, and reliable Scriptures. Protestants argue for the *completeness* of the Scriptures, while many Roman Catholic apologists insist that the Bible is *not* complete in and of itself, and therefore needs supplementation, either in oral

traditions that carry further inspired revelation,[7] or in a traditional source of interpretation.

5. *Sola scriptura does not entail the rejection of every kind or form of "tradition."* There are some traditions that are God-honoring and useful in the Church. *Sola scriptura* simply means that any tradition, no matter how ancient or venerable it might seem to us, must be tested by a higher authority, and that authority is the Bible.

6. *Sola scriptura is not a denial of the role of the Holy Spirit in guiding and enlightening the Church.* The doctrine does not amount to a "muzzling" of the Holy Spirit. It recognizes that the Spirit will give us understanding in everything (2 Timothy 2:7). We are not saying that a person with a Bible, but without the Spirit, has everything he needs. No indeed. The role of the Holy Spirit in enlightening the mind and giving guidance to the understanding is inherent in the very doctrine itself.

To summarize, *sola scriptura* is *not* a

1. claim that the Bible contains all knowledge;
2. claim that the Bible is an exhaustive catalog of all religious knowledge;
3. denial of the Church's authority to teach God's truth;
4. denial that God's Word has, at times, been spoken;
5. rejection of every kind or use of tradition;
6. denial of the role of the Holy Spirit in guiding the Church.

What *Sola Scriptura* Is

1. *The doctrine of sola scriptura, simply stated, is that the Scriptures alone are sufficient to function as the regula fidei, the infallible rule of faith for the Church.* The emphasis here is on the nature of Scripture. The Scriptures are, as God-breathed revelation, sufficient to provide the "rule of faith" necessary for the Church's mission in this world. Further, the Scriptures provide an *infallible* rule of faith, one that cannot err, one not affected by personal whims, social trends, or any other outside force. While the Church faces a myriad of challenging situations over time, the Scriptures themselves do not change and therefore provide the Church with a firm foundation.

2. *All that one must believe to be a Christian is found in Scripture,*

and in no other source. This is not to say that the necessary beliefs of the faith could not be summarized in a shorter form. However, there is no necessary belief, doctrine, or dogma absolutely required of a person for entrance into the kingdom of heaven that is not found in the revelation of God in the pages of Scripture. The corollary of this positive statement is presented in the next statement.

3. *That which is not found in Scripture—either directly or by necessary implication—is not binding upon the Christian.* To be more specific, I provide the definition I used when I first defended this doctrine in public debate:

> The Bible claims to be the *sole and sufficient* infallible rule of faith for the Christian Church. The Scriptures are not in need of any supplement; their authority comes from their nature as God-breathed revelation; their authority is *not* dependent upon man, church, or council. The Scriptures are self-consistent, self-interpreting, and self-authenticating. The Christian Church looks to the Scriptures as the only infallible and sufficient rule of faith, and the Church is always subject to the Word, and is constantly reformed thereby.

The Westminster Confession of Faith, a key statement of the faith fought for in the Reformation, is entirely clear on these issues:

> The authority of the Holy Scripture, for which it ought to be believed, and obeyed, dependeth not upon the testimony of any man, or Church; but wholly upon God (who is truth itself) the author thereof: and therefore it is to be received, because it is the Word of God (1:4).

The role of the Holy Spirit is plainly presented in the next paragraph of the Confession:

> We may be moved and induced by the testimony of the Church to an high and reverent esteem of the Holy Scripture, and the heavenliness of the matter, the efficacy of the doctrine, the majesty of the style, the consent of all the parts, the scope of the whole, (which is to give all glory to God), the full discovery it makes of the only way of man's salvation, the many other incomparable excellencies, and the entire perfection thereof, are arguments whereby it doth abundantly evidence itself to be the Word of God; yet, notwithstanding, our full per-

suasion and assurance of the infallible truth, and divine authority thereof, is from the inward work of the Holy Spirit, bearing witness by and with the word in our hearts (1:5).

The heart of the doctrine of *sola scriptura* is then laid out in the next two paragraphs:

> The whole counsel of God, concerning all things necessary for His own glory, man's salvation, faith and life, is either expressly set down in Scripture, or by good and necessary consequence may be deduced from Scripture: unto which nothing at any time is to be added, whether by new revelations of the Spirit, or traditions of men. Nevertheless, we acknowledge the inward illumination of the Spirit of God to be necessary for the saving understanding of such things as are revealed in the word; and that there are some circumstances concerning the worship of God, and government of the Church, common to human actions and societies, which are to be ordered by the light of nature, and Christian prudence, according to the general rules of the word, which are always to be observed (1:6).
>
> All things in Scripture are not alike plain in themselves, nor alike clear unto all; yet those things which are necessary to be known, believed, and observed for salvation, are so clearly propounded, and opened in some place of Scripture or other, that not only the learned, but the unlearned, in a due use of the ordinary means, may attain unto a sufficient understanding of them (1:7).

4. *Scripture reveals those things necessary for salvation.* This great confession lays out the extent of the doctrine by saying that "all things necessary for His own glory, man's salvation, faith and life" that are part of the counsel of God are laid out in Scripture, either "expressly" or "by good and necessary consequence."[8]

This is not asserting that the Bible is an exhaustive catalog of *all* of known truth, as we pointed out previously. And we should be quick to note that this does not mean that the Scriptures are so simple and the truth of God so elementary that everything is to be found lying on the surface of the Scriptures.[9] Instead, "those things which are necessary to be known, believed, and observed for salvation" are to be found in Scripture so that not only the learned but the unlearned may "in a due use of the ordinary means" come to a sufficient understanding.

It is important to note this, for it is obvious that some measure of effort must be expended in reading and understanding the Scriptures, and surely many of the disagreements people have over the meaning of the Scriptures are due not to any lack of clarity in them, but to unwillingness of people to make use of these "ordinary means."

5. *All traditions are subject to the higher authority of Scripture.* We will note this truth when we examine Matthew 15:1–9, beginning on page 68.

To summarize *sola scriptura:*

1. Scripture is the sole infallible rule of faith.
2. No other revelation is needed for the Church.
3. There is no other infallible rule of faith outside of Scripture.
4. Scripture reveals those things necessary for salvation.
5. All traditions are subject to the higher authority of Scripture.

The Biblical Basis of *Sola Scriptura*

The doctrine of *sola scriptura* is based on the nature of the Scriptures as the *Word of God.* There can be no understanding of the *sufficiency* of Scripture apart from an understanding of the true *origin* and the resultant *nature* of Scripture. Indeed, one might well conclude that the de-emphasis of *sola scriptura* in Protestantism over the past century has been directly related to the frightful popularity of unbiblical views of the nature of Scripture, including the total denial of inspiration, the wholesale rejection of the concept of the supernatural in the writing and communication of the Bible, and the general lack of reverence and honor due the Word of God that is so prevalent today. Why bother defending the *sufficiency* of the Scriptures when you don't believe they are God's inspired written revelation to His people? The Reformers had the highest view of the Bible, and therefore had a solid foundation on which to stand in defending the sufficiency of the Scriptures.

Paul's Words to Timothy

The second of Paul's two epistles to Timothy contains the classic passage cited in most works regarding the definition of *sola scriptura*:

> But you remain in what you have learned and have become convinced of, knowing from whom you learned it, and that from your childhood you knew the holy Scriptures, which are able to make you wise unto salvation by faith which is in Christ Jesus. All Scripture is God-breathed, and is profitable for doctrine, for reproof, for instruction, for training in righteousness, in order that the man of God might be complete, fully equipped for every good work (2 Timothy 3:14–17, *author's translation*).

The reader will immediately recognize that the same passage is always cited when referring to the *origin and nature* of Scripture as well. This illustrates clearly the fact that the sufficiency of Scripture flows from *what Scripture is*.

Paul's words refer primarily to the Scriptures of the Old Testament, for it is obvious that Timothy would have had none of the New Testament writings at that time. Some have argued that this fact makes this passage irrelevant to any discussion of *sola scriptura*, since it speaks only to the Old Testament, and no one would wish to say that the Old Testament is wholly adequate and the New Testament is superfluous or unnecessary. However, such an objection misses the point, as the thrust of the passage is the *origin* and resultant *nature* of Scripture and its abilities, not the *extent* of the Scriptures (i.e., to the canon). That which is God-breathed is able, by its very nature, to give us the wisdom that leads to salvation through faith in Christ Jesus ("all things necessary for man's salvation") and to fully equip the "man of God" for the work of the ministry ("all things necessary for . . . faith and life"). Both sides in this dispute agree that the New Testament books are "God-breathed."[10]

Paul counsels Timothy to abide in what he has been taught, knowing from whom he learned it. The message he has received in the Gospel is to be found in the Sacred Scriptures themselves. The content of the teaching Timothy has received is identical with, not separate from, that found in the Word of God. Paul understands this, for he says that Timothy has known the "holy writings" from childhood. These would be, of course, the books of the Old Testament. Paul insists that these books "are able to make you wise unto salvation by faith which is in Christ Jesus."[11] Given that in all of Paul's writings faith in Christ Jesus is the supernatural operation of the Spirit of God, it is obvious that the character of the Scriptures themselves must differ greatly from any secular writing. These Scriptures must partake of the spiritual and be derived from the Spirit himself. And this is exactly what Paul goes on to assert in verse 16.

"All Scripture is God-breathed. . . ." The conventional translation of this passage uses the term *inspiratio*, which comes to us through the Latin. It is normally rendered "all Scripture is inspired" or "given by inspiration." However, this Latin term refers to "breathing into" something, and this is not the concept Paul is communicating at all. The Greek term[12] used here, *theopneustos*, is most expressive. It is literally translated as "*God*-breathed" (as in the NIV), and it does not refer to the idea of taking merely human words and breathing something special into them. What is more, the text says it is the *Scriptures*, not the writers themselves, that are "God-breathed." Paul is here referring to the origin of the Scriptures, and insists in the strongest terms that they come from God himself. The foundation of Scripture, the fountain of divine revelation, is God the Almighty.

The great Princeton theologian B. B. Warfield wrote a work at the end of the nineteenth century that dealt in depth with the doctrine of the inspiration of Scripture. Far from being innovative or new, Warfield's work was a response to the rising tide of liberalism that was sweeping through most Protestant denominations, resulting in a denial of the divine origin of Scripture. He was not formulating something that had not been believed before; rather, he was defending the view of Scripture held by Christians from the very beginning. Warfield's book demonstrated historically and linguistically that the texts of the New Testament claim and teach the same doctrine that he and those of the Reformed tradition believed: All Scripture comes from God and is authoritative for that single reason.

With reference to the meaning of *theopneustos*, Warfield, having written an extensive treatise on the subject, concluded,

> From all points of approach alike we appear to be conducted to the conclusion that it [*theopneustos*] is primarily expressive of the origination of Scripture, not of its nature and much less of its effects. What is *theopneustos* is "God-breathed," produced by

the creative breath of the Almighty. And Scripture is called *theopneustos* in order to designate it as "God-breathed," the product of Divine spiration, the creation of that Spirit who is in all spheres of the Divine activity the executive of the God-head. . . . What it affirms is that the Scriptures owe their origin to an activity of God the Holy Ghost and are in the highest and truest sense His creation. It is on this foundation of Divine origin that all the high attributes of Scripture are built.[13]

Paul's point should not be missed. Because of the origin of Scripture in God himself, the authority of Scripture is God's authority. You don't have different authorities in the Church: Scriptural authority over here, and God's authority over there. The authority of the Church is one: God's authority. And when God speaks in Scripture His words carry His authority.[14] They are "God-breathed." The Church is not left without the voice of God, for when the Church listens to Scripture, she is hearing her Lord speaking to her. The divine authority of the Church, then, in teaching and rebuking and instructing, is derived *from Scripture itself*, despite Roman Catholic claims to the contrary.

What is the result of this creative act of God whereby He brings the Scriptures into existence? Paul continues, ". . . and is profitable for doctrine, for reproof, for instruction, for training in righteousness, in order that the man of God might be complete, fully equipped for every good work." Verse 17 continues the thought of verse 16. The fact that the Church has God's voice always present with her in God-breathed Scripture means that the man of God might be complete, fully equipped for every good work. Though in the text he refers specifically to Timothy, I believe by extension he includes all those who belong to Christ and who are a part of His Body, the Church.

The first term to examine is the adjective translated "complete."[15] The term, according to Vine,[16] means "fitted, complete." Bauer, Arndt, Gingrich, and Danker[17] tell us the term means "complete, capable, proficient." That is, as they say, "able to meet all demands," giving the specific citation of 2 Timothy 3:17 as the reference. Louw and Nida's *Greek-English Lexicon Based on Semantic Domains* uses the term "qualified" as well.[18] I pause only long enough to note that Paul asserts that the man of God can be complete, capable, proficient, and qualified, because God's inspired Scriptures are always available to him. If another source of authority was necessary, surely Paul would have directed us to it in order that we might be complete, but he does not!

Paul was not satisfied to merely state that the man of God may be complete. He goes on to define what he means: "Fully equipped for every good work." Various lexical sources list as meanings "fit out," "to furnish completely," and "equip."[19] Most significantly we find the word "sufficient" used to define this term as well. Louw and Nida's *Greek-English Lexicon* says with reference to this term, "to make someone completely adequate or sufficient for something—to make adequate, to furnish completely, to cause to be fully qualified, adequacy."[20]

We see here, then, that Paul teaches the man of God is thoroughly or completely equipped for *every* good work. Now, what does it mean that the Scriptures are able to fully equip the man of God if not that they are *sufficient* for this task? If I am a store owner who can *fully equip* a hiker to hike the Grand Canyon—if I have the resources and abilities to provide everything he needs in the way of supplies, hiking gear, shoes, maps, food, etc.—does it not follow that I am a *sufficient* source of supply for the hiker? If he has to go next door to another shop for a few more things, and then to a third shop for some things that neither mine nor the other shop had, then none of us are *sufficient* to equip the hiker. But if that hiker can come to my shop *alone* and get everything he needs to accomplish his task, then I can rightly call myself a *sufficient* equipper of a hiker of the Grand Canyon.

In the exact same way the Scriptures are able to *fully equip* the man of God so that he is able to do *every good work*.[21] No one serving God has to search about for other sources. The inspired Scriptures are the sufficient source for a person's needs in ministry. Is there a doctrine we need to impress upon our congregation? We will find the Scriptures sufficient to provide the basis of this exhortation. Is there a temptation facing the members of our flock? The Bible will not fail in providing us the proper remedy.

We need to note how this applies to the particular situation regarding Roman Catholicism. There are doctrines that Rome teaches as divine truth that are not found in Scripture, either directly or by any logical deduction or implication. For example, Rome teaches that Mary was bodily assumed into heaven. The Roman Catholic

Church teaches that this doctrine is binding upon all Christians. Surely, if this is a divine truth, then it would be a "good work" for the man of God to preach and teach this truth, would it not? And yet the Bible does not provide even a hint of the doctrine, and does not equip the man of God to teach it. Hence, the Protestant says the doctrine is not binding upon the Christian; the Roman Catholic, having accepted the doctrine on the authority of the Roman Church, is forced to conclude the Bible is insufficient as a source of all divine truth.

The Lord Jesus on the Authority of Scripture

Before moving on to another passage that presents the sufficiency and supremacy of Scripture, we would do well to note how the Lord Jesus illustrated the truth of 2 Timothy 3:16 in His own words and ministry. When engaged in debate with the Sadducees in Matthew 22, the Lord drew their attention to a passage of Scripture in these words:

> But regarding the resurrection of the dead, have you not read what was spoken to you by God: "I am the God of Abraham, and the God of Isaac, and the God of Jacob"? He is not the God of the dead but of the living (vv. 31–32).

This passage is often cited as evidence that the Lord was willing to base an argument on the words of the text. He was assuring us that God takes care of the Scriptures and protects them from wholesale corruption, and indeed the passage does indicate this very thing. However, we should not miss the importance of the introductory phrase the Lord uses: "Have you not *read* (i.e., in the Scriptures), *What was spoken to you by God*. . .?" The Lord Jesus Christ *held his hearers accountable* for reading the Scriptures. In fact, He did not simply view these words of Scripture as something that God said *long ago* to someone else. Instead, the plain and inescapable meaning of His words informs us that in His divine and infallible opinion, what God said in the sacred text *God continues to say to this day*. People remain accountable for the words of Scripture—just as accountable as the day when God uttered the words, "I am the God of Abraham," etc. Just as His Apostle would later put it, Jesus viewed the Scriptures as "God-breathed."

Traditions and the Scriptures

Another passage that deals with the doctrine of *sola scriptura* is Matthew 15:1–9:

> Then some Pharisees and scribes came to Jesus from Jerusalem and said, "Why do Your disciples break the tradition of the elders? For they do not wash their hands when they eat bread." And He answered and said to them, "Why do you yourselves transgress the commandment of God for the sake of your tradition? For God said, 'HONOR YOUR FATHER AND MOTHER,' and, 'HE WHO SPEAKS EVIL OF FATHER OR MOTHER IS TO BE PUT TO DEATH.' But you say, 'Whoever says to *his* father or mother, "Whatever I have that would help you has been given *to God*," he is not to honor his father or his mother.' And *by this* you invalidated the word of God for the sake of your tradition. You hypocrites, rightly did Isaiah prophesy of you: 'THIS PEOPLE HONORS ME WITH THEIR LIPS, BUT THEIR HEART IS FAR AWAY FROM ME. BUT IN VAIN DO THEY WORSHIP ME, TEACHING AS DOCTRINES THE PRECEPTS OF MEN.' "

Here we find the Lord providing us with the example that we must follow. The Jewish leaders objected to the fact that the disciples did not follow the rigorous hand-washing rituals of the Pharisees. They identified this as a breaking of the *"tradition of the elders."* They firmly believed that this body of tradition was *authoritative*, and some even believed that it had been passed down from Moses himself, though this is without warrant. But does Jesus accept this claim of authority?

Not at all. Instead, He launches a counterattack against these leaders by pointing out how they nullify the command of God by their own traditions, specifically in this case with reference to the *corban* rule, whereby a man could dedicate his belongings to the Temple and not support his parents in their old age. The Lord Jesus holds this traditional teaching up to the light of Scripture and finds it wanting.

It is vital to realize that the Jews viewed the *corban* rule as part of the "tradition of the elders." To them this was a divine tradition with divine authority. They did not simply view it as a "tradition of men," but as a concept revealed by God and passed down into the body of those teachings entrusted to the elders of the faith.

The parallels to the Roman claim regarding Sacred Tradition are many. Rome claims divine authority for her Sacred Traditions, and even subjugates Scripture so as to make it a part of Sacred Tradition along with the supposedly Apostolic, unwritten traditions, and the authority of the Magisterium of the Church. Yet the person who wishes to follow the example of Christ will hold such traditions up to the light of Scripture, knowing how fearful it is to be found guilty of nullifying the Word of God for the sake of mere human traditions. The Lord Jesus subjugated even this allegedly "divine tradition" to the supreme authority, the Scriptures. This is vitally important, for the most common response to the citation of this passage with reference to Roman tradition is, "Well, the passage refers to testing human traditions, not divine traditions." Yet, when it comes to authority, *any* tradition, no matter what its alleged pedigree, is to be tested by the known standard, the Holy Scriptures.

Having explained the doctrine and its basis,[22] we now turn to the difficult task of figuring out the many different Roman Catholic viewpoints on these issues.

6

THE THOUSAND TRADITIONS

One of the great ironies in dealing with the Roman Catholic rejection of *sola scriptura* and the corresponding positive claim of "Sacred Tradition" involves the oft-repeated claim that the Scriptures are liable to many interpretations and therefore we need a clear, defining voice to cut through the confusion and make the truth manifest. What makes the claim ironic is that most of the time the statements of Rome are not only equally as liable to various interpretations, but often *more* liable. There are many passages in the Scriptures that are *much* simpler and easier to understand than some of the explanations put forth by the Roman authorities. Even on the issue of tradition itself there are a thousand "traditions," a thousand different ways of understanding the "final" word on the matter.

The Council of Trent has been called the great "Counter-Reformation Council." Trent's dogmatic canons and decrees defined the Roman response to the Reformation in no uncertain terms. Despite what many modern Roman Catholics believe, Trent's words and teachings remain fully binding on them today. Not only did Vatican I and Vatican II reiterate and verify the authority and teaching of Trent, but one often finds the new *Catholic Catechism* drawing from it as well. With reference to the relationship of Scripture and tradition, Trent said in the *Decree Concerning the Canonical Scriptures* (Fourth Session):

> It also clearly perceives that these truths and rules are contained in the written books and in the unwritten traditions which, received by the Apostles, from the mouth of Christ him-

self, or from the Apostles themselves, the Holy Ghost dictating, have come down to us, transmitted as it were from hand to hand. Following then, the examples of the orthodox fathers, it receives and venerates with a feeling of piety and reverence all the books both of the Old and New Testaments, since one God is the author of both; also the traditions, whether they relate to faith or to morals, as having been dictated either orally by Christ or by the Holy Ghost, and preserved in the Catholic Church in unbroken succession.

The meaning of these words would *seem* to be rather straightforward. However, as we will see, controversy surrounds some of the phrases, with differing and contradictory views derived from the very same words. Before looking into this, let us note some modern dogmatic statements from Rome regarding the same issue. Because some feel Trent is outdated, it is necessary to make sure the modern Roman Church is saying the same things. The second great Vatican Council, Vatican II, which opened in 1962, produced a number of important documents. One of these, *Dei Verbum*, the *Dogmatic Constitution on Divine Revelation* (November 18, 1965), is vitally important for our purposes here. In the Prologue, the council indicates that this document sets forth the "authentic teaching about divine revelation and about how it is handed on." It will not do to relegate most of this document's statements to endnotes. Instead, I have compiled a conflation of citations from this important source in the hopes that the intention and teaching of the Roman Catholic faith at this point is both forcefully and accurately represented. It is material worth reading carefully.

(8) This tradition, which comes from the apostles, develops in the Church with the help of the Holy Spirit. . . . Through the same tradition the Church's full canon of the sacred books is known, and the sacred writings themselves are more profoundly understood and unceasingly made active in her. . . . (9) Hence there exists a close connection and communication between Sacred Tradition and Sacred Scripture. For both of them, flowing from the same divine wellspring, in a certain way merge into a unity and tend toward the same end. For Sacred Scripture is the word of God inasmuch as it is consigned to writing under the inspiration of the divine Spirit. To the successors of the apostles, Sacred Tradition hands on in its full purity God's word,

which was entrusted to the apostles by Christ the Lord and the Holy Spirit. Thus, led by the light of the Spirit of truth, these successors can in their preaching preserve this word of God faithfully, explain it, and make it more widely known. Consequently, it is not from Sacred Scripture alone that the Church draws her certainty about everything that has been revealed.[1] Therefore both Sacred Tradition and Sacred Scripture are to be accepted and venerated with the same sense of devotion and reverence. (10) Sacred Tradition and Sacred Scripture form one sacred deposit of the word of God, which is committed to the Church. . . . The task of authentically interpreting the word of God, whether written or handed on, has been entrusted exclusively to the living teaching office of the Church, whose authority is exercised in the name of Jesus Christ.[2] It is clear, therefore, that Sacred Tradition, Sacred Scripture, and the teaching authority of the Church, in accordance with God's most wise design, are so linked and joined together that one cannot stand without the others and that all together and each in its own way, under the action of the Holy Spirit, contribute effectively to the salvation of souls. . . . (12) For all of what has been said about the way of interpreting Scripture is subject finally to the judgment of the Church, which carries out the divine commission and ministry of guarding and interpreting the word of God. . . . (21) She has always regarded the Scriptures together with Sacred Tradition, as the supreme rule of faith and will ever do so. . . . (24) Sacred theology rests on the written word of God, together with Sacred Tradition as its primary and perpetual foundation.

The careful reader will readily see the vitally important statements and how consistent the document is in making close distinctions. First, we are told that the tradition that comes from the Apostles "develops in the Church with the help of the Holy Spirit." Obviously, if this tradition develops over time, then we are referring here to something *extrascriptural*, for the Scriptures are in no way "developing," even if our understanding of them increases. According to Rome, it is through this tradition the canon may be known, and the Scriptures themselves are "more profoundly understood." Again, the *extrascriptural* aspect of this tradition is plain. While a close connection is taught, the distinction is maintained throughout. This tradition makes possible the handing on of the Word of God in purity, which would lead us to believe that *without* this tradition, the Word of God would be impure. Vatican II then states plainly that the Roman Catholic Church does not depend *solely* upon the Scriptures for "her certainty about everything which has been revealed" because it is Scripture plus tradition that makes up the "one sacred deposit of the Word of God."

This sacred deposit, then, is entrusted to the Church, so that only the Church can handle the task of "authentically interpreting the Word of God, whether written or handed on." This is extremely important, for not only is Rome claiming the exclusive right of interpretation of the Scriptures but the exclusive right of both definition and interpretation of tradition, as well. When we ask to see the contents of tradition, we have to depend upon the veracity of the same Church that bases her doctrines (including her claim to interpretive authority) on those very traditions! This leads to the problem of circular reasoning that we discussed in Chapter 4. Because Rome defines tradition itself, you have "Scripture and Church," not "Scripture and tradition." In fact, Vatican II directly states, "Sacred Tradition, Sacred Scripture, and the teaching authority of the Church . . . are so linked and joined together that one cannot stand without the others."

Here is the "three-part" view of authority found so often in Roman Catholic writings: the Scriptures, tradition, and the Magisterium (the Church's teaching power). Since the Magisterium defines the extent of the Scriptures (by defining the canon), claims sole right of interpretation of the Scriptures, tells us what is and what is not tradition, and defines doctrines on the basis of this self-defined tradition, in reality we see that the only one of the three "legs" of this system that is not defined by one of the others is the Magisterium itself. Because of this fact, the reasoning behind the often repeated Protestant assertion that the Scriptures are not the ultimate authority in Roman Catholic teaching is clear. While Rome loudly proclaims her fidelity to the Scriptures and insists that the Church is *subject to* the Scriptures, she at the same time makes statements that plainly elevate her own Magisterium to the highest position of authority.[3] When Vatican II states that the Roman Catholic Church "has always regarded the Scriptures together with Sacred Tradition as the supreme rule of faith and will ever do so," the claim rings a bit hollow upon examination. Because the Catholic Church claims no one else can properly interpret those Scriptures, and she herself claims to be the sole guardian of "Sacred Tradition," no external checks and balances exist that could correct her should she err. It is less than helpful to say that Rome has a "supreme rule of faith" when in fact that rule of faith does not exist outside of her own realm of authority. The Roman Catholic Church defines and interprets the rule as she sees fit.

The newly released *Catholic Catechism–1994* provides the same viewpoint, frequently citing from the very same passages quoted above. Section 76 of the *Catechism* says that the Gospel is handed on in two ways: orally and in writing. This "apostolic preaching" is "continued in apostolic succession." Section 77 says that "the apostolic preaching, which is expressed in a special way in the inspired books, was to be preserved in a continuous line of succession until the end of time." This leads us to section 78, which specifically makes the claim, "This living transmission, accomplished in the Holy Spirit, is called tradition, since it is distinct from Sacred Scripture, though closely connected to it." The *Catechism* then quotes at length from the same passages cited above from Vatican II, and then moves on to distinguish the tradition under discussion from "the various theological, disciplinary, liturgical, or devotional traditions, born in the local churches over time."[4] These types of lesser traditions may be changed over time "under the guidance of the Church's Magisterium" (section 83). Note again how the definition of what is and what is not real tradition is left up to the Magisterium. The *depositum fidei*, the "sacred deposit," made up of "Sacred Scripture and tradition," is then entrusted to the whole Church (section 84), with section 85 repeating Vatican II's claims regarding Rome's exclusive right of interpretation of this deposit. Sensing what such a claim means, section 86 is quick to assert:

> (86) Yet this Magisterium is not superior to the word of God, but its servant. It teaches only what has been handed on to it. At the divine command and with the help of the Holy Spirit, it listens to this devotedly, guards it with dedication, and expounds it faithfully. All that it proposes for belief as being divinely revealed is drawn from this single deposit of faith.

And so we conclude our review of these *official* statements from the Roman perspective with Rome's own claim to be in subjection to the Word of God. She says she is only teaching what has been handed on to her. I believe a review of such doctrines as the Immaculate Conception, the Bodily Assumption of Mary, and Papal Infallibility will demonstrate that this is not a true claim at all. Such doctrines were not "handed on" by the Apostles, and they were unknown to the early Christians. It is obvious that Rome has drawn from tradition doctrines that are not Apostolic. Thus, we must question the validity of the above statement and insist that the Magisterium, by its own teachings, cannot logically maintain that it is a servant of the Word of God. Given the claims the Magisterium makes concerning its position and authority, it is not logically possible for it to take any other position than "overseer" of the Sacred Scriptures, a position that demands a superior authority than that vested in the Bible itself.

Differing Viewpoints

Despite the fact that the preceding citations *seem* rather clear, as with any written communication there are differences of understanding expressed within the broad spectrum that makes up Roman Catholicism. In fact, the two primary positions set forth regarding the nature, extent, and authority of tradition are, logically speaking, mutually exclusive. Yet they exist side by side in Roman Catholic theology. One of the great ironies of this entire conflict is that while Rome claims ultimate authority in teaching and interpretation of divine truths, and while her defenders constantly point to the "doctrinal chaos" that exists in denominations that hold to *sola scriptura*, she allows her followers to hold to perspectives completely at odds with each other on points as basic as the extent and authority of tradition itself.[5]

It should be remembered that *both views deny sola scriptura*. Neither view affirms the sufficiency of Scripture that I have outlined in the previous pages. In fact, the second view, though it may sound a little *closer* to the truth, does not, in fact, come close to affirming the truth about the Bible. In many ways it is more difficult to discuss and expose than the first.

Roman theology speaks with two voices concerning the concept of the sufficiency or insufficiency of Scripture. The older and, I believe, far louder voice advocates the traditional concept of two "modes" or "sources" of revelation: Scripture and oral tradition. In this concept the oral traditions *actually exist*; that is, there are oral traditions that were passed on to the successors of the Apostles long ago. These traditions have been guarded and passed down through the episcopate to this day. The term "Apostolic tradition" has meaning in this viewpoint, as it is believed that there is a real substance, a real existence, to these traditions. They are identifiable things that existed in history. This perspective is expressed clearly in the first draft of the decree on the Scriptures issued by the Council of Trent, which said that revelation is passed on "partly in written books, partly in unwritten traditions."

This viewpoint, which we will call the *partim-partim* view (*partim* being Latin for "partly"), teaches that *part* of God's revelation is found in Scripture, *but not all of it*, and *part* of God's revelation is found in the oral traditions, *but not all of it*. In order to have all that God intends you to have, you must have *both*. One separated from the other will only lead you to chaos and confusion. Those who hold to this view would say the Bible is "materially insufficient," for all of those truths God has revealed and desires us to have are *not* found in the Bible *alone*. The New Catholic Encyclopedia says regarding this view:

> A generation after the council some of the leading theologians who retained this teaching were Melchior Cano, OP (*De locis theologicis*, 1563), St. Peter Canisius, SJ (*Catechism*, 1555), St. Robert Bellarmine, SJ (*De controversiis*, 1586). In a series of articles (Greg, 1959–61) H. Lennerz, SJ, vigorously defended the *partim . . . partim* theory and opposed it to the Protestant "scripturistic principle." Neither tradition nor Scripture contains the whole Apostolic tradition. Scripture is materially (i.e., in content) insufficient, requiring oral tradition as a complement to be true to the whole divine revelation.[6]

The final version of the decree from the Council of Trent reflected the protest of the minority of participants, for instead of directly asserting the *partim-partim* terminology, it reads, "contained in the written books and in the unwritten traditions," a rendering that allows one to interpret the Council as teaching the *partim-partim* viewpoint, but does not *demand* it. The document still affirms that these unwritten traditions were passed down from the Apostles, were dictated by the Holy Spirit, and are to be the object of veneration in the Church.

In many ways this viewpoint is the easiest to deal with from a Protestant perspective. It is the most straightforward and clear. The traditions can be dealt with biblically and historically. The Roman Catholic who holds this perspective will cite various passages of the Bible (such as 2 Thessalonians 2:15) that refer to oral traditions, and will assert that the Bible is referring to this concept of extrabiblical, revelational traditions that we must hold to in order to have everything God intended for the Church. It is the boldest of the two positions, for it is actually saying that the traditions that have been made into dogmas—such as the Bodily Assumption of Mary or Papal Infallibility—are actually Apostolic in origin and historical in nature.

This *partim-partim* viewpoint carries with it insurmountable problems. Aside from the fact that the passages cited from the Bible do not support the entire concept of extrabiblical revelation in the form of oral traditions (see chart on page 80), the Roman apologist cannot demonstrate the existence of this kind of tradition in history. The novel concepts that have been made dogma in later years were not in any way a part of the record of the early Church. Though Roman Catholic historians view the writings of the early Fathers as a witness to this tradition, those writings present the single most telling objection to this theory concerning the oral traditions. It is not possible to defend the idea that such doctrines are directly, actually, historically, *Apostolic* in origin.

The Material Sufficiency View

The second viewpoint put forth by Roman Catholics does not have to deal with this kind of historic criticism, since it is not nearly as bold in its claims. Instead, it affirms the *material sufficiency* of the Bible. These theologians assert that divine revelation is contained entirely in Scripture and entirely in tradition, *totum in Scriptura, totum in traditione*. It is vital to immediately point out that these Roman Catholic theologians are *not* affirming *sola scriptura*. Instead, they are saying that all of divine revelation can be found, *if only implicitly*, in Scripture. That means that such doctrines as the Immaculate Conception, the Bodily Assumption of Mary, and Papal Infallibility are, from this perspective, *implicitly* found in Scripture. There is a passage here, a phrase there, that, *when viewed in light of the teaching of the Church*, might lead one to believe in these doctrines.

This second viewpoint involves a different view of tradition itself. For most who take this perspective, tradition becomes a framework, a system of interpretation, rather than concrete revelational material that can be examined and found in historical sources. The tradition can be as solid as Apostolic *interpretations* of the Bible or as nebulous as a general concept of the understanding of the Church over time. Different authors give different spins to the concept. But in any case, the oral tradition does not contain any revelation that is not to be found, *at least implicitly*, in the Scriptures.[7]

While it may appear that this alternate viewpoint is not as objectionable as the first, in reality little is gained by embracing this view outside of an apologetic advantage. Surely it is easier to present a rather nebulous concept of tradition without the inherent difficulties of claiming a real, historical origin with the Apostles. Those who hold to the "development thesis" that was put forward most clearly by Cardinal Newman, the celebrated convert to Roman Catholicism, will naturally follow his lead in holding to this second view of tradition and the "material sufficiency" of Scripture. Newman, one of the leading scholars of the Roman Catholic Church of the last century, gladly admitted that many Roman Catholic doctrines (including the Papacy) were not present in their full form in the early history of the Church. Instead, these doctrines were present as a seed is present in the soil, so that through the process of time they can be seen growing and developing into their modern forms. In the same way, tradition becomes something that grows and changes as well. Rather than the static boundaries set by the older viewpoint (the traditions come from the Apostles and are guarded—unchanged—by the Church), this second perspective allows for the explanation of some of the more radical developments in Roman Catholic doctrine and practice over time. Tradition becomes a sort of theological putty, a moldable material that can fit into the parameters of a changing and evolving theological system.

The most dangerous aspect of this perspective is that its adherents are saying almost nothing different than those who hold to the *partim-partim* view, at least as far as it concerns *sola scriptura*. It just *sounds* as though they are.[8] The end result is the same: they deny the sole sufficiency of Scripture, and in its place establish an authoritarian system that has no means of self-correction. Since there is no *external* and *unchanging* rule of faith for the Roman Catholic Church, then there is no real means of reformation when she goes astray in doctrinal matters. Surely throughout Roman Catholic history there have been reformations where certain problems were addressed (such as the abuse of indulgences for profit at the time of the Reformation). Yet, theologically, once Rome has defined a doctrine, there is no way of going back and undoing a proclamation. There is no means of correcting past errors because Rome views herself as infallible and the Scriptures as either materially insufficient or as simply one part of a broader "Sacred Tradition." Let's summarize:

Partim-Partim Viewpoint	Material Sufficiency Viewpoint
Oral tradition is a separate and different revelation	Oral tradition does not contain other revelation
Oral tradition is necessary, in-spired revelation	Oral tradition is necessary for proper interpretation
The Bible is materially insuffi-cient	The Bible is materially sufficient

Both viewpoints on tradition boil down to an argument not for "Scripture plus tradition" but for "Scripture as taught by the Church." In both cases tradition is defined and revealed by the Church alone. It cannot be said, even in the first viewpoint, that tradition exists separately from the Roman Catholic Church, its guardian and protector. Therefore, tradition functionally becomes in *both* systems another word for the teaching of the Church, so that the Church's teaching authority becomes supreme over *both* Scripture and tradition. When all the smoke is cleared and all the fancy words are reduced to their simplest form, Protestants believe in *sola scriptura* and Catholics believe in *sola ecclesia*, the Church alone. And when the special claims of Rome are mixed in, the best description of the resultant position is *sola Roma*.

What About "Development"?

We come now to consider the issue of the "development of doctrine." John Henry Cardinal Newman wrote *An Essay on the Devel-*

opment of Christian Doctrine. This concept of the development of doctrine over time was central to Newman's thought and to his apologetic for many of the distinctive Roman Catholic beliefs. Karl Keating devotes an entire chapter to the subject in his defense of Catholicism,[9] following closely on the heels of Newman's views.

Much of the material produced in modern times that is designed to share the biblical Gospel with Roman Catholics falls far short of properly addressing the issue of the "development of doctrine." A common view among evangelicals is that "any and all development is wrong, and is probably the work of Satan rather than the work of God by His Spirit." Some of this attitude comes from not knowing anything at all about the writings of the early Church or the opinions and views of those men we call the "Fathers" of the Christian Church.

The Roman Catholic position is basically this: God has given His revelation in Jesus Christ. Revelation, in the scriptural sense, has ceased. The canon of Scripture is complete and not open for further additions. However, God has promised certain things to the Church. The Spirit is her guide, and the leadership of the Church, the Magisterium, has the Apostolic authority to teach the truth about the Christian faith. Over time, as questions arise, the Magisterium is guided in its answers to these questions. Frequently, the questions are more than simple. They are outright heresies, such as that of Arius in the fourth century. Arius denied the deity of Christ, and he began teaching his heretical views to anyone who would listen. Prior to this, no one had been forced to specifically address the issues that Arius was presenting. This does not mean that prior to Arius no one believed in the deity of Christ, for they most certainly did, but since it was not the burning issue of the day, exact formulations of the doctrine were not needed. The more exact formulations that arose to combat heresy were not new doctrines or new revelations, but simply developments and explanations of previously held beliefs. Nothing new is added by this clarification process. The foundations were there from the very beginning in the revelation of God. But the further development of those basic building blocks took time. For some concepts, especially the Marian doctrines, it took millennia.

There is much about this Roman view that is correct. The example of Arius speaks the truth despite the fact that it is certainly not demonstrable that the Church of the days of Athanasius (bishop of Alexandria, defender of orthodoxy) can in any way be said to be identical to, or even closely related to, modern Roman Catholicism. As time passed, questions about the Christian faith arose that required answers, and many times those answers required new and original thinking on the "once-for-all-delivered-to-the-saints faith" of which Jude speaks (Jude 3). As the Gospel spread out into the world, it encountered new cultures and new philosophies. These people asked questions that were not directly addressed in the Holy Scriptures. The Greeks asked questions, and though some of these questions are addressed by Paul in his epistles, others are not. The early Fathers felt it was proper to answer those questions, and they did not feel that they had to limit themselves solely to the language of Scripture. When a Greek asked a question couched in Greek philosophical language, men such as Justin Martyr answered the question—in Greek philosophical language, so that the person who asked could understand the answer. We may rightly assert that Justin and others went too far and became enamored with Greek philosophy at the expense of the biblical revelation. But the point is this: over the years Christian men and women have thought upon the revelation of God, and under the influence of the Spirit of God they have gained insight into the truths contained in Scripture. This is the proper development of doctrine.

Though it may seem surprising to some, in many aspects the Christian scholar of today is closer to the original writings of the Apostles than people who lived as little as two centuries later. Why is this true? First, we have ready access to not only the entire Bible but to many of the secular writings of the day that give us important historical, cultural, or linguistic information. We have the Bible available to us in the original tongues (the vast majority of the early Church Fathers, for example, were not able to read both Hebrew and Greek, and many in the Western Church could not read either one!) as well as many excellent translations. We also have access to a vast amount of writing from earlier generations. We can read the works of men like Spurgeon or Warfield or Hodge or Machen and glean insights from these great men of God that were not available in years past. While a person living in the sixth century might have been chronologically closer to the time of Paul, he would not have had nearly as much opportunity to study the writings of Paul as we have today. We can include in our studies the historical backgrounds of the cities to which Paul was writing; we can read his letters in their original Greek. Today we can sit at a computer and with the click of the mouse have it list all the aorist passive participles in the letter to the Romans (there are 18)! These advantages allow us to be far more biblical in our teaching and doctrine.

Real Development of Doctrine

So we agree with Rome that doctrine does develop. But we strongly disagree about *how* it develops. For the Roman Catholic Church, the guiding force in development is the teaching Magisterium of the Church itself. The Magisterium claims full interpretive control over the Bible, and because it is the sole guide to the development of doctrine, it can steer its own course. Historically, this is just what happened. Many doctrinal formulations that Rome claims "developed" over time, which Protestants point out are not only nonbiblical but downright antibiblical, came about as a result of a process—that is granted. But it was not a process of the development *of* Christian doctrine but rather a process of slowly departing *from* Christian doctrine.

We said earlier that development does indeed take place. And what is the guiding factor? The guiding factor for development of Christian doctrine is the Bible itself! The text of Scripture provides the grounds, and most importantly, *the limits* for this development over time. Rather than bringing in outside influences such as Roman tradition, Protestants recognize that no one has ever plumbed the depths of the revelation of God contained in the Bible. No one has ever come close to exhausting what is to be found in the pages of the Scriptures, which the writer of Hebrews called "living" (Hebrews 4:12). Therefore, real development of Christian doctrine is simply the ever-increasing understanding of the Word of God. It involves the recognition of how one passage is related to another, one truth to another. When Christian scholars discover more and more about the languages of the Bible, the meanings of words, the forms of expression, this brings about development of our understanding, and thus the further definition of doctrine. On the spiritual level, it comes about through the Spirit's illumination of men and women of God who humbly submit themselves to the authority of the Bible.

The example of Arius cited earlier points this out. Anyone who has read the treatises of Athanasius or Augustine concerning the Trinity and the deity of Christ knows that these men used the Scriptures as their sole source. They exegeted passages from the Bible, showing how their opponents' position was inconsistent with the entirety of the biblical revelation. And this process has continued to this day. For example, in the late eighteenth century a man by the name of Granville Sharp formulated a rule of Greek grammar that today bears his name: "Granville Sharp's Rule." (Greek grammarians are not known for creativity in naming rules.) This rule states that if you have two nouns, the first with an article before it, the second without, and they are connected by the word "and," both nouns are describing the same person.

What is the significance of this? Titus 2:13 contains a "Granville Sharp" construction. Since this rule was recognized as being valid for the Greek language after the translation of the King James Version, those translators did not follow the rule. They were more influenced by the Latin and translated the verse as follows: "Looking for that blessed hope, and the glorious appearing of the great God and our Saviour Jesus Christ." Now, it's not that the translation is *wrong*. It's just not as *clear* as it could be. One could misconstrue the text to be differentiating between the terms "God" and "Savior." But when Granville Sharp's rule is taken into account, the rendering is much clearer: "Looking for the blessed hope and the glorious appearing of our great God and Savior, Jesus Christ." Therefore, the recognition of this rule of Greek grammar has increased our understanding of the doctrine of the deity of Jesus Christ, for here Paul readily equates the term "God" with the Lord Jesus. This is true, biblically based development that is guided not by a group of men claiming Apostolic authority, but by the text of Scripture itself.

Another example is the Atonement of Christ. History tells us that the early Fathers had some very interesting views of the Atonement. Hardly one agreed with another on the subject. Their writings, however, show a great lack of clarity on the whole council of God on the matter, and consistent, in-depth exegesis of the relevant passages is lacking in many patristic sources. Part of this may be due to the extensive energy and time that was spent in defending the doctrine of Christ's Person rather than His work. Whatever the reason, some completely nonbiblical doctrines regarding the nature of the Atonement have been popular in the past and continue to this day. Yet as those committed solely to the authority of the Word of God have studied the Bible's teaching on the subject, many of the false impressions that have been prevalent in the past have been put aside, and the truth of the atoning work of Christ is much more readily available to someone today than it was only four centuries ago. This, again, is proper doctrinal development. It is not change, for the limitations of the proper use of development are set by the very words of Scripture itself. It is not an imposition of external concepts or authorities on the teaching of the Bible, as we see in Roman doctrine. Rather, it is a digging ever deeper into the revelation of God, a prayerful seeking of His guidance and direction.

We cannot emphasize enough the importance of the guiding principle in doctrinal development and how it differs between the Roman view and the Protestant view. From Rome's view, the guiding principle is the Church itself—how else could it be? The Bible is not a safe guide, Roman leaders tell us, and it is not complete in itself. Sacred Tradition must be allowed to speak as well. But through whom does it speak? The Magisterium of Rome? How could the Bible define the boundaries of development if it is not a complete, sufficient revelation? We have already discussed the sufficiency of Scripture and will not go back to it now. It is clear from Rome's perspective, given what she teaches about the Bible, that the Protestant concept of a biblically defined realm of doctrinal development is not logical or possible. But when one rejects Rome's concept of revelation and her claims over the interpretation of Scripture, the concept of a continuing process of study and enlightenment based upon God's Word is not only logical but beautiful.

In conclusion, we see that when Roman apologists use the concept of doctrinal development as a defense for the various teachings of Rome, they are using a true principle incorrectly. One cannot speak of doctrinal development when attempting to defend the Marian doctrines, for example, or the concept of Papal Infallibility. They are not developments based upon a further study of the Bible but a departure from Scripture based upon exterior sources of authority.

7

SOLA SCRIPTURA VS. SACRED TRADITION

We now have an idea of what *sola scriptura* is, and what the Roman Catholic position on Sacred Tradition is. How do we settle the issue? In this chapter we will examine some of the more popular arguments presented by Rome in defense of her own position, and in denial of *sola scriptura*.

An Apology for This Chapter

I want to point out that I use the term "apology" here in the classical sense of a "defense," not an expression of regret. Why should we take the time to work through the arguments concerning this topic? Isn't it enough to define the two positions and get on with our discussion of the Gospel? Some might think so. But if you have listened to the words of those who are going into Roman Catholicism from evangelical churches these days, you will realize how vitally important it is to honestly and directly face the challenges presented by Rome. A few examples will suffice to illustrate my point.

Scott Hahn is one of the most celebrated converts to Roman Catholicism in quite a while. A graduate of Gordon-Conwell Seminary and formerly a staunch Presbyterian, Hahn is an exceptionally bright man with a tremendous ability to persuade and convince. The story of his conversion, *Rome Sweet Home*, has found a niche in the Roman Catholic community as a warmhearted if less than theologically convincing testimonial to the attracting power of "Sacred Tradition." I first met Scott Hahn when I debated a friend of his, Gerald Matatics, in Phoenix in December of 1990. I had heard the story of his conversion on cassette tape. This tape has been widely distributed, judging by the number of people I have met who also have heard his story.

As with so many other converts to Roman Catholicism, he claims he could not find any basis for *sola scriptura* in the Bible. In his book he recounts one of the events that began his trek toward Rome. During a church history class he was teaching, a student asked him, "Where does the Bible teach that 'Scripture alone' is our sole authority?" The conversation that followed is most revealing:

> I looked at him and broke into a cold sweat. I had never heard that question before. In seminary I had a reputation for being a sort of Socratic gadfly, always asking the toughest questions, but this one had never occurred to me.
>
> I said what any professor caught unprepared would say, "What a dumb question!" As soon as the words left my mouth, I stopped dead in my tracks, because I'd sworn that, as a teacher, I would never say those words.
>
> But the student was not intimidated—he knew it wasn't a dumb question. He looked me right in the eye and said, "Just give me a dumb answer."
>
> I said, "First, we would go to Matthew 5:17. Then we would look at 2 Timothy 3:16–17, 'All Scripture is inspired by God and profitable for teaching, for reproof, for correction and for training in righteousness that the man of God may be complete, equipped for every good work.' And we'd look at what Jesus says about tradition in Matthew 15."
>
> His response was penetrating. "But, Professor, Jesus wasn't condemning all tradition in Matthew 15, but rather corrupt tradition. When 2 Timothy 3:16 says 'all Scripture,' it doesn't say that 'only Scripture' is profitable. Prayer, evangelizing, and many other things are also essential. And what about 2 Thessalonians 2:15?"
>
> "Yeah, 2 Thessalonians 2:15," I said weakly. "What does that say again?"[1]

Hahn goes on to relate how he got off the hook with the student, but afterward he was deeply troubled by the conversation. "Lord, what's happening? Where *does* Scripture teach *sola scriptura*?" he records himself saying that night. As a result he recalls, "There were

two pillars[2] on which Protestants based their revolt against Rome—
one had already fallen, the other was shaking. I was scared."

Scott Hahn then represents nameless scholars and theologians as
being utterly unprepared to even begin to present a discussion of
sola scriptura, let alone a defense of it. He later discusses a meeting
with the great Reformed theologian John Gerstner in which he again
does not receive a satisfying answer.[3]

Hahn is not alone. Tim Staples is a former Baptist who presently
crisscrosses the land giving seminars in defense of Roman Catholic
teaching. His story, too, is filled with references to his being out-
debated by a Roman Catholic on the topic of *sola scriptura*.[4] One of
the areas we will discuss next is the canon of Scripture. Staples reports that he could not respond to his Roman Catholic friend on the
issue of the canon, and he had to admit that he was trusting in the
witness of the Church regarding the very inspiration of Scripture.
His friend's assertions against the ultimate authority of Scripture are
presented as plain facts, and it is obvious Staples had no reply.

The list could go on for quite some time. One compilation of
eleven testimonials of converts to Roman Catholicism presents arguments against *sola scriptura* in no less than eight of the eleven stories.[5] It is obvious that an answer needs to be given, so we will now
examine some of the common arguments presented against the sufficiency of Scripture as the sole infallible rule of faith for the Church.

Doctrinal Chaos Revisited

We are now in a position to revisit the argument that is often
proposed by Roman Catholic apologists regarding the idea that *sola
scriptura* can't possibly be true for the simple reason that "it doesn't
work." They say that God could not have designed His Church to
function in the mire of consistent confusion that is evidenced by
Protestantism. The Bible simply isn't *clear enough* to do what Protestants want it to do.

How should we respond to this argument, which is finding many
a listening ear in our world today? First, it is an inconsistent argument. It refutes the position of the one using it. It presupposes the
idea that if (in the case of Protestantism) the Scriptures are meant to
be the sole infallible rule of faith for the Church, then it follows that
the Scriptures will produce an external, visible unity of doctrine on

all fronts. I say this is an inconsistent argument because the solution offered to us by Rome—namely, the teaching Magisterium of the Roman Catholic Church, replete with oral tradition and Papal Infallibility—has not brought about the desired unity even among Roman Catholics. I have spoken with and corresponded with Roman Catholics—individuals actively involved in their parishes, regular attendees at Mass, etc., who have held to a *wide* range of beliefs on a *wide* range of topics. I've been witness to debates between Catholics on canon laws, excommunications, Father Feeney,[6] and other subjects that rival any debates I've seen among Protestants, and that doesn't include the liberal wing of the Roman Church! If *sola scriptura* is disproven by the resultant disagreements among people outside of Rome, then Roman claims regarding the Magisterium are equally disproven by the same argument.

Dr. Cornelius Van Til often commented on the errors of Rome regarding their view of man,[7] and how these errors impacted every aspect of their theology, and he was quite right. Rome's view of man leads her to overlook what is a very fundamental issue. Let me give you an illustration: Let's suppose someone writes the *perfect* textbook on logic. It is clear and easy to understand. It is fully illustrated, completely consistent, and it provides answers to all the tough questions in plain, understandable terminology. It covers all the bases. Now, would it follow that every person who consulted this textbook would agree with every other person who also consulted this textbook on matters of logic? Of course not. Some folks might read only one chapter. Others might read too quickly and not pay close attention to the author's fine explanations. Others might have read other less-well-written textbooks, and they might import their understandings into the words of the perfect textbook, resulting in misunderstandings. It is possible people might lack the mental capacity to follow all the arguments, no matter how well they are expressed. Folks end up clueless about the subject, despite having read the entire work.

Now the question I ask is this: Is there something wrong with the textbook if it does not produce complete unanimity on questions of logic? Is the problem in the *textbook* or in the people *using* the textbook? In the real world it is often a combination of both: a lack of clarity on the part of the textbook and a problem in understanding or comprehension on the part of the reader. But if the perfect textbook existed, would it result in absolute unanimity of opinion? No, because any textbook must be read, interpreted, and understood.

The Bible is absolutely clear in the sense that the Westminster Confession states: "Those things which are necessary to be known, believed and observed for salvation, are so clearly propounded and opened in some place of Scripture or other, that not only the learned, but the unlearned, in a due use of the ordinary means, may attain to a sufficient understanding of them." Does it follow, then, that there must be a unanimity of opinion on infant baptism? Does the above statement of the Confession even say that there will be a unanimity of opinion on the items that "are necessary to be known, believed, and observed for salvation"? No, it does not. And why not? Because people—sinful people, people with agendas, people who want to find something in the Bible that isn't really there—approach Scripture, and no matter how perfect it is, *people are fallible.*

Now, Roman apologists may well say, "See, you've proven our point! You need an infallible interpreter to tell you what the Bible says because you are a sinful person, and you need a sinless, perfect guide to tell you what to believe!" Aside from the fact that such a concept is absent from Scripture, and is in fact countermanded by Scripture (did not the Lord Jesus hold men accountable for what God said to *them* in Scripture?), we need to observe that Rome has hardly solved the problem of fallible people. Once Rome speaks, the fallible person must still interpret the supposed infallible interpretation. As noted in the previous chapter, the element of error remains, no matter how much Rome may think it has been removed. Indeed, beyond the problem of interpreting the infallible interpreter, you still have the fallible decision of following *Rome's* claimed absolute authority rather than Brooklyn's, or Salt Lake City's, or Mecca's, or whoever's. That remains a *fallible* decision, and the longing for those infallible fuzzies that come from turning your responsibilities over to an infallible guide remain as unfulfilled as ever.

Finally, the argument put forth is even more pernicious because it attacks the sufficiency of Scripture itself. It implies that the Holy Spirit did such a poor job of inspiring and producing Scripture that although the Psalmist thought God's Word was a lamp to his feet and a light to his path, he (the Psalmist) was in fact quite deluded, and was treading dangerous ground. Instead of the glorious words of God spoken of in Psalm 119, we are told that such basic truths as the nature of God, including the deity of Christ or the personality of the Holy Spirit, *cannot* be derived solely from Scripture but require external witnesses.

Lest the reader think I am being harsh, I offer two representative citations, the first from a popular Roman Catholic writer, John O'Brien, author of a widely read work titled *The Faith of Millions*. In an earlier pamphlet titled "Finding Christ's Church," he wrote, "Great as is our reverence for the Bible, reason and experience compel us to say that it alone is not a competent nor a safe guide as to what we are to believe." This kind of bold claim is rather startling to the ear of the person trained to believe the Bible to be sufficient. The second example is far less striking, *though no less strident*, in what it says. Karl Keating provides us with the following paragraph with reference to the Holy Spirit's status as revealed solely in Scripture:

> If we imagine ourselves as ancient pagans or as present-day non-Christians, coming across the Bible for the first time, we realize that the status of the Holy Spirit is by no means clear. If we think of ourselves as having no recourse to divine Tradition and to the Magisterium of the Church, we can appreciate how easy it must have been for the early pneumatological heresies to arise.[8]

Are we to believe that the Bible is so unclear and self-contradictory that we cannot arrive at the truth through an honest, wholehearted effort at examining its evidence? It seems that is what Rome is telling us. But because the Scriptures *can be misused*, it does not follow that they are *insufficient* to lead us to the truth. Such an argument is flawed in its reasoning no matter how often it is repeated. The reason that Rome tells us the Bible is insufficient, I believe, is so we will be convinced of Rome's ultimate authority and abandon the God-given standard of Scripture.

The Argument From the Canon

The single best argument presented by Roman Catholicism against the concept of *sola scriptura* is based on the assertion that without some kind of extrabiblical revelation it is not possible for us to know the canon[9] of Scripture. Without such an infallible revelation we have a fallible list of infallible books, so to speak, and how can anyone live with that? Therefore, if we as Protestants are dependent on some outside source for our knowledge of the canon, that outside source by itself violates the sufficiency of Scripture. In other words, if the Scriptures are not self-definitional, then they are insufficient. Or to put it even more plainly, unless God gives us a golden index, the Bible is incomplete. Of course, Rome claims that the canon depends for its certainty on the entirety of Sacred Tradition, including the teaching Magisterium of the Church. As one Roman Catholic apologist recently expressed it to me, "The Roman Catholic Church is the publisher of the Bible."[10]

How are we to understand the issue of the canon? Despite the importance of the subject, it is rarely the topic of discussion in Sunday morning sermons. Are we dependent on Rome for the canon? Does the need for an infallible revelation of the canon violate *sola scriptura?* This is not an easy question, and the answers are not simple. I believe some careful consideration, however, will help us to see the problem with the Roman Catholic assertion.

The difficulty of the question is that it views the canon as a separate entity from Scripture. This extrascriptural view of the canon makes it itself an object of revelation. In other words, we have here what I have called in the past the "golden index syndrome." Unless the Protestant can produce *the* golden index to the Scriptures, like what Joseph Smith produced for the Mormons, then we have here the refutation of *sola scriptura*. Without such an index, the Protestant cannot know what the Scriptures actually *are*. But is the canon an extrabiblical revelation? I do not believe it is. The canon is a *function* of Scripture, or, to be more specific, it is a *result* of the inspiration of Scripture itself. It is not an object of revelation *separate from* Scripture, but is revealed *and defined* by God's action of inspiration. This is a crucial point that I have rarely heard addressed by Roman Catholic or Protestant apologists.

The canon is a function of the Scriptures themselves. The canon is not just a listing of books; it is a statement about what is *inspired*. The canon flows from the work of the Author of Scripture, God himself. To speak of canon outside of speaking of what is "God-breathed" is to speak nonsense. Canon is not made by man. Canon is made by God. It is the result of the action of His divine inspiration. That which is "God-breathed" is canon; that which is not "God-breathed" is not canon. It's just that simple. *Canon is a function of inspiration, and it speaks to an attribute of Scripture.*

The canon of Scripture tells us something *about* Scripture: that is, the canon speaks to the *extent* of the work of God in inspiring Scripture. God defines the canon not by giving some revelation outside of the *scriptura* but by giving the *scriptura* itself! The Roman error lies in creating a dichotomy between two things that cannot be separated, and then using that false dichotomy to deny *sola scriptura*.

Often two separate but related issues get confused when this topic is discussed: (1) the canon's nature, and (2) how people came to know the *contents* of the canon. An illustration might help. I have written eight books. The action of my writing those books creates the canon of my works. If a friend of mine does not have accurate or full knowledge of how many books I have written, does that mean there is no canon of my books? No, of course not. In fact, if I was the *only one* who knew how many books I had written, would that mean that the canon of my books does not exist? The point is clear. The canon is one issue, and it comes from God's action of inspiring the Scriptures. Our knowledge of the canon is another. Our knowledge can grow and mature, as it did at times in history. But the canon is not defined by us nor is it affected by our knowledge or ignorance.[11]

While the Roman Catholic argument about the canon might appear to have some validity with reference to the New Testament, it falls apart when applied to the Old Testament. I have often asked Roman Catholics, "How did a Jewish man who lived fifty years before the time of Christ know that Isaiah and 2 Chronicles were Scripture?" The question is meant both to define their particular viewpoint as well as illustrate a point. If it is asserted that one must have an *infallible* knowledge of what Scripture is and what it is not, then how did a Jewish man attain this kind of *infallible* knowledge back then? If the answer is that he gained such knowledge from the Jewish leadership, then one has to wonder why we no longer follow that particular guide if indeed God had an infallible guide on earth fifty years before Christ. When did this guide become fallible? What is more, the *corban* rule we spoke of earlier in our discussion of Matthew 15 came from the same source, and yet Christ rejected it as a tradition of men that contradicted the Scriptures. And finally, that same source would say that Rome has erred in its Old Testament canon, since it is quite obvious that the Jewish people did not hold to the canon Rome has infallibly defined! So it will not do to go that direction.

Some have replied that our Jewish man living fifty years before Christ *couldn't* infallibly know that Isaiah and 2 Chronicles were Scripture.[12] Yet, as we have seen, Jesus held men responsible for the Scriptures and their teachings (Matthew 22:31). To say that such a person did not *need* to have an *infallible* knowledge, but only a *sufficient* knowledge—based upon the overall acceptance of God's people and the internal consistency and integrity of the Scriptures as a body—is to say nothing more than what Protestants say about *all* the Bible. It admits there is no need for the "golden index" in this case, or any other.

While much more could be said about the canon, we must move on. I close with the observation of the Psalmist recorded in Psalm 119, "Forever, O LORD, Your word is settled in heaven" (v. 89). How did the Psalmist know this? His entire psalm is a long tribute to the worth and power of the Scriptures, but how could he write such a psalm so many centuries before there was a bishop in Rome to tell him that the Scriptures were inspired, or which books belonged to the canon? And if the Jewish believer who was moved by the Spirit of God to write these words—words which have thrilled the hearts of believers for more than two thousand years—could *know* the Scriptures then, why can't I today? The answer is clear: I *can* have a *sufficient* knowledge, just as the Psalmist had, *without* subjecting myself to the authority claims of the bishop of Rome.

The Scriptural Argument

We close our discussion of *sola scriptura* by examining the principal passages offered by Roman Catholics in defense of their concept of oral tradition and, therefore, in denial of *sola scriptura*. Remember, however, that the following passages must be interpreted differently by adherents to the two Catholic positions on tradition: (1) those who hold to the *partim-partim* view, seeing one thing in the Scriptural term "tradition," and (2) those who hold to the "material sufficiency" view, which is something rather different.

The most common passage cited *against* the doctrine of *sola scriptura* and in *support* of the Roman position is 2 Thessalonians 2:15. Let's look at the preceding verses as well to get the context:

But we should always give thanks to God for you, brethren beloved by the Lord, because God has chosen you from the beginning for salvation through sanctification by the Spirit and faith in the truth. It was for this He called you through our gospel, that you may gain the glory of our Lord Jesus Christ. So then, brethren, stand firm and hold to the traditions which you were taught, whether by word of mouth or by letter from us (vv. 13–15).

Verse 15 contains the key terms. Paul speaks of "the traditions" that were passed on in one of two ways: by letter from us (i.e., 1 Thessalonians), or "by word of mouth," as the NASB puts it. That is, orally, by teaching. The most common use of the verse goes like this: "Here you have a positive command to hold to *both* the written tradition, which is Scripture, *and* the oral tradition as well. Protestants hold to the one, but not to the other. Only Roman Catholics do both." The underlying assumption, however, is that this oral tradition is somehow *different* or *separate* from the written tradition.[13] But is this the case? Does an honest look at the context of the passage support this use by Rome?

The first thing we note is that this is a command to stand firm and hold fast to a *single body of traditions already delivered to the believers*. There is nothing *future* about this passage at all. Does Paul say to stand firm and hold fast to traditions that *will* be delivered? Does he say to hold on to interpretations and understandings that have not yet developed? No, this oral teaching which he refers to has already *been* delivered to the entire Church, not just to the episcopate, not just to the bishops, but to *everyone* in the Church at Thessalonica.

This *single* body of traditions was taught in two ways. First, orally, when Paul was personally with the Thessalonians, and then by epistle, the first letter of Paul to the Thessalonians. Now, what does the term "orally" refer to? We first note that the context of the passage is the Gospel. The verses that immediately precede verse 15 speak of the Gospel and its work among the Thessalonians. The traditions Paul speaks of are not traditions about Mary or Papal Infallibility. Instead, the traditions Paul refers to have to do with a single topic, one that is close to his heart. He is encouraging these believers to stand firm—in what? In oral traditions about subjects not found in the New Testament? No, he is exhorting them to stand firm *in the Gospel.* Note what Paul said to them in 1 Thessalonians concerning what he orally preached to them: "For this reason we also constantly thank God that when you received the word of God which you heard from us, you accepted it not as the word of men, but for what it really is, the word of God, which also performs its work in you who believe."

We have further evidence that Paul is speaking here of the Gospel, not of some separate oral tradition that exists outside of Scripture. When Paul exhorts the believers to "stand firm," he uses a term[14] that is found elsewhere in his writings. For example, we read in 1 Corinthians 16:13, "Be on the alert, *stand firm* in the faith, act like men, be strong" (emphasis mine). The phrase "stand firm" comes from the same Greek term Paul uses in 2 Thessalonians 2:15. He exhorts the Corinthians to "stand firm" in "the faith" that he himself has delivered to them. Who can possibly claim that the faith is not found *explicitly* in Scripture? And what defines "the faith" for Paul but the phrase, "the Gospel of Jesus Christ"? From a simple exegesis of the passage, it is clear there is nothing in this passage *in its own context* that is supportive of either of the Roman positions regarding tradition.

Are there not other references to tradition in the Bible? Yes, there are. For example, Paul wrote to the Corinthians:

> For I received from the Lord that which I also delivered to you, that the Lord Jesus in the night in which He was betrayed took bread (1 Corinthians 11:23).

The phrase "delivered to you" speaks of the passing on of a tradition,[15] in this case, the words of the Lord Jesus regarding the Last Supper. This provides little support for the specific and unique claims put forward by Rome, as this tradition is obviously recorded for us in Scripture. While it does illustrate the reality that for a time the early Christians were dependent on the transmission of this information in an oral manner, it does not logically follow that God intended Christians to *always* remain dependent in this way. Nor does it provide support for the idea that Paul taught the Christians things that, *while important for salvation and proper belief*, are nowhere recorded for us in Scripture. Instead, we find passages that indicate a harmony and identity between the preaching of the Apostles and their written epistles and gospels. For example, note Paul's words to the Thessalonians:

> Do you not remember that while I was still with you, I was telling you these things? (2 Thessalonians 2:5)

Often the Apostles indicate that they are repeating in written form what they taught orally. Peter likewise reminded his readers in 2 Peter 1:12–15 that it was good for him to refresh their memory in some of the basic truths of the Gospel, since we all need to do this from time to time.

Examining 2 Timothy 2:2

Another passage referred to by those who present a concept of a separate oral tradition that exists outside of Scripture is 2 Timothy 2:2:

> The things which you have heard from me in the presence of many witnesses, entrust these to faithful men who will be able to teach others also.

Here the aged Paul, facing the end of his ministry, exhorts young Timothy to entrust his teaching to faithful men who will be able to teach others as well. Some would say that this supports the idea of a separate oral tradition, for Paul does not say, "entrust my letters to these men" but "entrust my teaching to these men." To believe that this is the case assumes that what Paul *taught* in the presence of many witnesses is different than what he *wrote* to entire churches.

This assumption is manifestly untrue. The deposit of teaching that has been given to Timothy is not different from what we have in Acts, Romans, or Galatians. It is important to point out that Paul speaks of his teaching as being *done in public*. This is significant to note because this passage has been pressed into duty more than once by groups seeking to defend a hidden or secret tradition, passed down in such a way that it is virtually unknown until it is brought to light by a particular group. The early church Father Tertullian faced men who did just this, and who used this passage as support. These teachers insisted that the Apostles had two different teachings, one that was open and known to all, and a second, secret doctrine known only to a few. Tertullian refutes this idea in the following words:

> But here is said the same madness: their allowing that the Apostles were ignorant of nothing and preached no doctrines that contradicted one another, but at the same time insisting that they did not reveal all to all men. But that they proclaimed some openly and to all the world, and others they disclosed in secret and to a few, because Paul addressed to Timothy: "O, Timothy, guard thou which is entrusted to thee," and again, "That good which is committed unto thee, keep." What is this deposit? Is it so secret as to be characterized as a new doctrine, or is it a part of that charge referred to when he says, "This charge I committed unto thee, son, Timothy," and also that priesthood to which he says, "I charge thee in the sight of God who quickeneth all things, and before Jesus Christ who witnessed a good confession under Pontius Pilate, that thou keep this commandment." Now what is this commandment and what is this charge? From the preceding and succeeding context it will be manifested there is no mysterious hint darkly suggested in this expression about some far-fetched doctrine, but rather that a warning is given against receiving any other doctrine than that which Timothy had heard from himself [Paul], as I take it, "publicly before many witnesses," is his phrase.[16]

When we recall that such doctrines as the Bodily Assumption of Mary and Papal Infallibility have been defined on the basis of tradition, we can see the weight of Tertullian's words about "some far-fetched doctrine." It is quite obvious that when Paul spoke before many witnesses, he was not speaking about such doctrines but about the message of Christ in the Gospel.

"Moses' Seat" and Matthew 23

> Then Jesus spoke to the crowds and to His disciples, saying: "The scribes and the Pharisees have seated themselves in the chair of Moses; therefore all that they tell you, do and observe, but do not do according to their deeds; for they say things and do not do them. They tie up heavy burdens and lay them on men's shoulders, but they themselves are unwilling to move them with so much as a finger. But they do all their deeds to be

> noticed by men; for they broaden their phylacteries and
> lengthen the tassels of their garments" (Matthew 23:1–5).

The final passage we will examine presents the idea of "Moses' seat." Some modern Roman Catholics present this passage as proof that a source of extrabiblical authority received the blessing of the Lord Jesus. It has been alleged that the concept of "Moses' seat" is in fact a refutation of *sola scriptura*, for not only is this concept not found in the Old Testament, but Jesus seemingly gives His approbation to this extrascriptural tradition. But is this sound exegesis? Is this passage being properly understood?

First, we note that the passage has spawned a number of differing understandings among scholars. But a few items immediately remove the Roman apologist's interpretation and application from consideration. The "Moses' seat" refers to a seat in the front of the synagogue on which the teacher of the Law sat while reading from the Scriptures. Synagogue worship, of course, came into being long after Moses' day, so those who attempt to make this an oral tradition going back to Moses are engaging in wishful thinking. Beyond this, we are only speaking of a position that existed at this time in the synagogue worship of the day. Are we truly to believe that this position was divine in origin and therefore binding upon all who would worship God? It certainly doesn't seem that the New Testament Church understood it that way.

Some interpreters view this passage as engaging in biting irony. The Jewish leaders have *presumed* to sit in Moses' seat. They sat themselves in this place, but improperly. Such an understanding is certainly in line with the biting attack that follows immediately in the rest of the chapter.

I am more prone to accept Gundry's understanding, in which he rejects the satirical interpretation and instead notes,

> So long as sitting in Moses' seat qualifies the speaking of the
> scribes and Pharisees, "all things whatever" does not include
> their interpretative traditions, but emphasizes the totality of the
> law. "Therefore" establishes the qualification. They *do* keep their
> traditions. But they do *not* practice what they speak while sitting
> on Moses' seat. Hence their traditions are not in view. Though
> elsewhere Matthew is concerned with criticizing the scribes' and
> Pharisees' interpretations of the law, here he is concerned with

stressing the necessity of keeping the law itself. As usual, his eye is on antinomians in the church.[17]

Indeed, the Lord's unwillingness to become an "ecclesiastical rebel" is in perfect harmony with the Scriptural teaching on the subject of authority in the Church. There was nothing in the tradition of having someone read from the Scriptures while sitting on Moses' seat that was in conflict with the Scriptures. Unlike the *corban* rule that we saw earlier in Matthew 15, Jesus does not reject this traditional aspect of Jewish synagogue worship. He does not insist upon anarchy in worship in the synagogue any more than the Apostle Paul would allow for it in the worship of the church at Corinth. It is quite proper to listen to and obey the words of the one who reads from the Law or the Prophets, for one is not hearing a man speaking in such a situation, but is listening to the very words of God. Indeed, when Ezra read the Law to the people in Nehemiah, chapter 8, the people listened attentively and cried, "Amen! Amen!" at the hearing of God's Word. And who can forget the result of Josiah's discovery of the Book of the Covenant in 2 Chronicles 34? It is proper to have leaders in positions of authority in the synagogue, just as in the Church. But Jesus points out that the listener is still to exercise a critical eye, for he is not to imitate the evil behavior of those who have been entrusted even with the sacred duty of leading the people of God in worship.

To move from Jesus' refusal to overthrow the form of synagogue worship that was present in His day to a total endorsement of extrascriptural, oral traditions is to make a leap of monumental proportions. And in light of the passages we have already examined that refute the need for such an extrascriptural rule of faith, I suggest that the use of this passage by Roman apologists is in error.

Sola Scriptura Defended

There is much more that could be said concerning the subject of *sola scriptura*, both in a positive way (i.e., evidence establishing its truthfulness), as well as by way of review of the Roman Catholic denial of the doctrine. But the preceding discussion will have to suffice, so that we can move on to the final aspect of the issue of authority: the Papacy. We have seen Rome's denial of the sufficiency of Scripture, but what of her own teachings? What makes them better, or more trustworthy? To that we now turn.

8

THE CLAIMS OF THE PAPACY

Our discussion of Rome's claims of authority would not be complete if we did not at least briefly examine Roman assertions regarding the Papacy.[1] If *sola scriptura* is not true, what does Rome offer in its place? As we saw in the previous chapter, Rome offers the teaching Magisterium of the church, and the pinnacle of the Magisterium is the Pope. As the new *Catholic Catechism* put it, "The task of interpreting the Word of God authentically has been entrusted solely to the Magisterium of the Church, that is, to the Pope and to the bishops in communion with him."[2]

The claims of the Papacy are extensive. There is no need to quote any of the personal statements of the various Popes who have spoken highly of themselves and their position. Plenty of official, dogmatic statements exist from which to draw to carefully and honestly define the claims of the Roman Catholic Church regarding the office and person of the Pope. For example, I offer as evidence the words of the First Vatican Council's Dogmatic Constitution entitled *Pastor aeternus*, given April 24, 1870:

> We, therefore, for the preservation, safekeeping, and increase of the Catholic flock, with the approval of the sacred Council, do judge it to be necessary to propose to the belief and acceptance of all the faithful, in accordance with the ancient and constant faith of the universal Church, the doctrine touching the institution, perpetuity, and nature of the sacred Apostolic Primacy.

Please note that the Council claims that the teaching it will present is in full accord with the "ancient and constant faith of the universal Church." We continue:

> We therefore teach and declare that, according to the testimony of the Gospel, the primacy of jurisdiction over the universal Church of God was immediately and directly promised and given to blessed Peter the Apostle by Christ the Lord. For it was to Simon alone, to whom he had already said, "Thou shalt be called Cephas," that the Lord after the confession made by him, saying, "Thou art the Christ, the Son of the living God," addressed these solemn words: "Blessed art thou, Simon Bar-Jona, because flesh and blood have not revealed it to thee, but my Father who is in heaven. And I say to thee that thou art Peter; and upon this rock I will build my Church, and the gates of hell shall not prevail against it. And I will give to thee the keys of the kingdom of heaven. And whatever thou shalt bind on earth, it shall be bound also in heaven; and whatsoever thou shalt loose on earth, it shall be loosed also in heaven." And it was upon Simon alone that Jesus after his resurrection bestowed the jurisdiction of chief pastor and ruler over all his fold in the words: "Feed my lambs; feed my sheep." At open variance with this clear doctrine of Holy Scripture as it has been ever understood by the Catholic Church are the perverse opinions of those who, while they distort the form of government established by Christ the Lord in his Church, deny that Peter in his single person, preferably to all the other Apostles, whether taken separately or together, was endowed by Christ with a true and proper primacy of jurisdiction; or of those who assert that the same primacy was not bestowed immediately and directly upon blessed Peter himself, but upon the Church, and through the Church on Peter as her minister.
>
> If anyone, therefore, shall say that blessed Peter the Apostle was not appointed the Prince of all the Apostles and the visible Head of the whole Church Militant; or that the same directly and immediately received from our Lord Jesus Christ a primacy of honor only, and not of true and proper jurisdiction: let him be anathema (*anathema sit*).

This position remains valid to this day. The Second Vatican Council borrowed directly from the language of the first in saying,

> In order that the episcopate itself might be one and undi-

vided, He placed blessed Peter over the other apostles, and in-
stituted in him a permanent and visible source and foundation
of unity of faith and fellowship. And all this teaching about the
institution, the perpetuity, the force and reason for the sacred
primacy of the Roman Pontiff and his infallible teaching authority, this sacred synod again proposes to be firmly believed
by all the faithful.

The Roman Catholic writer Cardinal Gibbons wrote regarding
the Papacy:

> The Catholic Church teaches that our Lord conferred on St.
> Peter the first place of honor and jurisdiction in the government
> of his whole church, and that same spiritual authority has al-
> ways resided in the popes, or bishops of Rome, as being the
> successors of St. Peter. Consequently, to be true followers of
> Christ all Christians, both among the clergy and laity, must be
> in communion with the See of Rome, where Peter rules in the
> person of his successor.[3]

What do these statements mean? What is Rome claiming concerning the Papacy? We will limit ourselves to an examination of the
claims Rome makes regarding what she asserts to be the alleged biblical basis for the Papacy. Since the concept of the Papacy is central
to a denial of *sola scriptura*, we need to examine any proposal that
the Bible actually teaches or supports the concept itself. Also, an examination of the methods of biblical interpretation utilized by Rome
in pressing the claims of the Papacy will show what is meant by the
assertions that those teachings are at least "implicitly" contained in
Scripture. Vatican I claimed that this is the "*clear* doctrine of Holy
Scripture as it has been *ever* understood by the Catholic Church"
(emphasis added). This document gives us an excellent opportunity
for finding out how Rome comes to such "clear" conclusions based
upon the biblical text.

The Roman Catholic Position

The Roman Catholic Church claims that Peter was placed in a
position of primacy by the Lord Jesus. This primacy is one of honor,
jurisdiction, and rulership.

According to the dogmatic teachings of the Church of Rome, this primacy given to Peter is presented in Matthew 16:18–19 and John 21:15–17. Peter is the rock of Matthew 16, and Christ, in conferring a primacy upon Peter, intends this to be understood to apply to Peter's successors as well. They claim Christ is, in this passage, instituting the office of the Pope for the Christian Church. Rome further teaches that when Christ spoke to Peter and said "feed my sheep," He was setting Peter apart as the pastor of all Christians in a manner different from all the other Apostles.

Further, Roman Catholicism teaches that Peter was the first bishop of Rome. Because of this, they avow that this primacy was passed on to his successors, the succeeding bishops of Rome.

And finally, this viewpoint has presumably been the ancient and constant faith of the Christian Church. Supposedly the Church has *always* believed this to be true. Anyone who would express a different perspective is holding to perverse opinions, and is, in fact, anathema. This is crucial: Roman Catholic theology makes this statement in an infallible document that places the curse of God upon anyone who would say otherwise. If we find that the Church has *not* always understood this doctrine as Rome now defines it, and that the modern Roman Catholic doctrine of the Papacy is the result of centuries of theological and political development, we find an obvious and glaring error in an allegedly *infallible* pronouncement.[4] And if the claim that the Papacy is the ancient and constant faith of the Church is in error, what other claims of Rome are likewise contradicted by the historical evidence?

The Burden of Proof Falls on Rome

In light of the preceding claims, it seems obvious that Rome must bear a tremendous burden of proof if it is to substantiate such broad and sweeping assertions. I feel it is incumbent upon the defender of Roman Catholic teaching to demonstrate the following:

(1) Jesus is without question speaking to Peter in Matthew 16, and in so doing is identifying him as the rock upon which the Church is built.

(2) The words the Lord Jesus speaks establish Peter as the "prince of the Apostles," the very first pope, the head of the Christian Church.

(3) These words of Jesus *necessarily* indicate the creation of an office of Pope, replete with successors and the associated powers.

(4) And finally, that the Christian Church has always held this to be her constant and unchanging faith.

We must note that defenders of the Roman Catholic Papacy cannot merely demonstrate that the Roman position is *probably* true, or that it is *likely* to be true, but that it is true *beyond question*. Rome claims absolute authority in spiritual matters over all believers in Jesus Christ. She claims infallible teaching authority. The Papacy is not an issue about which one can be neutral. Pope Boniface made this quite clear in the papal bull, *Unam Sanctam*, promulgated November 18, 1302:

> Consequently we declare, state, define, and pronounce that it is altogether necessary to salvation for every human creature to be subject to the Roman Pontiff.

A few moments of reflection on this statement will reveal how tremendously wide the claims of Rome for the Papacy are, and how, in reality, the denial of *sola scriptura* is absolutely *necessary* in order to establish this claim of absolute religious authority centralized in the person of the bishop of Rome, the Pope.

Examination of the Roman Position

Before addressing the few passages cited by defenders of the Papacy, we must step back and ask the first and most necessary question: Does the New Testament as a whole lead us to believe that Peter was considered the head of the Church? Was Peter viewed as the Vicar of Christ on earth? Did Christians of his day think of him as the Holy Father? Did the other Apostles recognize Peter as their spiritual head and leader? Did they instruct people to obey Peter as the Pope? Does the New Testament lead us to believe that there was an office of Pope to which all Christians looked for guidance and on which the Church's unity itself was founded? And do we find in the words, actions, and writings of Peter evidence that he interpreted Jesus' words in Matthew 16:18–19 in the way modern Roman Catholics do?

We begin our brief New Testament survey by recognizing those truths that are not in dispute. Peter's name is prominent in the Gospel accounts. He is clearly the leading disciple. His name occurs more often than any other and almost always appears first in any listing given, which may simply reflect his being the oldest, or the first called. He is impetuous, often the first person to open his mouth—sometimes with God's blessing, sometimes to Peter's detriment.

For example, immediately after receiving the revelation from the Father concerning the identity of Jesus Christ in Matthew 16, Peter demonstrates his great fallibility by standing in the way of God's very plan of salvation. When the Lord Jesus begins to speak to His disciples concerning His coming death, Peter takes Him aside and begins to rebuke the Lord! Jesus' bold rebuke of Peter shows us Peter was not one to think through what he had to say before speaking.

The same thing happens on the Mount of Transfiguration. Luke records in the ninth chapter of his gospel that Peter spoke up in the presence of the glory of God, and of Moses and Elijah, saying, "Master, it is good for us to be here; let us make three tabernacles: one for You, and one for Moses, and one for Elijah." Luke is kind to report at this point that Peter did not realize what he was saying (v. 33). If speaking up carelessly in the presence of Moses, Elijah, the transfigured Christ, and the glory of the Father is not indicative of impetuosity, I don't know what is.

No one disputes that Peter takes a prominent role in the Gospel records. However, to leap from prominence to primacy is wholly unwarranted on two counts. First, the Gospels themselves deny that any of the Apostles held a position of primacy. Secondly, the rest of the New Testament shows that Peter did not actually end up taking any supposed position of primacy.

In support of the first point, I call our attention to Luke 22:24–30. In this passage we are told that even as the disciples walked toward the Garden of Gethsemane on the night of Christ's betrayal, they got into an argument about who among them would be considered the greatest. This discussion comes right on the heels of the establishment of the Lord's Supper. Might the argument have arisen because John, the disciple whom Jesus loved, had been leaning on the Lord's breast immediately prior to this? Indeed, if the course of history had been different, and political and geographical factors had turned out to favor a church established by the Apostle John rather than one claiming Peter as its founder, we might be debating whether the description of John as the "disciple whom Jesus loved" does not establish Johannine primacy rather than Petrine.

Be that as it may, in light of the recurring arguments about who would be the greatest, it does not seem that the disciples understood the words of Matthew 16 to establish Peter as the foundation of the Church, the first Pope, the Vicar of Christ on earth. If that were indeed Christ's meaning, the argument would for all practical purposes be over. And we would find the Lord rebuking the remaining disciples and informing them that He had already chosen Peter as the first Pope, the head of the Church, the prince of the Apostles. But we do not hear this. Instead, He treats all the disciples alike and speaks of conferring on them all—not on Peter alone—a kingdom in which they would judge the twelve tribes of Israel. Indeed, immediately after this we find the Lord specifically praying for Peter's faith, because Peter, more obviously than any of the other disciples, would dishonor his Lord that evening in betrayal.

The second reason that leaping from Peter's prominence in the Gospel accounts to the Roman concept of primacy is improper and illogical is because the rest of the New Testament does not give us a hint of Peter's supposed supremacy. Let us look briefly at some of this evidence.

First, nowhere in the epistles of Paul or John or James or Jude do we find them ever referring their readers to Peter as a Pope, by name or description. At no time do they give us any indication whatsoever of the existence of an institution known as the Papacy. Peter, in his own letters, fails to give us the slightest suggestion that he views himself as a Pope, as the head of the Church on earth. On the contrary, he says in his first epistle:

> Therefore, I exhort the elders among you, as your fellow elder and witness of the sufferings of Christ, and a partaker also of the glory that is to be revealed, shepherd the flock of God among you, exercising oversight not under compulsion, but voluntarily, according to the will of God; and not for sordid gain, but with eagerness (1 Peter 5:1–2).

Peter does not speak as a Pope, but as a fellow elder. He does not speak as the chief pastor, but as a fellow pastor. There is no reference to Rome, the Papacy, or any other element of Roman Catholic claims in this epistle.

In Peter's second epistle the same is true. One would expect to find Peter, writing at the end of his life, directing Christians to follow his successor in the office of Pope, if indeed the Roman position were true. But no such exhortation appears. We have no evidence from Peter's pen that he views himself as a Pope or that he was even the bishop of Rome, for that matter. When Paul wrote to the Church at Rome in A.D. 55–57, it is plain that Peter was not there. When Paul was in Rome and was writing the prison epistles, he never mentioned Peter. In fact, in one place, those epistles make it clear that either Peter was not in Rome, or he had actually abandoned Paul! In 2 Timothy 4:16, written close to the end of his life, Paul writes that "no one supported me" at the first defense—a devastating charge against Peter *if* Peter had been at Rome at this time, for Paul asks that the Lord "not hold it against them." Indeed, if we take the view that Peter was the bishop of Rome, but was absent from the Church much of the time, it seems strange that either Peter never wrote to his own church, for we have no such letter, or that they did not think enough of the letter to keep it around as in the case of Paul's epistle to the Romans.[5]

If there is no evidence for the Papacy from Peter himself, we should hardly be surprised that none exists in Paul's writings. Instead, we find statements and actions that are contrary to the Roman position had it existed in the primitive Church. For example: Paul indicates that he was in no way inferior to the very chiefest Apostles in 2 Corinthians 12:11. Even if Paul had in mind here someone other than the real Apostles of Christ, we can see plainly that he did not have any concept of the Papacy in the structure of the Church, for he wrote to the Corinthians that God had placed in the Church "first apostles, second prophets, third teachers . . ." (1 Corinthians 12:28). First the Pope, Peter, and *then* the Apostles is simply not the biblical order. We hardly need to be reminded that in all of Paul's letters, in which we find discussions of Apostles, bishops, deacons, and all sorts of other positions of ministry in the Church, never is a word said about the most important office of all, the supposed office of the Pope. And the reason is plain: no such office existed.

Paul provides further evidence that he did not view Peter as Roman Catholics do today when he says in 2 Corinthians 11:28 that "apart from such external things, there is the daily pressure on me of concern for all the churches." If the care of all the churches was in fact Peter's responsibility, Paul would have been meddling in another man's work. But, of course, we see from his epistles that Paul had no concept of Peter as the appointed universal pastor of all Christians.

·We might take Paul's epistle to the Galatians as a test case and ask, "Does this letter lead us to believe the Roman claim that Peter functioned as a Pope in the early Church?" The answer seems too obvious for comment. We begin by noting Paul's statement in Galatians 2:7: "But on the contrary, seeing that I had been entrusted with the gospel to the uncircumcised, just as Peter had been to the circumcised . . ." In this verse we have a specific delineation of Peter's calling as an Apostle, and it is as an evangelist to the Jews. Had he not been used also to speak to the Gentiles? Indeed he had, but God was using Paul in that role at this time, and Peter was content to speak to the Jewish people. Nothing in this passage even hints that Peter is viewed as the prince of the Apostles, the Vicar of Christ on earth.

This is seen even more clearly in Galatians 2 in Paul's willingness to directly rebuke Peter's errant behavior at Antioch, when Peter withdrew from table fellowship with the Gentiles. Surely if Paul viewed Peter as the Pope, the head of all Christians, he would be far out of line to publicly rebuke him and accuse him of not walking in accord with the truth of the Gospel. But this is fully in line with all of the Pauline writings, in which you will not find a shred of evidence to support Roman claims concerning Peter. Epistle after epistle can pass in review without the slightest evidence of Petrine primacy. Even the Pastoral Epistles, with their extensive instruction on ecclesiastical matters, speak not a word about the Papacy or Peter or anything even remotely similar to Rome's assertions.

We cannot pass by the most crucial evidence with regard to Roman claims: The Book of Acts gives us the clearest insight into the function of the early Church. Here if anywhere we would find clear and unequivocal evidence of Petrine primacy and the function of the Papacy. Is such evidence there? No, we find just the opposite.

When the need arises to investigate what has happened in Samaria, is Peter acting as a Pope and directing the actions of the Church? No. In Acts 8:14 we read, "Now when the apostles in Jerusalem heard that Samaria had received the word of God, they sent them Peter and John. . . ." Here Peter does not function as Pope, but as one of the apostles who is *sent* to investigate the situation.

In Acts 11 Peter is called to answer for his actions in going to Cornelius' house. Does he give evidence of Papal prerogatives here? Does he answer as Innocent III would have answered, or Alexander VI? Hardly. There is no mention of his position as Pope. Instead, rather than pleading his position as Vicar of Christ, Peter relates the supernatural vision and direction that had been given to him to proclaim the Gospel message to the Gentiles. This no more makes Peter a Pope than Paul's guiding vision in Acts 16.

In Acts 15 we read about a council of the early Church held at Jerusalem. Much has been made of this council and its relevance for claims of Petrine primacy. Let us note the important features of this account. In verse 6 we read, "The apostles and the elders came together to look into this matter." It does not say that the Pope and the apostles and the elders met. Peter is plainly considered an Apostle, as all the rest. The council is not under the direction of Peter. As the bishop of Jerusalem, James directs the proceedings. Peter addresses the group not as a Pope, but as an Apostle used by God to bring the Gospel to the Gentiles. He concludes his speech as follows: "We believe it is through the grace of our Lord Jesus that we are saved, just as they are" (v. 11, NIV).

The deliberations do not end with Peter's speech. Instead, we read in verse 12, "All the people kept silent, and they were listening to Barnabas and Paul as they were relating what signs and wonders God had done through them among the Gentiles." Paul and Barnabas address the group and confirm Peter's opinion by relating God's wondrous work in their own ministries. At this point James speaks up and, using the imperative mode (v. 13),[6] commands the assembly to listen to his words. He confirms Peter's words through the citation of Scripture, then gives his judgment in verse 19. Here we have the conclusion of the affair. The letter is written at James' suggestion, but again in the name of the Apostles and elders, not in the name of Peter the Pope.

The words of Peter in Acts 15:11 are his final ones in this book. In fact, from this point on no mention is made of him who is said to be the very head of the Church Universal, the founder of the Church at Rome! Even when Paul's arrival in Rome is mentioned at the end of the book, Peter is not around.

And so we conclude our initial overview of the New Testament evidence with the plain fact before us that the concept of a Papacy, with Peter as its initial office holder, is nowhere to be found. Not only does the term itself not appear, but the office is not mentioned at all. Instead we find data from the pages of inspired Scripture showing that the early Christians did not look to Peter or to any bishop of Rome as the head of all Christians.

In light of the testimony of the entire New Testament, the Roman apologist must be able to prove beyond a shadow of a doubt that the few passages to which he appeals prove the establishment of the Papacy. We cannot accept the mere *possibility* that the Roman position is correct. Given the absence of the Papacy from all the rest of the New Testament, the few passages cited by Roman apologists such as Matthew 16 and John 21 *must* plainly and unequivocally establish Petrine primacy and succession in the office of the Pope. But do these passages accomplish this?

John 21:15–17

> So when they had finished breakfast, Jesus said to Simon Peter, "Simon, son of John, do you love Me more than these?" He said to Him, "Yes, Lord; You know that I love You." He said to him, "Tend My lambs." He said to him again a second time, "Simon, son of John, do you love Me?" He said to Him, "Yes, Lord; You know that I love You." He said to him, "Shepherd My sheep." He said to him the third time, "Simon, son of John, do you love Me?" Peter was grieved because He said to him the third time, "Do you love Me?" And he said to Him, "Lord, You know all things; You know that I love You." Jesus said to him, "Tend My sheep."

Cyril of Alexandria (c. 370–444) demonstrates that the earliest and most logical understanding of this passage is that held by Protestants, not Roman Catholics. In commenting on this passage he said,

> If anyone asks for what cause he asked Simon only, though the other disciples were present, and what he means by "Feed my lambs," and the like, we answer that St. Peter, with the other disciples, had been already chosen to the Apostleship, but because meanwhile Peter had fallen (for under great fear he had thrice denied the Lord), he now heals him that was sick, and

exacts a threefold confession in place of his triple denial, contrasting the former with the latter, and compensating the fault with the correction.[7]

Here we have the gracious Lord restoring the Apostle who, in his brash impetuosity, had promised to follow Him even to death yet had denied Him three times. The threefold question of Peter, followed by the command to feed or shepherd Christ's sheep, is restorative in nature. Nothing in the passage even begins to suggest that Jesus' words mean that the other Apostles were not likewise commissioned to feed and pastor Christ's flock on an equal basis with Simon Peter. There is no indication that *only* Peter is told to shepherd God's flock. Indeed, if such were the case, Paul seems to have been ignorant of this injunction, for he instructed the Ephesian elders in Acts 20:28: "Be on guard for yourselves and for all the flock, among which the Holy Spirit has made you overseers, to shepherd the church of God which He purchased with His own blood."

Paul does not say, "Since Peter is the chief shepherd, you act as undershepherds of the flock of God." Let me reiterate. The only way that such an understanding can be found is if we take a much later development and read it back into the texts, as our Roman Catholic friends are forced to do. This passage in no way sets Peter apart as the prince of the Apostles. Instead, it shows that he was in need of special pastoral care on the part of Christ.

Luke 22:31–32

The next passage said to teach the concept of the Papacy is Luke 22:31–32, which reads:

> "Simon, Simon, behold, Satan has demanded permission to sift you like wheat; but I have prayed for you, that your faith may not fail; and you, when once you have turned again, strengthen your brothers."

Again we see that Peter's denial of the Lord is mentioned. The Lord warns Peter specifically that he is in danger, yet Peter replies rashly in verse 33, "Lord, with You I am ready to go both to prison and to death!" To which the Lord replies that Peter will, in fact, deny Him three times. Roman Catholics have cited this passage as confirming once again the preeminence of Peter. Some have even gone so far as to say that the Lord's prayer for Peter's faith extends to Peter's successors, the bishops of Rome, so that their dogmatic teachings are infallible! This passage, like John 21, shows us nothing more than that Peter needed pastoral care by the Lord due to his impetuosity. The Lord's prayer was fulfilled, for even having denied Christ, Peter, unlike Judas, went out and wept bitterly. But his faith did not fail completely, and he was restored and humbled, but wiser. To take this as indicating Petrine primacy, however, goes beyond anything the text says.

Some have said that Peter is set apart from the others by the phrase "and when you have turned back, strengthen your brothers." Yet even here we find no basis for reading Papal prerogatives into the passage, for such terminology is common in the New Testament. For example, the term used here[8] (14:22; 15:32; 15:41; 18:23) is used of Paul's confirming the churches of Syria and Cilicia, of Judas and Silas's confirming the brethren at Antioch, and of Timothy's confirming the Thessalonian Church. Amazingly, Paul uses the same Greek term in writing to the Church of Rome: "For I long to see you so that I may impart some spiritual gift to you, that you may be established" (Romans 1:11). And in Romans 16:25 Paul praises God, who is able to strengthen them according to *his* [Paul's] gospel! No mention is made of Peter at all!

So Peter is simply being instructed to strengthen his brothers after he himself is restored and strengthened by Christ. We all know that we are better able to share with others when we ourselves have gone through trials, which Peter most assuredly did after being restored to fellowship after his fall. No primacy or Papacy is found here.

The Key Passage and Final Refuge

Few would argue that the foundational passage on which the entire Roman Catholic claim for the Papacy rests is found in Matthew 16:13–20, verses 18–19 in particular. We are told that their *plain* meaning supports the concept. It should be noted that Rome has *infallibly* interpreted these verses in the words of Vatican I. It is one of the few passages of Scripture that have in fact been *infallibly* interpreted by the Roman Catholic Church (John 21:25–27 being another). Let's look at Matthew's record.

> He said to them, "But who do you say that I am?" Simon
> Peter answered, "You are the Christ, the Son of the living God."
> And Jesus said to him, "Blessed are you, Simon Barjona, because
> flesh and blood did not reveal this to you, but My Father who
> is in heaven. I also say to you that you are Peter, and upon this
> rock I will build My church; and the gates of Hades will not
> overpower it. I will give you the keys of the kingdom of heaven;
> and whatever you bind on earth shall have been bound in
> heaven, and whatever you loose on earth shall have been loosed
> in heaven."

No one will deny that this is a singularly important passage. Here the Lord Jesus leads His disciples to a confession of faith in himself; the Father from heaven reveals the true nature of His Son, Jesus Christ.

Yet we find these verses being used to support a concept seen nowhere else in Scripture. We are asked to believe that not only is the impetuous and frail Peter made the very foundation of the Church itself, but that this foundational position creates an office of Pope, and that this office involves successors who will sit in the seat of bishop in the city of Rome, 1,500 miles distant.

Before we can discuss this passage, it is necessary to address the claim often made by Roman Catholic apologists: They say that we should imagine how Matthew's words would appear in Aramaic, assuming that they were spoken in that language. Some even go so far as to say that Matthew was originally written in Aramaic, though the modern opinion on the subject has changed over the past decades. We could spend much time arguing about whether Matthew was written in Aramaic; I could cite Alexander Bruce,[9] G. H. Schodde,[10] D. A. Carson,[11] and Robert Gundry.[12] But I shall simply allow the leading New Testament textual scholar, Kurt Aland, to summarize my position: "There is no longer any doubt that Greek was the language in which all the parts of the New Testament were originally written. . . ."[13]

Much has been said by Roman Catholic apologists about what Matthew 16:18 would read in Aramaic. Some have asserted with complete confidence that they can tell us exactly what the Aramaic would be. Yet, is it not strange that when dealing with the central passage used to support the Papacy, they must appeal to a nonexistent, unknown "Aramaic original" that no one—no matter how great their scholarship—can possibly claim to be able to re-create with certainty?[14]

Anyone familiar with the comments of scholars on this passage is aware of the multitude of differing positions taken about it. I would first like to provide a straightforward interpretation of the verses, and then discuss some of the areas of dispute.

The central theme is the Messiahship of Jesus Christ. Any interpretation that takes the focus off of Jesus as Messiah is missing the point. Jesus' questions to the disciples about the opinions of the multitudes, and then their own viewpoints, are all directed toward His own person, His own identity. When Peter speaks up and confesses that Jesus is the Christ, the Son of the living God, he is confessing the faith of all the disciples, not merely his own. He often spoke for them all. Jesus' pronouncement of blessing upon Peter is not because of any inherent goodness in Peter but rather his being the recipient of a great blessing from the Father. To Peter has been revealed the true identity of Jesus Christ. And, of course, this revelation was given to the other Apostles as well. We can hardly think that they all sat there amazed at Peter's words, never having thought that Jesus was the Christ, the Son of the living God. The point of Jesus' words is that to reveal the Son requires the enlightening work of the Father. The same theme is seen in John 6, where no man can come to the Son unless drawn by the Father. In that same context, when all the disciples turned away from Jesus, save the twelve, it was Peter who spoke for the disciples again, saying, "Lord, to whom shall we go? You have words of eternal life. We have believed and have come to know that You are the Holy One of God" (John 6:68–69, emphasis added).

When the Lord says, "I tell you that you are Peter, and on this rock I will build my church, and the gates of Hades will not overcome it," the focus does not change. The subject of the passage remains the identity of Christ, found in the confession of Peter. Jesus is not speaking of the identity of Peter; He is still talking about himself and His Church. This is evident by continuing on through verse 20, where we read, "Then He warned the disciples that they should tell no one that He was the Christ." Some modern scholars, having missed the fact that the focus remains on Christ all the way through, are so puzzled by this passage that they suggest that it is not original! But such conjecture is not necessary.

The rock of which the Lord speaks is that common confession made by all who are part of the Church: Jesus is the Christ, the Son of the living God.[15] This is seen, I believe, in the fact that while the Lord is addressing Peter directly, He changes from direct address to the third person, "this rock," when speaking of Peter's confession. He does not say, "Upon you, Peter, I will build my church." Instead, you have a clear distinction between Peter, the Πέτρος (*Petros*), and the demonstrative pronoun preceding πέτρα (*petra*), the confession of faith, on which the Church is built.

This statement is followed by the promise to give the keys of the kingdom of heaven to Peter at some time in the future, so that what he binds on earth will be bound in heaven, and whatever he looses on earth will be loosed in heaven. I emphasize this is a promise, for the verb is future in tense.[16] Yet when we see this authority given in Matthew 18:18, it is given not to Peter alone or even primarily to him. It is conferred on all the Apostles, using the *exact* same language[17] regarding binding and loosing. If someone wishes to say that Peter receives the keys in distinction from the other Apostles, as their superior, they are also forced to admit that the actual giving of this keys is never recorded for us anywhere in Scripture, a strange thing indeed for something supposedly so fundamental to the constitution of the Church.

Now, a Roman Catholic may disagree with my interpretation. But my interpretation makes perfect sense. It does not require giant leaps of illogic to see how I have come to my conclusions. This position has been held by Christians from the earliest days of the Christian faith. If the Roman Catholic Church can present an equally likely interpretation, I believe it would fail. Because, as we have seen, Matthew 16 is the last bastion[18] of the Roman cause. If concrete support for the Papacy is not here, then it is nowhere at all. And Rome cannot simply provide a possible alternative. She must be able to prove, beyond all question, the *impossibility* of all other interpretations. And she cannot do this.

The Early Church's Understanding

Rome's claim regarding John 21 and Matthew 16 is that these passages clearly teach Petrine primacy *in the sense given that phrase by Rome*. I note again the words of Vatican I: "At open variance with this clear doctrine of Holy Scripture as it has been ever understood by the Catholic Church are the perverse opinions of those who . . . deny that Peter in his single person . . . was endowed by Christ with a true and proper primacy of jurisdiction." Is this the understanding of everyone down through Church history?

We begin with Luke 22:31–32, where the Lord prays for Peter's faith and instructs him, when he has turned back, to strengthen his brothers. We see that the New Testament does not indicate that this made Peter a Pope, or the prince of the Apostles. Dr. Salmon notes with reference to the patristic aspect of the interpretation of this passage:

> This prayer to Peter is so clearly personal that some Roman Catholic controversialists do not rely on this passage at all. Neither can they produce any early writers who deduce from it anything in favor of the Roman See. Bellarmine can quote nothing earlier than the eleventh century, except the suspicious evidence of some Popes in their own cause, of whom the earliest to speak distinctly is Pope Agatho in his address to the sixth general council, A.D. 680.[19]

We do not find the modern Roman interpretation of this passage in any of the writings of the early Church. But what of John 21? We have read the words of Cyril of Alexandria written in commentary on this passage, who provided not the Roman interpretation but the Protestant one. Remember that Vatican I tells us that the Catholic Church has *always* understood these passages, specifically Matthew 16 and John 21, in the way presented by Rome today. This is manifestly untrue. The existence of different interpretations, without the slightest evidence that those giving those interpretations were attempting to rebel against Apostolic doctrine, or to be perverse in their opinions, refutes the Roman contention. It also shows that these commentators did not find the constitution of the Church itself in these passages, as later claimed by Rome.

When we examine the early church writings that address the pivotal passage of Matthew 16:18–19, we find just as wide a variety of interpretations as we find in scholarly literature.[20] It is easy to understand why many Roman Catholic scholars felt it necessary to leave communion with Rome following Vatican I. Those who were even slightly familiar with patristic interpretation and concerned about truth could never say that the Church has *always* interpreted this passage as it is interpreted by that council. But before documenting this, I wish to quote an important passage from Dr. Salmon. After going through the various interpretations found in the patristic sources, he writes,

> But none of these can be reconciled with the interpretation which regards this text as containing the charter of the Church's organization. A charter would be worthless if it were left uncertain to whom it was addressed or what powers it conferred. So that the mere fact that Fathers differed in opinion as to what was meant by "this rock," and that occasionally the same Father wavered in his opinion on this subject, proves that none of them regarded this text as one establishing a perpetual constitution for the Christian Church.[21]

It is vital to note, then, that when the Roman Catholic advocate makes Matthew 16 the charter of the Papacy, he is separating himself from the early Church, which saw no such thing in this passage but instead allowed for a multiplicity of interpretations.

The French Roman Catholic Launoy surveyed the patristic evidence and found seventeen citations supporting the concept that Peter is the rock of Matthew 16. Please note that this does not mean that all sixteen of these Fathers also felt that this meant that the bishop of Rome was a Pope, but only that they saw Matthew 16 and the phrase "this rock" as referring to Peter. However, Launoy found sixteen citations that identified the rock as Christ. He found eight that identified all the Apostles together as forming the rock of Matthew 16. And he found forty-four citations indicating that the rock of Matthew 16 was the confession of faith made by Peter in Jesus Christ. If we add these numbers together, we find that the Roman position, which claims to have *always* been the faith of the Catholic Church, in Launoy's survey actually represents twenty percent of the Fathers. Eighty percent of the time, then, the early Fathers expressed, in Vatican I's words, "perverse" opinions at the very best.[22] I might note that even as late as the Council of Trent it was said this passage was referring to the faith that Peter expressed.

Should one Roman Catholic's survey not be enough, we turn to the Jesuit Maldonatus, who writes,

There are among ancient authors some who interpret "on this rock," that is, "on this faith," or "on this confession of faith in which thou hast called me the Son of the living God," as Hilary, and Gregory Nyssen, and Chrysostom, and Cyril of Alexandria. St. Augustine, going still further away from the true sense, interprets "on this rock," that is, "on myself Christ," because Christ was the rock. But Origen "on this rock," that is to say, "on all men who have the same faith."[23]

Was Maldonatus correct? Most definitely so. Let's look, for example, at Hilary's statement regarding Matthew 16:18, as found in his work *De Trinitate*, book 6, chapter 37, written between A.D. 356 and 359:

> This faith it is which is the foundation of the Church; through this faith the gates of hell cannot prevail against her. This is the faith which has the keys of the kingdom of heaven (p. 112).

Indeed, as one reads all of chapter 37, one finds Hilary referring to each of the prime texts on which the Papacy is built, including John 21 and Luke 22, and yet not once mentioning the Papacy! Can you imagine a modern Roman apologist citing all three of these passages and *not* mentioning the Papacy? How could Hilary be ignorant of such a basic truth? And how could he be joined by the likes of John Chrysostom or Gregory Nazianzus? How could these great men and preachers be ignorant of such a basic truth? Where does this "perverse notion" come from that the passage refers to the faith of Peter's confession, and not to Peter himself? Was it not the common belief of Christians for centuries before that this passage referred to Peter, thus establishing the Papacy? Unless, perhaps, it was not a basic truth at all?

And what of the great Augustine? His most famous commentary on the passage is found in his *Retractiones*, written toward the end of his life. He writes,

> I have somewhere said of St. Peter that the church is built upon him as the rock. . . . But I know that I have since frequently said that the word of the Lord, "Thou art *Petrus*, and on this *petra* I will build my church," must be understood of him, whom Peter confessed as Son of the living God; and Peter, so

named after this rock, represents the person of the church, which is founded on this rock and has received the keys of the kingdom of heaven. For it was not said to him: "Thou art a rock" (*petra*), but, "*Thou art Peter*" (*Petrus*); and the rock was Christ, through confession of whom Simon received the name Peter. Yet the reader may decide which of the two interpretations is the more probable.[24]

I would point out that Augustine left his readers to decide how they would interpret the passage. We should think seriously about what it means that Augustine, the great bishop of Hippo, could think that how one views this passage is a matter of freedom, when Vatican I tells us it is a matter upon which the *anathema* can and should be used. Notice the huge movement in thought that has taken place between the early part of the fifth century and the latter part of the nineteenth.[25]

A Brief Word on the Issue of Papal Infallibility

The great Princeton theologian Charles Hodge wrote regarding Papal Infallibility:

> There is something simple and grand in this theory. It is wonderfully adapted to the tastes and wants of men. It relieves them of personal responsibility. Every thing is decided for them. Their salvation is secured by merely submitting to be saved by an infallible, sin-pardoning, and grace-imparting Church. . . . We know that when Christ was on earth men did not believe or obey him. We know that when the Apostles were still living, and their authority was still confirmed by signs, and wonders, and divers miracles and gifts of the Holy Ghost, the Church was distracted by heresies and schisms. If any in their sluggishness are disposed to think that a perpetual body of infallible teachers would be a blessing, all must admit that the assumption of infallibility by the ignorant, the erring, and the wicked, must be an evil inconceivably great. The Romish theory, if true, might be a blessing; if false, it must be an awful curse.[26]

And yet there is a great attraction toward the concept of an infallible guide in the person of the Pope. The idea that God has a "spokesman" of a sort on earth, to which the really tough questions can be addressed, attracts many faithful followers. The terminology used of the Pope reveals how deeply this desire is found in the heart of humankind. For example, the Pope is called the "Vicar of Christ on earth." A vicar is a substitute, as in the term *vicarious*. The Pope functions in the place of Christ as the *earthly* head of the Church as Christ is the *heavenly* leader. This idea at first sight provides a sense of security and assurance. But when one considers it in the light of biblical teaching, one is struck by the fact that the "Vicar of Christ" on earth, according to the Lord himself in John 14 and 16, is the Holy Spirit, not the bishop of Rome.

What of the concept of infallibility on the part of the Pope? The official declaration of this concept came out of the first Vatican Council that convened in 1870. The idea that the Church as a whole could not err is far older; only after the idea of the Pope as the universal head of the Church became fully established could the concept of infallibility move toward fulfillment in the person of the Pope. The specific claim limits the Pope's infallibility to teachings addressed to the whole Church on matters of faith and morals. Some apologists use this to so limit the concept as to reduce the number of infallible teachings to a bare handful. Others recognize that this makes the entire concept rather meaningless and allow for a much wider application of Papal Infallibility.[27]

If the biblical evidence for the Papacy is nonexistent, we should not be overly surprised that the concept of Papal Infallibility is likewise without support in the inspired Scriptures. It is, to borrow a phrase, a *theological novum* in the history of the Church, a concept unknown to the Apostles and the early Fathers of the Church. What is more, it stands inalterably opposed to the facts of history. Though space does not allow even a discussion of the historical reality of errors on the part of the Pope,[28] such is the case, and the attempts of Roman apologists to find ways of excusing these errors is most instructive.

Papal Infallibility is really the capstone of the entire denial of *sola scriptura*. We are told we can find an infallible guide in the person of the Pope, one who can speak for the Church without question on matters of faith and morals. It is impossible not to point out the simple fact that in this doctrine one finds the final step in a process that began with the first addition of a human tradition to the Scriptures: the process of replacing the Holy Spirit of God with a structure of man's making. Before one reacts too strongly to that statement, consider well to what I refer. Who is to take Christ's place when He ascends to heaven? The Holy Spirit. Who is to teach Christians and lead them into truth? The Holy Spirit. Who is to guide Christians and enlighten their minds to the truths of God? The Holy Spirit. It is not enough to say, "Well, the Church does all these things with the help of the Spirit." The truth of the matter is that the Holy Spirit's role has been taken over by the hierarchy of the Church, and the individual Christian is subject to that authority as a matter of his eternal salvation.

But the person who is subject to the authority of the Word of God cannot be subject to the Pope, having seen that the Papacy as an institution has no real basis in the Scriptures. I invite the individual Roman Catholic to look to the Scriptures *as the sole infallible source of God's revealed truth* so as to determine just how he or she *can* have peace with God. We come back, then, to the Gospel of peace, and we seek to come to the Scriptures not to find in them what we *want* to find, or what we are *told* to find by a Church, but what the Holy Spirit of God placed there when He breathed out those sacred words. To these we now turn, praying with the Psalmist,

Open my eyes, that I may behold wonderful things from Your law (Psalm 119:18).

9

JUSTIFIED BEFORE GOD: ROME'S VIEW

Quite often the Roman Catholic/Protestant dialogue is marred by miscommunication and misunderstanding. As in so many other areas, differences in terminology and meaning cause great confusion and frustration. This is especially the case when discussing salvation in the Roman Catholic context. "Nuance" is a term that often arises when discussing this issue. There are so many nuances to the various elements of the Roman Catholic viewpoint that much of the time both parties end up talking right past each other.

Therefore, we must briefly define some terms. While we will normally seek to draw directly from official statements, we will also allow Roman Catholic scholars and theologians to have their say when they can assist in clarifying a point. Obviously, entire books have been written on each of the aspects we note below. Any brief definition is in danger of being said to be inaccurate by *someone* who has a little different "take" on a subject. But in light of the necessity of providing *some* background to the topic, we risk the charge, hoping the benefit outweighs the risk. Before we can discuss the differences between Protestants and Roman Catholics on justification we must define Rome's position on other issues that are so closely related that they cannot be ignored. We will therefore look briefly at Rome's definition of sin as well as her concept of sacraments before moving into justification.

The Nature of Sin

The basic concept of sin being rebellion against God and God's law is not disputed in Roman Catholic teaching. Neither is it contested that sin separates man from God, though the extent of the separation and the results for the "natural" or lost man is an issue of disagreement. The important issue here, however, revolves around the *kinds* of sin and the penalties of sin, along with how sin is forgiven.

Roman Catholic theology separates sin into two main categories: *venial* and *mortal*. Theologian John Hardon defines venial sin:

> An offense against God which does not deprive the sinner of sanctifying grace. It is called venial (from *venia*, pardon) because the soul still has the vital principle that allows a cure from within, similar to the healing of a sick or diseased body whose source of animation (the soul) is still present to restore the ailing bodily function to health.[1]

On the other hand, mortal sin is:

> An actual sin that destroys sanctifying grace and causes the supernatural death of the soul. Mortal sin is a turning away from God because of a seriously inordinate adherence to creatures that causes grave injury to a person's rational nature and to the social order, and deprives the sinner of a right to heaven.[2]

A person enters into a state of "sanctifying grace" through baptism, which the Council of Trent called the "laver of regeneration."[3] So it is seen that venial sins, "daily sins" as they are often called, do not destroy sanctifying grace but impede spiritual progress. It is not even necessary to confess venial sins in the sacrament of confession to the priest,[4] but these can be "expiated" by means of "sorrow, prayer, works of charity and abstinence, reception of Holy Communion. . . ."[5] There is no clear and infallible guide as to just what is and what is not venial sin, and the line between venial and mortal sin is difficult to trace with absolute certainty from Roman writings. Mortal sins destroy sanctifying grace and, unless they are confessed, bar one from entering into heaven. In fact, as the Council of Florence said,

> Moreover, the souls of those who depart in actual mortal sin or in original sin only, descend immediately into hell but to undergo punishments of different kinds.[6]

When a Roman Catholic confesses to the priest, the priest (by his power of ordination, coming to him through the Church) absolves the penitent person of the guilt and the eternal punishment of the sin; however, he does not necessarily remove the temporal punishment of the sin. Rather, he assigns works of penance or contrition, by which the person then provides "satisfaction" for his sins, thereby removing the penalty. This is a vital point for our discussion and needs to be fully understood:

> Finally, in regard to satisfaction . . . the holy council declares that it is absolutely false and contrary to the word of God, that the guilt is never remitted by the Lord without the entire punishment being remitted also. . . . And it is in keeping with divine clemency that sins be not thus pardoned us without any satisfaction. . . . Neither was there ever in the Church of God any way held more certain to ward off impending chastisement by the Lord than that men perform with true sorrow of mind these works of penance. Add to this, that while we by making satisfaction suffer for our sins, we are made conformable to Christ Jesus who satisfied for our sins, from whom is all our sufficiency. . . . Neither is this satisfaction which we discharge for our sins so our own as not to be through Christ Jesus; for we who can do nothing of ourselves as of ourselves, can do all things with the cooperation of Him who strengthens us . . . no Catholic ever understood that through our satisfactions the efficacy of the merit and satisfaction of our Lord Jesus Christ is either obscured or in any way diminished.[7]

The claim that the concept of satisfaction does not detract from the satisfaction derived from the atoning work of Christ is very important. No representation of Roman Catholic doctrine is accurate if it does not honestly state that Rome tries to safeguard the work of Christ with such claims. Rome is certainly concerned about this issue. The important question for the honest inquirer, as we will see, is whether Rome succeeds or fails in her attempt to avoid obscuring or diminishing the efficacy of the merit and satisfaction of Jesus Christ.

Returning to the issue of the punishment of sin, another theologian notes,

> All temporal punishments for sin are not always remitted by God with the guilt of sin and the eternal punishment.[8]

In Roman Catholic theology, there is a difference between guilt and the temporal punishment of sin. The atoning work of Christ, applied by the "laver of regeneration" (i.e., baptism), cleanses from the guilt of sin (including original sin) and results in justification. However, as the Council of Trent explains,

> If anyone says that after the reception of the grace of justification the guilt is so remitted and the debt of eternal punishment so blotted out to every repentant sinner, that no debt of temporal punishment remains to be discharged either in this world or in purgatory before the gates of heaven can be opened, let him be anathema.[9]

According to Trent, the temporal punishments of sins committed before baptism are remitted by baptism; but if one sins after baptism, even when these sins are forgiven through the sacrament of confession, the temporal punishments remain. These punishments are then "expiated" by works either in this life, or, if a person dies with unexpiated punishments remaining, they are satisfied in purgatory by suffering. Men's actions, including suffering, tears, prayers, pilgrimages, acts of charity, etc., are considered in Roman Catholic theology to have merit in God's eyes. As one writer puts it,

> Man, for his part, in order to arrive at full sanctification, must cooperate with the grace of the Holy Spirit through faith, hope, love of God and neighbor, and prayer; but he must also perform other "works." It is a universally accepted dogma of the Catholic Church that man, in union with the grace of the Holy Spirit must merit heaven by his good works. These works are meritorious only when they are performed in the state of grace and with a good intention. . . . We have shown that according to Holy Scripture the Christian can actually merit heaven for himself by his good works.[10]

So, "good works" are meritorious, not only positively in regards to earning eternal life but negatively in making "satisfaction" before God in expiating one's sins, specifically the temporal punishment due those sins.

The Sacraments—Channels of Grace

Roman Catholicism is inherently sacramental. In fact, it could be rightly said that salvation is mediated through the Sacraments of the

Church. But just what is a Sacrament? Roman Catholic John O'Brien answers:

> [Christ] likewise established the sacraments which serve as so many channels through which the graces and blessings of the Redemption reach the soul of each individual recipient. The administration of the sacraments was entrusted to the Church to which Christ gave complete jurisdiction over the deposit of divine truth and over the means of sanctification. In a very true sense the Church may be said to be the extension of the Incarnation. . . . A sacrament is an outward sign of inward grace. . . . The sacraments and the holy Sacrifice of the Mass are the chief channels through which the fruits of the Redemption, the blessings and graces of God, are applied to individual souls. . . . Christ by His suffering and death gained vast spiritual riches for us; they may be said to constitute a huge spiritual reservoir. It is necessary that some means be devised to tap the reservoir and carry its riches to our souls. The sacraments are such means: channels of divine grace to the souls of men.[11]

Sacraments, then, are "channels of grace," the means by which the grace of God is applied to individuals. According to modern Roman Catholic teaching, the Sacraments number seven: Baptism, Confession, Holy Eucharist, Confirmation, Holy Orders, Matrimony, and Extreme Unction. We have already seen that the Sacrament of Baptism forgives sins; it "makes us heirs of heaven and co-heirs with Jesus Christ." It is said to unite us with Christ, to make us a part of the body of Christ. Baptism is an absolute necessity for salvation, for as Canon 5 of the "Decree Concerning the Sacraments" from the Council of Trent says, "If anyone says that baptism is optional, that is, not necessary for salvation, let him be anathema." And if anyone disagrees with this view of baptism they are condemned by anathema as well (Canon 3).[12]

The other two Sacraments that bear directly on the discussion of salvation are Confession and Holy Eucharist. We will address the Holy Eucharist in another chapter. Ludwig Ott provides a brief definition of confession:

> The Sacrament of Penance . . . is that Sacrament by which the sinner, who repents of his sins, acknowledges them sincerely and has the will to render atonement, has his sins, com-

mitted after his Baptism, remitted in the absolution pronounced by the priest. The word penance is also used to designate a particular part of the Sacrament of Penance, i.e., the satisfaction.[13]

The Sacrament is made up of three parts: contrition, confession, and satisfaction. Contrition is the sorrow for sin; confession the action of confessing those sins to the priest to receive absolution for them (an action that is absolutely necessary for salvation for anyone who would commit a mortal sin after their baptism); satisfaction is undergoing some kind of penance, normally assigned by the priest, to expiate the temporal punishment for the sin(s).

The Reformers rejected the concept of Roman penance, confession, and satisfaction because they felt all of these in one way or another denied the sufficiency of the atoning work of Jesus Christ: (1) *penance*, because it asserts that Christ's death does not cleanse from all of sin, including the temporal punishments; (2) *confession*, because it affirms the existence of a sacramental priesthood in the New Testament Church; and (3) *satisfaction*, because it asserts that man by his undergoing of some kind of penance can "satisfy" justice. It is in the sacrament of penance where some of the most basic differences between Roman Catholicism and the biblical view espoused by the Reformers can be seen.

A Word on "Works-Salvation"

It is common for Protestants who are involved in discussions with Roman Catholics to say, "Rome teaches a works-salvation system." It is important that this kind of allegation be understood correctly, both by those who use the phrase and by Roman Catholics. First, Catholics assert that they do not believe that they are saved by their works alone or primarily, and there are numerous Roman Catholic dogmatic statements that deny just this thing. Most Protestants are not asserting that Catholics give no place at all to Christ. It is obvious that the Catholic doctrine speaks of the work of Christ and asserts that without the Atonement of Christ, salvation would be impossible.

Having said that, it is important that the Roman Catholic understand what the Protestant is trying to say as well. "Works-salvation" would refer to the concept that human works are *necessary* for salvation; that is, that the work of Christ, *in and of itself*, without human works, actually saves no one at all. If it is asserted that Christ's work is dependent upon the actions of humankind, and that God has simply made a way of salvation available that is still dependent upon works (whether these be penances, baptism, whatever), this is "works-salvation." Works are a necessary part of this kind of doctrine, and it is this that Protestants say is in direct contradiction to the Word of God. It is not necessary that God's grace or mercy be absent in salvation for a teaching to be branded "works-salvation." The key issue is whether those works are necessary and determinative to salvation.

Justification According to Rome

The Reformers rightly emphasized the biblical term "justification." They preached that justification was by faith alone, or, as they put it, *sola fide*. Forced to respond to this constant emphasis in Reformed proclamation, the Council of Trent early on addressed the doctrine of justification.

The dogmatic decree that resulted from the Council of Trent contained sixteen chapters and thirty-three canons condemning various teachings, including, of course, those presented by the Reformers. It has been rightly said that the Council of Trent did not fully understand what the Reformers were saying on a number of counts. Some who insist that Rome has "changed" point to this reality. It is difficult, however, to see how this changes things, as the Council of Trent is still considered infallible in its teaching by the Vatican, and such a view cannot change without a rejection of the entire concept of the infallibility of the Church.[14] The decree opened,

> Since there is being disseminated at this time, not without the loss of many souls and grievous detriment to the unity of the Church, a certain erroneous doctrine concerning justification . . . the holy, ecumenical, and general Council of Trent . . . to expound to all the faithful of Christ the true and salutary doctrine of justification . . . strictly forbidding that anyone henceforth presume to believe, preach or teach otherwise than is defined and declared in the present decree.

The Council continues by asserting that though Christ died for all, "yet all do not receive the benefit of His death, but those only to whom the merit of His passion is communicated," which is "effected . . . through the laver of regeneration. . . ."—that is, by baptism. It then asserts that God gives "predisposing grace" to the individual that is in no way "merited" by anyone; yet it continues on to say that they "may be disposed through His quickening and helping grace to convert themselves to their own justification by freely assenting to and cooperating with that grace. . . ." Next, repentance is said to be a necessary action. After all of this preparation, one is finally justified:

> This disposition or preparation is followed by justification itself, which is not only a remission of sins but also the sanctification and renewal of the inward man through the voluntary reception of the grace and gifts whereby an unjust man becomes just and from being an enemy becomes a friend . . . the instrumental cause is the sacrament of baptism, which is the sacrament of faith, without which no man was ever justified finally. . . . Wherefore, when receiving true and Christian justice, they are commanded, immediately on being born again, to preserve it pure and spotless, as the first robe given them through Christ Jesus in place of that which Adam by his disobedience lost for himself and for us, so that they may bear it before the tribunal of our Lord Jesus Christ and may have life eternal.

This definition of justification, however, should be carefully distinguished from what many Protestant readers would understand as justification. The Roman concept of "being justified" is hardly permanent, for it can be "undone" by the commission of a mortal sin. It is in the clearest sense of the term a "conditional" justification, one that is not permanent but dependent on the continued faithfulness of the person. The "incompleteness" of this justification can be seen in Chapter 10 of this decree, where it asserts that one can "increase" in justification: "through the observance of the commandments of God and of the Church, faith cooperating with good works, increase in that justice received through the grace of Christ and are further justified. . . ." Various denials of Protestant doctrines are put forth: a denial of justification by faith and faith alone follows quickly.[15]

Roman Catholic scholar Ludwig Ott, in his book *Fundamentals of Catholic Dogma*, said the following concerning the idea of "achieving justification":

The reason for the uncertainty of the state of grace lies in this, that without a special revelation nobody can with certainty of faith know whether or not he has fulfilled all the conditions which are necessary for achieving justification.[16]

Must we fulfill all the conditions Roman Catholicism says to be necessary in order to achieve justification? Or are we made right with God by His free and merciful grace, not on the basis of what we do in a state of grace, but upon the basis of what Christ did as our Perfect substitute on the cross? That is the issue before us.

The Role of Faith and Grace in Justification

Turning again to the Council of Trent, we read,

Faith is the beginning of human salvation, the foundation and root of all justification. . . . We are therefore said to be justified gratuitously, because none of those things that precede justification, whether faith or works, merit the grace of justification.[17]

Notice what is said here: according to Trent, we can say that we are justified by grace, or "gratuitously," solely because those things that precede justification, faith and works, are prompted and aided by God's grace. The process of justification is based on God's grace—but it is not completely of God's grace, and it cannot be said that God's grace alone is sufficient without human works to bring about full and complete justification!

Roman Catholicism teaches that the "grace of justification" can be gained and lost, gained and lost. Trent said,

Those who through sin have forfeited the received grace of justification can again be justified when, moved by God, they exert themselves to obtain through the sacrament of penance the recovery, by the merits of Christ, of the grace lost. . . .[18]

Justification, in Roman Catholic theology, involves an infusion of grace—the grace of justification—into the individual. This involves a subjective change in the person. Because of this, he or she is enabled through the power of grace to do good works. These works are, according to the Council of Trent, meritorious in God's sight. This is a vitally important point. Notice carefully the words of Trent:

> Hence, to those who work well unto the end and trust in God, eternal life is to be offered, both as a grace mercifully promised to the sons of God through Christ Jesus, and as a reward promised by God himself, to be faithfully given to their good works and merits . . . we must believe that nothing further is wanting to those justified to prevent them from being considered to have, by those very works which have been done in God, fully satisfied the divine law according to the state of this life and to have truly merited eternal life, to be obtained in its [due] time, provided they depart [this life] in grace. . . .[17]

It must be emphasized that eternal life is *merited* by the good works performed by the person *in the state of grace*. We must remind ourselves that these words are part of the dogmatic teaching of the Roman Catholic Church. While many today might wish to minimize their impact, they remain the inviolable teaching of the Roman Church all the same. Trent said that a person is justified by baptism; that this justified person then does good works ("works which have been done in God"); and that these good works fully satisfy the divine law according to the state of this life. Moreover, the person who has done them has "truly merited eternal life," provided, of course, he departs this life in that same state of grace. The basis, then, of one's final salvation is *not* solely the work of Christ. Dr. Ludwig Ott wrote,

> By his good works the justified man really acquires a claim to supernatural reward from God.[20]

Karl Keating likewise comments,

> The Catholic Church, not surprisingly, understands justification differently. It sees it as a true eradication of sin and a true sanctification and renewal. The soul becomes objectively pleasing to God and so merits heaven. It merits heaven because now it is actually good.[21]

The new *Catechism of the Catholic Church* says that justification "has been merited for us by the Passion of Christ" (section 1992). It is important to recognize that what is being said is not that the death of Christ actually *justifies* us, but that the grace of justification itself is merited by Christ by His death, so that we are able to obtain this grace through the Sacrament of Baptism. Note well the words of the *Catechism:*

> **2010** Since the initiative belongs to God in the order of grace, *no one can merit the initial grace* of forgiveness and justification, at the beginning of conversion. Moved by the Holy Spirit and by charity, *we can then merit* for ourselves and for others the graces needed for our sanctification, for the increase of grace and charity, and for the attainment of eternal life.

Roman Catholic apologists are quick to deflect such citations by asserting that any work we do in the state of grace cannot be said to detract from the glory of Christ, because outside of that grace our works would not be meritorious.[22] Since it is God who by grace enables us to do the good and therefore meritorious works, the entire scheme is said to avoid the charge of "works-salvation."

Grace: Necessary or Sufficient?

While we will have much to say about this in the following chapter, it is important to note while the citations of the Roman position are fresh in our minds that the issue has *never been* the mere *necessity* of grace. The Reformers were not saying that Rome wholly denied grace in the matter of salvation. Such would be silly in light of the frequent mention of the term in the liturgy of the Church. The issue never has been and probably never will be the *necessity* of grace. Unless Rome changes its views (something impossible in the current teaching of the Church) the matter will always be the *sufficiency of grace.* Both sides agree on the *necessity* of grace.

The issue is whether grace is *sufficient* in and of itself to accomplish the salvation of God's people—or if something else must be added to grace to complete that salvation. The Reformers summarized this issue under the term *sola gratia,* by grace *alone.* Not grace mixed with merit (an impossible mixture, we will argue in the next chapter), not grace mixed with works of law, works of charity, works of anything else, but grace *alone.* Can grace, by itself, accomplish the salvation of the human soul? The Reformers said yes. Rome said, *and continues to say,* no. Most importantly, the Apostles said yes.

It is essential that the reader recognize the difference in the two positions. Rome will say that salvation *cannot take place without God's grace*. In fact, the new *Catechism* says of this,

> **1996** Our justification comes from the grace of God. Grace is *favor*, the *free and undeserved help* that God gives us to respond to his call to become children of God, adoptive sons, partakers of the divine nature and of eternal life.

But it is two completely different things to say that salvation cannot take place *without* grace and to say that salvation can take place *by grace alone*. In the first, grace is *necessary* but not *sufficient*; in the second it is both *necessary and sufficient*.[23] If it helps to illustrate the difference, it is much like the earlier discussion of *sola scriptura:* Rome says the Scriptures are *necessary* but not *sufficient*. She adds something to those Scriptures, her tradition in its many forms. As a result, the teaching of the Scriptures is altered in accordance with Roman tradition. While Rome confesses the *necessity* of the Scriptures, she refuses to acknowledge the *sufficiency* of them. In the same way, Rome confesses the *necessity* of grace, but refuses to acknowledge the *sufficiency* of it.

This is the great divide that separated Protestants and Roman Catholics at the time of the Reformation. Time has surely blurred some of the once clear lines of demarcation. One finds, especially in the United States, men and women who fellowship in the Roman Catholic Church who will affirm such phrases as *sola gratia* and *sola fide*. And, at the same time, one will find Protestants who are, as I like to put it, "treading water in the Tiber,"[24] denying some of the very doctrines that once gave form and substance to the Protestant position. But the issues have not changed over the course of more than four centuries.

Some Questions to Consider

In light of Roman Catholic teaching, we might do well to consider some questions before moving to the next point. For example, if a Christian believes that the righteousness that is his is a perfect righteousness because it is not his *own* but is rather the righteousness of *Christ* imputed to him by faith (the Protestant position), does this not invoke the anathema of the Twenty-Fourth Canon of the Sixth Session of the Council of Trent, which reads,

> If anyone says that the justice received is not preserved and also not increased before God through good works, but that those works are merely the fruits and signs of justification obtained, but not the cause of its increase, let him be anathema.

If a Christian is convinced by such Scriptural passages as Ephesians 2:8–10 that the good works he does are truly the "fruits and signs of justification" but not a means of the *increase* of justification (our righteousness, being that of Christ, being perfect and not liable to increase), does this person then fall under the anathema of Rome?

If a person takes Romans 5:1 and, realizing that the action of justification spoken of here is *past tense*, believes himself to be justified by this kind of living faith, how can this person then understand Ott's reference to the necessity to fulfill "all the conditions which are necessary for achieving justification"? Or if this same person reads Paul's words in 1 Corinthians 1:30–31, wherein he is told that it is by God's doing that we are in Christ Jesus, who has become to us wisdom from God and righteousness and sanctification and redemption, so that our boast is only in Him and not ourselves, does this not put such a person under the anathema of Canon 32, which reads,

> If anyone says that the good works of the one justified are in such manner the gifts of God that they are not also the good merits of him justified; or that the one justified by the good works that he performs by the grace of God and the merit of Jesus Christ, whose living member he is, does not truly merit an increase of grace, eternal life, and in case he dies in grace, the attainment of eternal life itself and also an increase of glory, let him be anathema.

And finally, if a person believes that the righteousness of Christ has been imputed to him by faith on the basis of Romans 4:1–8, how can he at the same time believe the words of Canon 32, which states, "We must believe that nothing further is wanting to those justified to prevent them from being considered to have, *by those very works which have been done in God, fully satisfied the divine law according to the state of this life and to have truly merited eternal life*, to be obtained in its [due] time, provided they depart [this life] in grace" (emphasis added)? These are crucial questions that must be addressed by anyone who seeks to find Roman Catholic teaching to be in harmony with the Scriptures.

No Salvation Outside of the Church

One of the major questions faced by Roman Catholics is whether there is salvation outside of the Roman Catholic Church, the topic of *extra Ecclesiam nulla Salus*. In reality, prior to this century—and even today in most Roman Catholic nations around the world—this was not really an issue. The traditional view continues to be taught. But in the United States and in various European countries the issue is hotly debated, not only in Protestant/Roman Catholic discussions but between Roman Catholic theologians and laypeople of various stripes and temperaments. Quite honestly, the strongest disagreements between Protestant denominations get no hotter than the conflict that exists between various views within the Roman communion itself. Charges of apostasy fly hot and heavy *inside* the broad spectrum that makes up Roman Catholicism in the United States. For example, it took me only a few moments with access to the Internet to track down file after file arguing this issue from *both* sides—files filled with strident language and heated emotion. And it is easy to see why this is. Note just a few of the available statements from the past:

> Pope Innocent III (December 18, 1208): "With our hearts we believe and with our lips we confess but one Church, not that of the heretics, but the Holy Roman Catholic and Apostolic Church, outside which we believe that no one is saved."[25]
> Pope Pius IX (December 9, 1854): "It must be held by faith that outside the Apostolic Roman Church, no one can be saved; that this is the only ark of salvation; that he who shall not have entered therein will perish in the flood."[26]
> Pope Leo XIII (January 10, 1890) Encyclical *Sapientæ Christianæ:* "He scatters and gathers not who gathers not with the Church and with Jesus Christ, and all who fight not jointly with Him and with the Church are in very truth contending against God."[27]
> Pope Saint Pius X (March 12, 1904) Encyclical *Iucunda Sane:* "It is our duty to recall to everyone great and small, as the Holy Pontiff Gregory did in ages past, the absolute necessity which

is ours to have recourse to this Church to effect our eternal salvation."

Pope Innocent III and Lateran Council IV (A.D. 1215): "One indeed is the universal Church of the faithful outside which no one at all is saved. . . ."[28]

Pope Boniface VIII in his Papal Bull *Unam Sanctam* (November 18, 1302): "We declare, say, define, and pronounce that it is absolutely necessary for the salvation of every human creature to be subject to the Roman Pontiff."[29]

Pope Eugene IV and the Council of Florence (February 4, 1442): "[The most Holy Roman Church] firmly believes, professes, and proclaims that those not living within the Catholic Church, not only pagans, but also Jews and heretics and schismatics cannot become participants in eternal life, but will depart 'into everlasting fire which was prepared for the devil and his angels' (Matthew 25:41), unless before the end of life the same have been added to the flock; and that the unity of the ecclesiastical body is so strong that only to those remaining in it are the sacraments of the Church of benefit for salvation, and do fastings, almsgiving, and other functions of piety and exercises of Christian service produce eternal reward, and that no one, whatever almsgiving he has practiced, even if he has shed blood for the name of Christ, can be saved, unless he has remained in the bosom and unity of the Catholic Church."[30]

These statements clearly demonstrate why many modern Roman Catholics have been forced to embrace the concept of the "development of doctrine." It takes a great stretch to reconcile the statements above with the words of Vatican II regarding Protestants as "separated brethren"[31] and an even greater stretch to accept words such as these:

Those also can attain to everlasting salvation who through no fault of their own do not know the gospel of Christ or His Church, yet sincerely seek God and, moved by grace, strive by their deeds to do His will as it is known to them through the dictates of conscience.[32]

While Vatican II does affirm that "the Church . . . is necessary for salvation"[33] and that "whosoever, therefore, knowing that the Catholic Church was made necessary by God through Jesus Christ, would refuse to enter her or to remain in her could not be saved,"[34] the Council manages to allow both traditional and modern viewpoints to exist side by side without really solving the obvious contradiction. For this reason, many are insisting that Vatican II was more of a "pastoral" Council and did not exercise dogmatic or infallible authority. Aside from illustrating the fact that having an allegedly infallible teaching authority does not result in a unanimity of opinion, it is important to realize the differing positions taken on this very fundamental issue. Any conversation on this topic will require both sides to understand what position is taken on the ultimate question of whether salvation can be found outside the walls of the Church.[35]

We now come to the point where we can ask the most important question: What do the Scriptures say? What is the Gospel? We have seen that Rome's attempt to add her traditions to the Scriptures fails, and we have now seen what Rome has to say about salvation itself. It is time to look to the Scriptures to find out what God has revealed in His Word about this critically important point.

10

JUSTIFIED BEFORE GOD: BY GRACE THROUGH FAITH ALONE

My pastor takes preaching seriously. He views it as a privilege and a high calling to stand before the people of God to open the Word of God. I well remember the first time I filled the pulpit in our congregation. When we met in the pastor's office prior to the service he asked, "Are you scared?"

"Yes, a bit" I replied.

"Good," he said. "It is an awesome thing to preach the Word of God to God's people." Then, as we went into the service, he said to me, "Play the man, Mr. Ridley."

I knew these words were spoken by Hugh Latimer to Nicholas Ridley, bishop of London, as they both went to the stake as martyrs under the reign of Queen Mary. I wasn't completely sure how I should apply those words at that particular point, but I got the basic idea.

I feel the same sense of awe and apprehension as I approach the topic of justification: the marvelous work of the Almighty God in making sinful, rebellious human beings right before Him through the awesome and gracious work of Jesus Christ. There is nothing more important, no subject more weighty than this one. In a flippant age of sound-bites and shallow thinking it calls for our best—indeed our all. We need to roll up our sleeves and do some work if we are to treat this topic with the respect it deserves.[1]

The Protestant, biblical doctrine of justification differs from the Roman Catholic view in four foundational aspects:

(1) We differ on the meaning and extent of the term "justifi-cation."
(2) We differ on the meaning of the term "impute" or "impu-tation."
(3) We differ on the means by which justification takes place. Is it faith alone, or faith plus works?
(4) Finally, we differ on the grounds or basis upon which sinful people can be justified.

These four areas will define our discussion. We cannot even begin to exhaust this topic in the brief space available.[2] Instead, we must focus on those aspects of the doctrine that are at stake when dealing with the teachings of Roman Catholicism.

Defining Terms

Let us begin with some definitions. We have seen the Roman Catholic view in brief. Now we provide the Protestant side of the debate. Let us first look at a statement of the doctrine from the 1689 Baptist Confession of Faith:

> Those whom God effectually calleth, he also freely justifieth, not by infusing righteousness into them, but by pardoning their sins, and by accounting and accepting their persons as righteous; not for anything wrought in them, or done by them, but for Christ's sake alone; not by imputing faith itself, the act of believing, or any other evangelical obedience to them, as their righteousness; but by imputing Christ's active obedience unto the whole law, and passive obedience in his death for their whole and sole righteousness, they receiving and resting on him and his righteousness by faith, which faith they have not of themselves; it is the gift of God.
>
> Faith thus receiving and resting on Christ and his righteous-ness is the alone instrument of justification; yet it is not alone in the person justified, but is ever accompanied with all other saving graces, and is no dead faith, but worketh by love.
>
> Christ, by his obedience and death, did fully discharge the debt of all those that are justified; and did, by the sacrifice of himself in the blood of his cross, undergoing in their stead the penalty due unto them, make a proper, real, and full satisfaction to God's justice in their behalf; yet, inasmuch as he was given

by the Father for them, and his obedience and satisfaction accepted in their stead, and both freely, not for anything in them, their justification is only of free grace, that both the exact justice and right grace of God might be glorified in the justification of sinners.[3]

The Baptist Confession of Faith is in full agreement with the Westminster Shorter Catechism,[4] which sums up this subject well by stating,

Q: What is justification?
A: Justification is an act of God's free grace, wherein he pardoneth all our sins, and accepteth us as righteous in his sight, only for the righteousness of Christ imputed to us, and received by faith alone.

Justification is said to be an act of God as *judge* wherein He *declares* the believer righteous. It is, therefore, a legal, *forensic* declaration on the part of God concerning the believer. Now the term "forensic" is hardly attractive at first glance. It seems distant and dry. But it serves a vital and, if I might be so bold, *exciting* purpose. It helps us to realize that God has done something about our lost condition. Sinners are condemned by God's just and holy law. How can the person who stands before the Judge of all the earth, plainly guilty and condemned, find full freedom and restoration? The language in which the New Testament discusses this issue is the language of the courtroom, and the term "forensic" simply tells us that God has done something *wonderful* in the realm of law, guilt, and forgiveness.

Justification is an act undertaken *by God*, and it is not based on anything done in or done by us as believers. *It is an act of sovereign grace*, because it is something *God does*, not something *we do*. This viewpoint is God-centered, not man-centered. This is not merely a plan that we work to gain something from God. It is God's work, and when God does something He does it well.

Next, we touch on the very heart of the Gospel, and in so doing, on the very heart of God. Justification is based solely and completely upon the merits of another—Jesus Christ. How can God, as a just and holy Judge, declare a sinner to be sinless? How can He rightly release the guilty prisoner? Because the Perfect Substitute has intervened. The basis of justification is the perfect work of Jesus Christ. Even though the term "merit" is not a biblical term, if we are to use it in this discussion it must be limited to the only One who possesses such a thing: Christ. All we have before God, due to sin, is demerit, nothing more. Christ, however, has perfect righteousness, so that the declaration of the righteousness of the believer is based upon *His* work *alone*.

Justification involves the imputation of the righteousness of Christ—both His perfect life as well as His perfect, all-sufficient atoning sacrifice—to the believer. On this basis the believer is called "righteous." God is the one who imputes this righteousness to the believer. Imputation is another one of those words that *should* cause the believer's heart to swell with praise, for it is an act of grace beyond comprehension, and without that term there would be no salvation, no peace with God. Imputation is different from both "infusion" and "impartation." How? If you infuse something into someone, you are making a change in that person. If you impart something to them, you are simply giving something to them to keep or hold. When God imputes the righteousness of Christ to us, He is again acting as sovereign judge, *crediting* us with the works of another: Jesus Christ. He is not merely handing us something, for we could drop such a precious gift or in some other way fail to properly handle it. He is not infusing something into us, making a change in us as a person. Instead, as judge, He imputes to our account the righteousness of another, so that He can properly and rightly look at us and say, "This person is righteous. He is free and has peace with me."

Justification is by grace, through faith. Faith is the instrument, the means of appropriating justification. This faith is a true, saving faith. This kind of faith is not just a bare intellectual assent to the facts of the Gospel; it is a faith that results in the person "believing and resting on Him and His righteousness."[5] This faith is supernatural in origin, for it is not of ourselves, "it is the gift of God." This is a living faith, one that looks to Christ alone for salvation. The second section of the Confession expands upon this, asserting that faith is the "alone instrument of justification." No works of human merit can bring about this justification. No religious rites or activities can justify. Faith—true, saving faith—is the only instrument of justification. Note, however, that faith is but the *instrument* and not the *basis* of justification.[6] We are not justified *because* we believe; we are justified *through* faith, faith being the "appropriating organ" by which justification comes. This kind of faith, the confession asserts, is "not alone" but is "ever accompanied with all other saving graces, and is no dead faith, but worketh by love." As has been said many times, faith alone saves, but a saving faith is never alone.

Justification, while distinct from sanctification, *cannot possibly be separated from it.* This is extremely important. In Roman Catholic theology justification and sanctification are synonymous; in Protestant theology a very important distinction is made between the two terms. God *changes* us in regeneration and sanctification; God *declares* us righteous in justification. Anyone who is justified *will be sanctified.* It is *impossible* to separate justification and sanctification, but it is *absolutely necessary* to distinguish them.

Finally, justification is a once-for-all action. Since it is based on the completed work of Christ, it cannot be undone or destroyed by the actions of any human. We *look back* upon our justification, as Paul said in Romans 5:1, *"having been justified by faith."*

The Freedom of Grace

Before we move to the demonstration of these truths on the basis of Scripture, I wish to emphasize something that is absolutely foundational. The Bible teaches that salvation is based on God's grace. Grace is not simply an aid that helps us to do certain things. Grace is free—absolutely free, completely based on the will and mercy of God, not on any action on our part. The Bible tells us that we are justified by grace in Titus 3:5–7, where we read,

> He saved us, not on the basis of deeds which we have done in righteousness, but according to His mercy, by the washing of regeneration and renewing by the Holy Spirit, whom He poured out upon us richly through Jesus Christ our Savior, so that being justified by His grace we would be made heirs according to the hope of eternal life.

We are also told that we are justified as a gift by His grace in Romans 3:24. But aside from being justified by free grace, we are also said to be justified by the blood of Jesus Christ. In Romans 5:9 we read,

> Much more then, having now been justified by His blood, we shall be saved from the wrath of God through Him.

So we see that the Bible speaks of our justification *by grace*, and our justification *by the blood of Christ*. And further, the Bible speaks of our justification *by faith*, as in Romans 5:1:

> Therefore, having been justified by faith, we have peace with God through our Lord Jesus Christ.

Justified by grace, justified by the blood of Christ, justified by faith. Are these three different things, or three aspects of one thing? Clearly, Paul is describing the great truth of justification by God's free grace. His grace is unmerited; we cannot earn it. The blood of Christ shed in behalf of His people was unmerited and free. And the faith that justifies—true, saving faith—is the gift of God's grace as well. So the real issue is this: is God's grace sufficient to bring about justification, or must human merit be added to the grace of God?

Using the Manual

How we interpret the Bible affects our understanding of justification. At this point I am not referring to the role tradition plays in the Roman Catholic reading of Scripture. My point is rather the fact that many times people build an entire theology on the *minority* of references to a subject while ignoring the *majority*.

Take for an example a person who wishes to learn about the headlights on his car. That person may pick up the owner's manual and begin looking through the information provided. Now, he may find a passing reference to the headlights under the topic of the "battery," and he may find something about them under "maintenance," and something else under "safety inspections." But if he really wants to know about the headlights, he will first look under the all-important topic "headlights." If he neglects to look there first, he may end up with an unusual understanding of headlights by drawing conclusions only from passing references found in sections dedicated to other topics.

While this scenario seems rather obvious to us, it is amazing how often such a simple truth is ignored when it comes to interpreting the Bible. Rather than going to the primary passages that specifically discuss a given topic, many people build their entire theology on a passing reference to a term or concept in passages that are not specifically about the belief under discussion. If you wish to know about the qualifications of the officers of the Church, for example, you go to the Pastoral Epistles, where Paul provides specific, direct instruction about elders and deacons. If you ignore those passages and attempt to draw together various references to elders and deacons from other sources, you run the danger of ending up with an unbalanced understanding of what the Bible, *as a whole revelation*, teaches on the topic. Surely it is true that once those *primary* passages are consulted, you can derive *additional* information from other sources. But to ignore the primary places of exposition and the primary expositors of a given belief is to mistreat the Bible and end up with a false understanding and a faulty theology.

This is especially true regarding the doctrine of justification. The family of terms that make up the concept of "justification" (the verb "to justify," the noun, "justification," and the adjective "just") are used in many ways throughout the Bible. Yet God has provided specific passages containing particular, direct, unquestionable discussion of exactly how a sinner is made just in God's sight. To build a theology from other references to these terms—and then try to import this into the primary passages—is to go at the subject backward. Instead, we must allow the primary expositor of this issue, in this case, the Apostle Paul, to speak first; his epistles to the Romans and the Galatians must define the issues, for it is in them that we have direct discussions of exactly how justification takes place. Once we have consulted these sources, we can then move on to garner other elements of the biblical revelation that are found in *tangential* ways elsewhere.

A frequent objection to this assertion goes along these lines: "You are making Paul a higher authority than Jesus or Peter or anyone else." This is simply not the case, however. The Lord Jesus did not choose to address every issue that His Church would need to know or understand. He left many things for His Apostles to address under the direction of the Holy Spirit. For example, Jesus almost never speaks directly of the Church—He leaves that for the Apostles to discuss and explain. Does this mean that the revelation given through the Apostles is somehow "less inspired" than that given by the Lord Jesus? Of course not. God has simply chosen different means of revealing His truth. We would have a lopsided view of things if we held only to the four Gospels. God has given us more than the four Gospels, and we dare not think that He did so without reason. It is not as if the Lord Jesus did not discuss the issue of how we are saved. He surely did. But He did not deem it proper to discuss the specifics of the issues prior to Calvary. In His sovereign will He left that to the Apostle Paul, who undertook that task with great energy and clarity in his epistle to the Romans and his epistle to the Galatians.

One other item needs to be addressed to avoid confusion. I have often asked classes, "What is the biblical difference between the terms "righteousness" and "justification"? Often the responses center on seeing "righteousness" as a *moral* attribute, and "justification" as a *legal* thing. In reality, there is absolutely no difference at all between the two words as they are used in the Bible. In fact, there are not two different terms in the New Testament that are translated as the two words "righteousness" and "justification." There is only one term which is translated by both of these words. To be righteous is to be justified; to make righteous is to make just, and so on.

Works and Faith

When Paul confronted Peter at Antioch for his hypocrisy, he reminded Peter of some basic truths of the Gospel message. Peter had seriously compromised the Gospel by withdrawing from fellowship with the Gentiles. In rebuking him, Paul said,

> Nevertheless knowing that a man is not justified by the works of the Law but through faith in Christ Jesus, even we have believed in Christ Jesus, so that we may be justified by faith in Christ and not by the works of the Law; since by the works of the Law no flesh will be justified (Galatians 2:16).

The works of the Law are contrasted with faith. The Law, of course, was the highest expression of God's holiness. The Law is just and good, Paul taught (Romans 7:12). But even the Law could not justify, for it was never intended to do so. He made the same point in Romans 4, where he sets forth one of the clearest, most obvious arguments for justification by faith. He concludes the first section of the book by saying,

> For we maintain that a man is justified by faith apart from

works of the Law (Romans 3:28).

Some modern Roman Catholic apologists attempt to limit Paul's argument to *only* the works of the Law, i.e., such things as circumcision. They say that works can still be a part of justification as long as they are not works of the Mosaic law itself, but are instead works of love, penance, etc. This argument fails on two accounts: first, if works of the *highest* Law are of no avail, surely works of some other law (which could not be any higher or more holy than the Mosaic) will not suffice either. More importantly, this attempt misses Paul's whole point. While he did indeed focus on the works of the Law due to his struggle against the Judaizers (those who wished to put Christians under the old Mosaic law, as in Acts 15:1–5), it is a terrible exegetical mistake to miss the contrast Paul is presenting between *working* and *believing*. Note how the works of the Law are nowhere to be found in Romans 4:4–5, where the very same issues are in view:

> Now to the one who works, his wage is not credited as a favor, but as what is due. But to the one who does not work, but believes in Him who justifies the ungodly, his faith is credited as righteousness.

Note well that Paul *contrasts* the concepts of working and believing. This is a *common concept* in the New Testament: there is a strong *antithesis* between belief and work when it comes to being made right with God. You must *either work* at doing the deeds of the Law (and that perfectly!), or you *must believe* in Christ; you simply *cannot* meld the two together. This passage parallels two phrases—those who do *not* work and those who *believe*—and says the two groups are one! The ones who receive righteousness are those who see that *believing* is different than *working for* something.[7] The antithesis between faith and works is central to all of Paul's discussion of how a man is made right with God. Prior to this Paul said in Romans 3:21–25:

> But now apart from the Law the righteousness of God has been manifested, being witnessed by the Law and the Prophets, even the righteousness of God through faith in Jesus Christ for all those who believe; for there is no distinction; for all have sinned and fall short of the glory of God, being justified as a gift

by His grace through the redemption which is in Christ Jesus; whom God displayed publicly as a propitiation in His blood through faith. This was to demonstrate His righteousness, because in the forbearance of God He passed over the sins previously committed.

Paul asserts that we are justified freely and by grace here in Romans 3:24, and again in Titus 3:7. Is Paul contradicting himself by saying that we are justified by grace, and that we are justified by faith? Not at all. As we stated before, justification is by faith so that it would be in harmony with grace, just as Paul said in Romans 4:16, "For this reason it is by faith, that it may be in accordance with grace." *Faith abandons all efforts at work or merit and realizes our complete dependence upon God, not just for the provision of a way of salvation, but for the entire action of salvation!*

For salvation to be of grace, it cannot possibly be of works. As Paul said in Romans 11:6, either it is on the basis of works or of grace; it cannot be both. *Saving grace, by definition, excludes the entire concept of human works or merit.* Grace cannot be merited, and cannot coexist with merit on the part of the one to whom it is given.

The contrast of faith and works as mutually exclusive concepts is continued in Paul's strong letter to the Galatians. He emphasizes again that it is impossible to combine works of the Law with faith in Christ. Note his strong words in Galatians 2:21:

> I do not nullify the grace of God, for if righteousness comes through the Law, then Christ died needlessly!

If you assert that righteousness is the result of God's grace and human action, then you are nullifying the work of Christ completely. No synergism is possible—it is either all of grace, or not of grace at all. Finally, Paul provides a clear antithesis when, in Galatians 3:10–11, he writes,

> For as many as are of the works of the Law are under a curse; for it is written, "CURSED IS EVERYONE WHO DOES NOT ABIDE BY ALL THINGS WRITTEN IN THE BOOK OF THE LAW, TO PERFORM THEM." Now that no one is justified by the Law before God is evident; for, "THE RIGHTEOUS MAN SHALL LIVE BY FAITH."

The impossibility of the Roman Catholic position is clearly seen:

faith plus works nullifies grace. Grace plus works is dead. But does not the Bible say that Christians are to do good works? Of course. *But the only one who can do good works is the one who has already been justified!* As Paul taught the Ephesians,

> For by grace you have been saved through faith; and that not of yourselves, it is the gift of God; not as a result of works, so that no one may boast. For we are His workmanship, created in Christ Jesus for good works, which God prepared beforehand so that we would walk in them (2:8–10).

Salvation is the gift of God—not just the bare plan of God, or even just the bare grace of God that prompts us to move toward God, but *all* of salvation is of God. Were this not the case, we would certainly boast! The purpose of God is clearly presented: we have been created in Christ Jesus *unto* good works—not by good works, not with the help of good works, but that we might perform good works! *First* comes full salvation from God, *then*, as a result, the works prompted by the Holy Spirit of God. *No human merit, even that supposedly produced by human works performed in a state of grace, will ever stand before the judgment throne of God.* Only the righteousness of Christ, apprehended by faith, will avail. And lest you think my words to be too strong, remember what Paul said in summing up his argument in Galatians 5:2:

> Behold I, Paul, say to you that if you receive circumcision, Christ will be of no benefit to you.

The Judaizers in Galatia were asserting that one act of obedience—circumcision—was absolutely necessary for justification. Paul made it crystal clear: it is either Christ alone as the perfect Savior, or it is works of the Law—no matter what law one might choose.[8] Christ will not share His Saviorhood with anyone!

Sola Fide—faith alone, that is, saving faith, resting solely in the perfection of the work of the Lord Jesus Christ in my stead. That is my hope. That is the Good News. Not justification by baptism, then rejustification after committing a mortal sin by sacramental forgiveness, penances, and satisfactions. No merit from good works done in a state of grace so as to receive eternal life.

No, justification is by faith alone, so that it can be by grace alone. That is the Gospel.

The Basis of Justification

What is the basis of justification? How can God declare someone who is unjust just? How can God declare sinners saints?

One of the fundamental differences between the Roman Catholic doctrine and the Protestant doctrine is simply this: the righteousness by which we stand before God, according to the Protestant, is the righteousness of Jesus Christ *alone*.[9] No one will *ever* stand before God clothed in the righteousness of Christ, Mary, the saints, and himself.[10] The righteousness of Christ is the actual and real possession of the believer. This is the righteousness a Christian pleads before the judgment throne of God. Christ is our Substitute. Our sins are imputed to Him; His righteousness is imputed to us. Christ does not simply merit for us grace so that we can then do good works to earn our way to heaven; by God's grace Christ's righteousness becomes ours, and we have eternal life because of Christ's righteousness, not because of our own.

There are far too many passages that teach this central truth to even begin to address all of them. However, a few representative samples must be presented. Paul taught the Corinthians,

> He made Him who knew no sin to be sin on our behalf, so that we might become the righteousness of God in Him (2 Corinthians 5:21).

Is this not what Isaiah had prophesied long ago?

> But He was pierced through for our transgressions, He was crushed for our iniquities; the chastening for our well-being fell upon Him, and by His scourging we are healed . . . by His knowledge the Righteous One, My Servant, *will justify the many*, as He will bear their iniquities . . . yet He Himself bore the sin of many, and interceded for the transgressors (Isaiah 53:5, 11–12).

Roman Catholicism speaks of our doing works—in a state of grace—that make satisfaction or atonement for sin.[11] Why? Christ bore all our sins, and since He did so, the Father can declare us righteous. This is truly the central difference between us: my justification is based completely and solely on the finished work of Christ. Roman Catholicism does not have a truly finished work of

Christ on which to base justification![12] Christ's merits are the Christian's merits by virtue of the union of the elect with their Head, Jesus Christ. When we are *in Him*, we have His life, His righteousness, and His "merits." And the union of the elect with Jesus Christ is not the result of human action or will. It is solely the result of God's merciful election in eternity past (Romans 9:16; Ephesians 1:4). From beginning to end, salvation is of God. May we all join with Paul's statement,

> So that I may gain Christ, and may be found in Him, not having a righteousness of my own derived from the Law, but that which is through faith in Christ, the righteousness which comes from God on the basis of faith (Philippians 3:8–9).

This is the only righteousness that will avail for us.

Christian justification does not result in a life filled with fear at falling from God's grace, or in a continual cycle of justification/fall/justification/fall. Instead, Paul, after presenting Abraham as the example of justification by faith, proclaimed:

> Therefore, having been justified by faith, we have peace with God through our Lord Jesus Christ, through whom also we have obtained our introduction by faith into this grace in which we stand; and we exult in hope of the glory of God (Romans 5:1–2).

We *have been* justified, and, because of this, we have peace with God through Christ! This is the peace we spoke of in Chapter 3. This is not a temporary cease-fire in a war that could erupt again at any moment at the whim of the will of man! This is a permanent peace, *true shalom!* And it can be true peace because it is based not on our merits, not on good works we produce while in a state of grace, but on the completed and finished work of Christ.

Righteousness as a Legal Concept

Next we turn to the examination of the term "righteousness." Abram believed God, and it was reckoned to him as righteousness. Christ became sin in our place, that we might be made the righteousness of God in Him. What do these terms mean?

The Hebrew term *zedekah*, normally translated in terms of "righteous" or "righteousness," carries two main thoughts. It is often used for what we normally consider as "moral righteousness" or uprightness. The New Testament uses the term in this way as well, for example, in describing Joseph as a "righteous man" (Matthew 1:19), and Zechariah and Elizabeth as "just" (Luke 1:6). But the Hebrew *zedekah*[13] also carries a forensic, or legal, concept of being right in the eyes of law; that is, of being in the proper relationship to the law. This is often the case when the verb form is used.

There are a number of examples of this usage from the Old Testament. These include Exodus 23:7 and Proverbs 17:15, but I shall use just one example, Deuteronomy 25:1:

> If there is a dispute between men and they go to court, and the judges decide their case, and they justify the righteous and condemn the wicked. . . .

Note the context: a law court. To justify the righteous obviously means to give a legal, forensic declaration regarding a person's proper standing before the law. This is clearly seen here by the term that is paralleled with the act of justifying: to condemn. Neither involves a subjective change of the individual; the righteous man was righteous inwardly even before the declaration of his righteousness, just as the guilty man was guilty before the proclamation of his guilt and condemnation.

This is the source of Paul's understanding of justification in the New Testament. Paul's use of the terms *demands* that this be so.[14] The conjunction of the two terms "impute" and "to justify" in Paul's teachings clearly shows that the Protestant understanding of God's declaration of the righteousness of the believer is the biblical one. I shall demonstrate this briefly by two passages from the New Testament. First, with reference to the imputation, we note again Paul's words in Romans 4:6–8:

> Just as David also speaks of the blessing on the man to whom God reckons righteousness apart from works: "BLESSED ARE THOSE WHOSE LAWLESS DEEDS HAVE BEEN FORGIVEN, AND WHOSE SINS HAVE BEEN COVERED. BLESSED IS THE MAN WHOSE SIN THE LORD WILL NOT TAKE INTO ACCOUNT."

Note the parallels that Paul presents: the imputation (reckoning) of righteousness and the non-imputation ("will not take into account") of sin are likened to forgiveness of those sins, and to their "covering." Where is the subjective change taught by Roman Catholic theology? It does not find support in the Scriptures because it doesn't exist there. The imputation of righteousness is a legal transaction based upon the authority of God as Judge. God can impute righteousness to those who have faith because of the full, complete, and *real* satisfaction that has been made on their behalf by Christ.[15]

The second passage relevant to the forensic or legal character of justification is Romans 8:33–34. Here we read,

> Who will bring a charge against God's elect? God is the one who justifies; who is the one who condemns?

Note the exact same contrast of the terms "to justify" and "to condemn" that is found in the Old Testament. God justifies His elect. Therefore, who can bring a charge against them? Note the legal language. Who can condemn those who have been justified—that is, who have been declared righteous by the Eternal Judge himself? No one.

What Does "Impute" or "Reckon" Mean?

The usage of the term translated "reckoned" or "imputed" in the Old Testament indicates that to impute something to someone does not involve a subjective change in the person. One example of this is Leviticus 17:4. Any man who did not bring an animal he had slaughtered to the door of the tabernacle as an offering to the Lord, as the Scripture says, "bloodguiltiness is to be *reckoned* to that man." Surely this guilt is not *infused* into the man, but he is *legally declared guilty* of blood.

I suggest that this is the proper background for Paul's understanding of the term in Genesis 15:6 as well. Paul cites Genesis 15:6 a number of times as a foundational passage indicating that salvation has *always* been by grace through faith (Romans 4:3, 9, 22; Galatians 3:6). To reckon something to someone's account does not involve a subjective change in that person. This is especially clear in a legal context, and that is what we have in Romans 3 and 4.

The Hebrew term *hashav*[16] has some interesting uses in the Old

Testament. We need to discover the background of Paul's use of the term as it is found relative to the imputation of righteousness.

In Genesis 31:14–15, Rachel and Leah, Jacob's wives, speak of their father and the treatment they have received at his hand. They say, "Do we still have any portion or inheritance in our father's house? Are we not *reckoned* (*hashav*) by him as foreigners?" Of course, Rachel and Leah were not foreigners, but they were *reckoned* as such by their father.

One other example is found in Leviticus 25:31 regarding the law concerning redemption rights. We read, "The houses of the villages, however, which have no surrounding wall shall be considered (*hashav*) as open fields; they have redemption rights and revert in the jubilee." The houses in unwalled villages were to be treated as if they were open fields; they were not, of course, open fields, but legally they were treated as if they were.

All of the examples listed above of this use of *hashav* are translated in the Greek translation of the Old Testament (the Septuagint) by the very same term[17] Paul uses in Romans 4 when he speaks of the imputation or reckoning of righteousness to the believer!

Why is this so significant? Because scholars recognize that Paul utilized the Septuagint as his main source of biblical citations, and his vocabulary is deeply influenced by it. Our understanding of what it means to impute something should take this into consideration.[18]

Luther's Dunghill

Martin Luther liked striking illustrations. One that frequently pops up when Roman Catholics and Protestants discuss justification is his idea of the "dunghill covered by snow." The illustration basically goes like this: We are a dunghill, repugnant to God, sinners worthy of condemnation. Justification is likened to a snowfall that covers over the dunghill. The dunghill is still a dunghill, but that which was once offensive to God is now covered over with a pure blanket so that the offense is no longer seen.

Luther was attempting in his own inimitable way to point out the difference between justification and sanctification. Justification does not change the dunghill into something else: it covers the dunghill with something that takes away the offensiveness that it has by nature. Then the process of sanctification begins, through which the dunghill is changed. Luther was trying to explain how we are both justified and sinful *at the same time*. The dunghill is still a dunghill: but it is covered over with a blanket of pure snow. In the same way, the believer is not changed subjectively by justification, but is covered over with an "alien righteousness," the "righteousness of another," that being the righteousness of Christ.

Roman Catholic apologists like to go after Luther, and his example of the dunghill is a prime target. "Surely God does not leave us as mere dunghills covered over with snow," they assert. "That would make justification mere legal fiction, empty words without meaning." Rarely do they admit that Luther was speaking to only one thing: the difference between justification and sanctification, and that he did not deny that the Spirit of God then works the miracle of sanctification in the life of the individual. His whole point was that what makes us acceptable before God is not anything done *in us* or *by us*. Instead, we are acceptable before God for only one reason: the pure snow that is the righteousness of our Savior, Jesus Christ.

One day when lecturing on this topic I turned the illustration around and used it to show the difference between the Roman Catholic position and the Protestant one. From Rome's viewpoint, the "grace of justification" actually changes the dunghill into a pile of gold, so that, since it is now pleasing to God, it merits eternal life. As we noted from Karl Keating,

> The soul becomes objectively pleasing to God and so merits heaven. It merits heaven because now it is actually good.[19]

Now surely it would seem that such an illustration is far more attractive than Luther's dunghill. However, if we probe a bit further, we realize the subtle danger that Luther saw so clearly. In Rome's concept, that pile of gold can, by the commission of a mortal sin, be instantly transformed back into a pile of dung! Through the commission of venial sins and through the imperfect performance of penances, the pile of gold can become impure, so that spots of dung again cling to its shiny surface. This impurity must be removed, *not by the application of the pure snow of Christ*, but by the suffering of the gold itself, in this life, or in purgatory after death. In light of Ott's statement about the "uncertainty of the state of grace," the pile of gold can never really know, outside of a supernatural revelation, whether it is a pile of dung or a pile of gold! In Luther's example, the dunghill is accepted by God because of the perfection of the work of the snow itself, which represents the righteousness of Christ. The centrality of human works in Rome's view is clearly seen when contrasted with the Savior-centered work presented by the Reformers based firmly upon the Scriptures.

Does It Really Matter?

The heart of every person who has been touched by the Holy Spirit of God knows intuitively that in truth they stand accepted before God solely on the basis of Jesus Christ. While many may deny the truth of justification by faith alone by their words, they cannot do so with their heart if they are truly one with the people of God. The faith that holds and clings to Christ and Christ alone, which pleads His righteousness, His perfect obedience, His all-sufficient death, will not allow the sinfulness of the heart to rear its ugly head and say, "I have done this or that to bring about my salvation." Christ is the believer's all—the one who has the divine gift of faith will not seek solace anywhere but in the Lord Jesus Christ.

Every time we bow in prayer, we are forced to realize the awesomeness of justification by faith. We draw near to a holy God, yet we do not do so in servile fear, but with a boldness that is based upon our full assurance of acceptance because of our union with Jesus Christ. We know we could never approach God on the basis of *anything* we might do. We know our own hearts well enough to realize that even our *best* work is tainted and stained with selfishness and pride. But we come near to God not on the basis of who we are or what we have done—we do not *dare* plead our own supposed "righteousness"—instead, we come before the throne of grace with hearts full of thankfulness and praise for our Lord Jesus Christ, who by His work has provided for us full and complete remission of sins and a perfect standing before the Father.

It is difficult for many to understand the fact that we cling to the righteousness of another and believe that Christ, as our perfect Substitute, has provided complete forgiveness of sins *and* has made it possible that His perfect righteousness—His sinless life—can be imputed to us as our present and precious possession. It is contrary to the natural religious impulses of fallen human beings to be so bereft of reason for boasting. It is not normal to give the glory completely to another. Yet this is the Gospel, and there is none other that truly saves. The beauty of the truth of justification by faith in Jesus Christ is clearly portrayed in the precious words of Lynnette Paasch:

It was a solemn afternoon
When he began to ponder
What could he bring to God
To merit favor from the King?
The works he cherished the most
Became as filthy rags
Before a holy God.
Nothing to his credit,
Save for the Cross.

Save for the Cross
He'd stand condemned.
Save for the Cross
He'd be dead in his sin.
But for the sacrifice
Of the Holy Lamb
He could not stand.

It was the moment of truth.
And he knew his life
Could never be the same.
For now he could clearly see,
That God was the author of his faith
By His glorious grace.

And save for the Cross
He'd stand condemned.
Save for the Cross
He'd be dead in his sin.
But for the sacrifice
of the Holy Lamb
He could not stand.

Save for the Cross,
Where His blood was shed,
Save for the Cross,
He knew destruction would be his end.
But for the sacrifice

of the Spotless Lamb,
He could not stand.
Save for the Cross
He could not stand.
Save for the Cross.
Save for the Cross.[20]

Only those who have realized what it means to give oneself completely to another can understand these words.

Peace with God is the present possession of the justified believer. This is not a peace that is transient; it is not a mere truce in a war that might again erupt at any time. This is a lasting peace, based upon the *permanent* cessation of hostilities. All that we could do could never bring about this condition of peace, even had we wanted to do so! But God has made peace, and each one who has faith in Christ Jesus and is declared just on that basis enjoys peace with his Maker, his Creator. What a tremendous blessing!

But if the Gospel is the power of God unto salvation, then we can see the reason why Paul warned so strenuously against a *false* gospel. A false gospel, quite simply, brings no salvation. It might assuage feelings of guilt—to a degree. It might give a person a feeling of peace—for a moment. But a false gospel lacks the power of God unto salvation, and that is why we find the strong warnings in Scripture concerning the need to maintain the purity of the Gospel message itself.

Does it matter?

When it comes to the Gospel, yes, it surely does.

On the most fundamental level the Gospel as presented by Rome differs substantively from that preached by the Apostles of Christ nearly two thousand years ago. If we did not go on to look at the Mass, at Purgatory, and at indulgences, we would still have more than enough in what we have seen thus far to proclaim the differences to be vital, important, and definitional. The Roman Catholic view of justification does not do what the biblical one does: it does not provide true peace. This alone would be enough. But there is much more. Rome adds to its view of a sacramentally mediated justification the concept of the Mass as a propitiatory (yet finite in value) sacrifice. To this is added the idea of Purgatory, wherein a person can undergo the "suffering of atonement." And beyond this we have indulgences and the "treasury of merit."

The issues are many, the import great.

11

WHAT OF THE MASS?

John O'Brien, in his popular work *The Faith of Millions*, wrote the following:

> When the priest announces the tremendous words of consecration, he reaches up into the heavens, brings Christ down from His throne, and places Him upon our altar to be offered up again as the Victim for the sins of man. It is a power greater than that of saints and angels, greater than that of Seraphim and Cherubim.
>
> Indeed it is greater even than the power of the Virgin Mary. While the Blessed Virgin was the human agency by which Christ became incarnate a single time, the priest brings Christ down from heaven, and renders Him present on our altar as the eternal Victim for the sins of man—not once but a thousand times! The priest speaks and lo! Christ, the eternal and omnipotent God, bows his head in humble obedience to the priest's command.
>
> Of what sublime dignity is the office of the Christian priest who is thus privileged to act as the ambassador and the vicegerent of Christ on earth! He continues the essential ministry of Christ: he teaches the faithful with the authority of Christ, he pardons the penitent sinner with the power of Christ, he offers up again the same sacrifice of adoration and atonement which Christ offered on Calvary. No wonder that the name which spiritual writers are especially fond of applying to the priest is that of *alter Christus*. For the priest is and should be *another Christ*.[1]

To Protestant ears, there are disturbing assertions in these comments. What of O'Brien's allegation that Christ is offered as a sacrifice upon the Roman altar? What of his statement that Christ, the omnipotent God, bows His head in "humble obedience to the priest's command" and comes down from heaven to be offered again and again in sacrifice? Is O'Brien simply going beyond what is really taught by Roman Catholicism?

The Council of Trent met in its thirteenth session in October of 1551 and promulgated a decree concerning "the Most Holy Sacrament of the Eucharist." At the end of the decree was a list of canons, providing anathemas for those who would reject the Council's teaching. Since these canons often provide short, succinct definitions of Roman teaching, we shall list some of them so that the position taken by Trent on the issue of the Eucharist—specifically, in this section, on the concept of "transubstantiation"—can be clearly understood:

> (Canon 1) If anyone denies that in the sacrament of the most Holy Eucharist are contained truly, really and substantially the body and blood together with the soul and divinity of our Lord Jesus Christ, and consequently the whole Christ, but says that He is in it only as in a sign, or figure or force, let him be anathema.

> (Canon 2) If anyone says that in the sacred and holy sacrament of the Eucharist the substance of the bread and wine remains conjointly with the body and blood of our Lord Jesus Christ, and denies that wonderful and singular change of the whole substance of the bread into the body and the whole substance of the wine into the blood, the appearances only of bread and wine remaining, which change the Catholic Church most aptly calls transubstantiation, let him be anathema.

> (Canon 8) If anyone says that Christ received in the Eucharist is received spiritually only and not also sacramentally and really, let him be anathema.

Eleven years later, in 1562, the twenty-second session was held. This time the decree promulgated was entitled "Doctrine Concerning the Sacrifice of the Mass." The second chapter of this decree says,

> And inasmuch as in this divine sacrifice which is celebrated in the mass is contained and immolated in an unbloody manner the same Christ who once offered Himself in a bloody manner

on the altar of the cross, the holy council teaches that this is truly propitiatory and has this effect, that if we, contrite and penitent, with sincere heart and upright faith, with fear and reverence, draw nigh to God, we obtain mercy and find grace in seasonable aid. For, appeased by this sacrifice, the Lord grants the grace and gift of penitence and pardons even the gravest crimes and sins. For the victim is one and the same, the same now offering by the ministry of priests who then offered Himself on the cross, the manner alone of offering being different. The fruits of that bloody sacrifice, it is well understood, are received most abundantly through this unbloody one, so far is the latter from derogating in any way from the former. Wherefore, according to the tradition of the Apostles, it is rightly offered not only for the sins, punishments, satisfactions and other necessities of the faithful who are living, but also for those departed in Christ *but not yet fully purified* (emphasis added).

Again a list of canons are found at the end of the decree, and some of them read as follows:

(Canon 1) If anyone says that in the mass a true and real sacrifice is not offered to God; or that to be offered is nothing else than that Christ is given to us to eat, let him be anathema.

(Canon 2) If anyone says that by those words, *Do this for a remembrance of me*, Christ did not institute the Apostles priests; or did not ordain that they and other priests should offer His own body and blood, let him be anathema.

(Canon 3) If anyone says that the sacrifice of the mass is one only of praise and thanksgiving; or that it is a mere commemoration of the sacrifice consummated on the cross but not a propitiatory one; or that it profits him only who receives, and ought not to be offered for the living and the dead, for sins, punishments, satisfactions, and other necessities, let him be anathema.

(Canon 4) If anyone says that by the sacrifice of the mass a blasphemy is cast upon the most holy sacrifice of Christ consummated on the cross; or that the former derogates from the latter, let him be anathema.

(Canon 5) If anyone says that it is a deception to celebrate masses in honor of the saints and in order to obtain their intercession with God, as the Church intends, let him be anathema.

(Canon 6) If anyone says that the canon of the mass contains errors and is therefore to be abrogated, let him be anathema.

We may summarize the teachings of the Roman Catholic Church on the Mass from the Council of Trent as follows:

(1) Jesus Christ is truly, really, and substantially present in the Sacrament of the Eucharist following the words of consecration.

(2) Transubstantiation involves the change of the whole substance of the bread into the substance of the body of Christ, and the change of the whole substance of the wine into the substance of the blood of Christ.

(3) Since Christ is said to be really present in the Eucharist, the elements themselves, following consecration, are worthy of worship.

(4) The Sacrifice of the Mass is properly called "propitiatory" in that it brings about pardon of sin.

(5) In the institution of the Mass at the Lord's Supper, Christ offered His own body and blood to the Father in the signs of the bread and wine, and in so doing ordained the Apostles as priests of the New Testament.

(6) The Sacrifice of the Mass is properly offered for sins, punishments, satisfactions, and other necessities, not only for the living but for the dead as well.

(7) Finally, anyone who denies the truthfulness of any of these proclamations is under the anathema of God.

If someone asks if this is *still* the teaching of the Church, a quick review of the new *Catechism of the Catholic Church* will make it quite plain that indeed Trent's teachings remain the official, dogmatic position of the Roman Catholic Church. While a scarce nine paragraphs are dedicated to the specific subject of justification,[2] a full eighty-four are dedicated to the Eucharist, not including fourteen summary paragraphs.[3] Trent is mentioned by name, quoted as authoritative, and its doctrines plainly presented as the Church's teaching. As an example, I cite only one paragraph from the *Catechism:*

1367 The sacrifice of Christ and the sacrifice of the Eucharist are *one single sacrifice:* "The victim is one and the same: the same now offers through the ministry of priests, who then offered himself on the cross; only the manner of offering is different." "In this divine sacrifice which is celebrated in the Mass, the same Christ who offered himself once in a bloody manner on the altar of the cross is contained and is offered in an unbloody manner."

Both quotations are directly from the Council of Trent and are the most modern expression of *official* Roman Catholic doctrine.

The Mass and the Gospel

One could fill an entire book with arguments concerning the teachings of Rome concerning the Mass. Our concern here, however, is to deal only with those issues that are relevant to our examination of the Gospel message. The Mass is obviously central to Rome's view of salvation. As the *Catechism* says in quoting Vatican II:

As often as the sacrifice of the Cross by which "Christ our Pasch has been sacrificed" is celebrated on the altar, the work of our redemption is carried out.[4]

Therefore we must, if only briefly, consider some of the main issues raised by the teachings we have just examined.

There are two major areas that I wish to focus our attention on. First, the idea that the Eucharist involves *transubstantiation*, that is, that the wafer and the wine are changed by the power of God into the actual flesh and blood of Jesus Christ.[5] No one denies the ability of God to do such a thing, if He revealed that He desired to do so. No one denies that Christ is truly present in the Lord's Supper just as He is truly present with believers on a daily basis. He promised to be with His Church until the end of the age, and we believe that He is with us. We accept that Christ truly encounters us in the Lord's Supper, and that this is a special time of communion with the Lord. But Christ can be with us truly and really without transubstantiation of bread and wine into flesh and blood. In our next section we see that this belief has no solid foundation in the Word of God.

The second aspect of the Roman doctrine of the Eucharist we will explore is that the Mass is viewed as a propitiatory sacrifice. Roman Catholicism teaches that when Christ is offered upon the altar by the priest, this is a truly propitiatory sacrifice, for it is the same sacrifice as that of the Cross.[6] However, at the same time, it must be pointed out that Rome admits that the *effects* of this propitiatory sacrifice are limited. Masses can be said for the same intention with no full guarantee that that intention will be fully accomplished. Dr. Ludwig Ott wrote,

> The sacrifice of the Mass effects the remission of the temporal punishments for sin which still remain after the forgiveness of the guilt of sins and of the eternal punishment, not merely mediately by the conferring of the grace of penance, but also immediately, because the atonement of Jesus Christ is offered as a substitute for our works of atonement and for the sufferings of the poor souls. *The measurement of the punishments of sins remitted is proportional, in the case of the living, to the degree of perfection of their disposition.* In the case of the suffering souls, the satisfactory operation of the Sacrifice of the Mass is applied by way of intercession. . . . As they are in the state of grace and thus oppose no obstacle, theologians generally teach that *at least part of their punishments for sins is infallibly remitted.*[7]

And on the same page he added,

> As a propitiatory and impetratory Sacrifice, the Sacrifice of the Mass possesses a finite external value, since the operations of propitiation and impetration refer to human beings, who as creatures can receive a finite act only. This explains the practice of the Church of offering the Holy Sacrifice of the Mass frequently for the same intention.[8]

Recall that this concept of a humanly limited effectiveness of the sacrifice of the Mass was mentioned by Trent earlier when it made reference to those saints who leave this life "not yet fully purified." My point is this: *in Roman Catholic theology, a person can attend a thousand masses and still leave this life "not yet fully purified."* The ramifications of this should not be missed, especially in light of the claim that the Mass is the *same* sacrifice as that of Calvary. Can a person approach Calvary a thousand times, seeking forgiveness, and yet die "impure," so as to have to suffer in purgatory before entering God's presence? If not, then the Mass cannot be the *same* sacrifice as that of Calvary.

Does the Bible Teach Transubstantiation?

Nearly every Roman apologist bases his defense of the concept of transubstantiation and the Eucharist upon Jesus' words in John chapter 6, specifically verses 53 through 57. Indeed, it is commonly said that here the Roman Catholic Church "takes the Bible for what it says," while Protestants are somehow seeking to *avoid* the "clear" teaching of the Lord Jesus. To dispel this thinking let's explore the passage together:

> So Jesus said to them, "Truly, truly, I say to you, unless you eat the flesh of the Son of Man and drink His blood, you have no life in yourselves. He who eats My flesh and drinks My blood has eternal life, and I will raise him up on the last day. For My flesh is true food, and My blood is true drink. He who eats My flesh and drinks My blood abides in Me, and I in him. As the living Father sent Me, and I live because of the Father, so he who eats Me, he also will live because of Me."

The Roman Catholic Church claims that any understanding that does not take these words literally spiritualizes the text to avoid an unwanted conclusion.[9] Is the literal meaning of the text supportive of Roman Catholic doctrine of the Eucharist? Does a person literally have to eat the flesh of the Son of Man and drink His blood to have life in himself?

First, we must point out that the *literal* meaning of the text is obviously not always the *clear* meaning. The term "literal" is capable of quite a range of definition. If it is pushed to mean absurd literalism, and we are forced to accept an absurdly literal understanding of a text, then obviously the whole Bible is full of complete nonsense. Jesus claimed to be the door of the sheep in John 10; literally this means Jesus is a door, replete with hinges, knob, and maybe even a lock! And, of course, this would also have to mean that only sheep will be saved, not human beings, for He is the door of the *sheep*. Everyone understands that Jesus is speaking figuratively, and the obvious *and hence the literal* meaning of the passage is the one that recognizes the symbolism of the language used. If the text shows us that the terms used by the speaker are meant to be taken in a figurative or symbolic way, the *truly* literal interpretation will take this into consideration.

John loved to pick up on the different ways the Lord Jesus communicated a point. He differs in this from the other Gospel writers, for in John the same teaching will be presented in a number of different ways. Jesus is "the Light of the world," (8:12), the "good shepherd" (10:11), and the "true vine" (15:1). Jesus is not literally the sun in the sky, a shepherd of sheep, or a living vine. Yet all of these descriptions tell us something about Jesus *when they are taken according to the plain intention of the text:* as symbols. So, too, John likes to use different phrases to say the same thing. One that is important in John 6 is his use of the phrases "have eternal life" and "shall be raised up on the last day." It would be an obvious mistake to differentiate between these two phrases. They mean the same thing and are used in parallel to each other.

With these things in mind, we come to the longest chapter in the Gospel of John, chapter 6. John begins by narrating the miracle of the feeding of the 5,000 with the five barley loaves and two fishes. The people respond to this by saying, "This is truly the Prophet who is to come into the world" (6:14). Jesus perceives that they are about to attempt to make Him king by force, so He goes away into the mountain by himself. This is followed by the miracle of Christ's walking upon the water and calming the storm, which brings Him and His disciples to shore near Capernaum. The crowd, which has stayed the night near the place of their miraculous feeding, comes to Capernaum also, seeking Jesus.

When they find Him, they ask Him how He got there, but the Lord brushes their question aside and gets to the heart of the matter. Jesus goes directly to their motivation for seeking Him. Remember that the night before they were going to make Him king by force. They are obviously mistaken about who Jesus is. The dialogue that follows centers on the person of Christ and His role in salvation. He turns their thoughts away from a secular kingdom to His person and the importance of their relationship to Him. Pressing the claims of Christ will result in many turning away from Him, but this is necessary to dispel false followers who are seeking nothing but their own benefit.

Drawing from the miracle performed the day before, Jesus in verse 27 says, "Do not work for the food which perishes, but for the food which endures to eternal life, which the Son of Man will give to you, for on Him the Father, even God, has set His seal." The crowd was looking for a meal, but Jesus was directing them to himself, the bread "which endures to eternal life." The crowd did not fully follow His meaning and asked what they should do to "work the works of God." Jesus replied that the work of God was to believe in the One whom God had sent, namely, himself. This was quite a claim, of course, and the crowd demanded a sign as evidence of His authority. They, too, grasped the aforementioned miracle and asserted that Moses had given them bread from heaven to eat. Can Jesus do the same? Moses had accomplished it for a long period of time, while Jesus did so only once. Can He do it again?

> Jesus then said to them, "Truly, truly, I say to you, it is not Moses who has given you the bread out of heaven, but it is My Father who gives you the true bread out of heaven. For the bread of God is that which comes down out of heaven, and gives life to the world" (vv. 32–33).

The quotation from Psalm 78:24 offered by the people specifically identifies Yahweh as "He" who gave them bread in the wilderness. Possibly they were indicating Moses here, either directly or by implication, and so Jesus corrects them. Or they are making the comparison between Him (of whom some had said "this is truly the Prophet . . .") and Moses, and Jesus quickly corrects their misunderstanding of His person. Rather, the one source of the "true bread" is the Father—He gave the manna in the wilderness but is now giving (present tense) the "true bread from heaven." He gives not a perishable food but rather a person—"the one coming down from heaven." Here, in the first mention of Jesus as the bread from heaven, the emphasis is upon the *present*. The institution of the Supper in the future is not the focus of the chapter. The present reality of the living Christ standing before them *is*.

There is also another parallel in this text (but an incomplete one, of course): Just as the manna came down from heaven and provided sustenance for the people of God during their sojourn, so too Jesus has come down out of heaven to be the sustenance of God's people— and their salvation. Jesus utilizes this kind of dualistic symbolism throughout this discourse, referring to the physical reality of the manna to represent the spiritual reality of faith in Him. This dualism has been missed by the Roman Catholic Church, which reads into this passage the doctrine of transubstantiation in the Mass—and in so doing reverses the direction the Lord is taking with the conversation. They, like the first-century listeners, cannot see past the symbol to the reality beyond.

> Then they said to Him, "Lord, always give us this bread." Jesus said to them, "I am the bread of life; he who comes to Me will not hunger, and he who believes in Me will never thirst" (vv. 34–35).

The crowd continues in its blindness, unable to see the real significance of Jesus' words. In response Jesus gets quite specific—He himself is this bread. The one who "comes to Me"—a clear reference to faith (as the parallel will show)—will not hunger (the bread is spiritual, not natural) and the one who "believes in Me" will never thirst. The reference to "thirsting" seems somewhat out of place here, given that only food has been mentioned up to this point; but in actuality there is no difficulty, as Jesus is not referring to actual physical consumption of food. He is referring to our spiritual need. We all have a need spiritually (symbol: hunger and thirst), and Jesus meets that need completely and eternally. "Coming" and "believing" will become "eating" and "drinking" in verse 54. There is a clear progression in these terms that leads to the *literal* and *obvious* meaning of the text. What is more, since this is the first time that "hunger" and "thirst" are presented, the definitions assigned to these terms by the Lord (being spiritual and symbolic, not literal and earthly) must be carried through the rest of the text.

Following this, Jesus moves into demonstrating that no man can come to Him outside the Father's drawing (vv. 36–46).[10] He then returns to the symbol of the bread in verses 47 and following.

> "Truly, truly, I say to you, he who believes has eternal life. I am the bread of life. Your fathers ate the manna in the wilderness, and they died. This is the bread which comes down out of heaven, so that one may eat of it and not die. I am the living bread that came down out of heaven; if anyone eats of this bread, he will live forever; and the bread also which I will give for the life of the world is My flesh" (vv. 47–51).

The one who believes, Jesus says, has (present tense—continuous action) eternal life. Eternal life is not simply duration of life, but quality of life as well—not something only for the future, but present, too. What is the person believing? Faith in the Bible always has an object—it never exists in a vacuum. Faith is not a separate entity with an existence of its own. In the context, the main object of faith is the person of Jesus Christ himself.

This is seen in a few ways. First, in verse 46, He speaks of being the "One who is from God." In verse 48, He speaks of being the bread of life. Both of these statements are assertions about who Jesus is and are fitting objects of faith. The fathers of the Exodus ate the manna in the wilderness and died, but the bread that comes down from heaven (Jesus) is vastly superior to the manna that was simply a picture of what was to come later in Christ. The one who "eats" of this bread will never die. The "eating" here is paralleled with the "believing" of verse 47—*any attempt to make this a physical action misses the entire point the Lord is making.* He who believes has eternal life—he who eats of the true bread from heaven will never die. Eating=believing. This is clearly the *literal* meaning of the text.

This faith is a personal one, because it involves the "eating" of this true bread—which is Jesus himself (v. 51). The eating of the true bread means eternal life, and this bread, Jesus says, is His flesh "which is given for the life of the world." It is not Jesus' flesh *per se* that is the object here. It is His flesh as given in sacrifice that brings eternal life. It is the sacrifice that gives life, not simply the flesh. In His giving of His life, the Son provides life for the world.

> Then the Jews began to argue with one another, saying, "How can this man give us His flesh to eat?" (v. 52).

The Jews, continuing to dwell simply on the physical plane, and refusing to follow Jesus above to the spiritual truth underlying the symbol of His words, begin to quarrel among themselves about this teaching. The men ask how Jesus can give His flesh for them to eat. Of course, Jesus is not saying that He is going to do so. He is speaking of His coming sacrifice and the resultant forgiveness of sins and eternal life for all who are united to Him.

> So Jesus said to them, "Truly, truly, I say to you, unless you eat the flesh of the Son of Man and drink His blood, you have no life in yourselves. He who eats My flesh and drinks My blood has eternal life, and I will raise him up on the last day" (vv. 53–54).

Jesus decides to come down to their level in an attempt to bring them up to His. He moves on with the metaphor, already firmly established, of "eating=believing." The only way to eternal life is through union with the Son of Man. This involves a vital faith relationship with Him, symbolized here by the eating of His flesh and the drinking of His blood. To make the equation complete, Jesus places "eating My flesh and drinking My blood" in the exact same position as: (1) hearing His word and believing on Him who sent Jesus (John 5:24); (2) being drawn by the Father (6:44); (3) looking to the Son and believing (6:40); or (4) simply believing (6:47). The result is the same in each case—eternal life, or being raised up at the last day. Taken all together, we have a clear indication of Jesus' usage of the metaphor of "eating His flesh and drinking His blood" in John 6. Graphically we would have:

Everyone who beholds the Son and believes (6:40). Those who are drawn by the Father (6:44). He who believes in Christ (6:47). He who eats My flesh and drinks My blood (6:54).	ALL EQUAL	"eternal life" or "being raised up"

Consequently, the Roman Catholic interpretation of this passage is left without a foundation. Jesus is obviously not speaking of a Sacrament of the Eucharist supposedly established years later. His referring to His body and blood is paralleled clearly with belief in the Son and the drawing of the Father. Consistency of interpretation must lead to the rejection of a sacramental interpretation of this passage. The literal meaning, given the parallelism already firmly established in this passage, has to refer to the union of the believer by faith with Jesus Christ, not a participation in the Roman Catholic Mass.

This Is My Body

On the night of His betrayal, the Lord Jesus left to His Church a memorial of His death, the Lord's Supper, so that by partaking in this supper we might "proclaim the Lord's death until He comes" (1 Corinthians 11:26). The believer is well aware of the solemnity of the celebration of the Supper and the closeness to his Lord that is experienced during that time. The "words of institution" of this ordinance of the Church are special to all who call upon the name of Jesus. Matthew records them for us as follows:

> While they were eating, Jesus took some bread, and after a blessing, He broke it and gave it to the disciples, and said, "Take, eat; this is My body." And when He had taken a cup and given thanks, He gave it to them, saying, "Drink from it, all of you; for this is My blood of the covenant, which is poured out for many for forgiveness of sins (Matthew 26:26–28).

We have already seen the Roman interpretation of these words in our examination of the doctrine of the Mass. The teaching goes so far as to say that at the time the Lord spoke these words, He was offering up a sacrifice to God, and the elements (the bread and wine) were already changed into His body and blood. Of course, the Roman Catholic Church asserts that anything but a literal interpretation of the phrases "this is My body" and "this is My blood" is an attempt to avoid acknowledging the plain teaching of Scripture. But again, is this the plain teaching? Does an honest reading of the Lord's words force us to believe that Christ changed the bread and the wine into His body at this time, and then instructed His followers to do the same?

The Apostle Paul also spoke of that night, and the institution of the Lord's Supper. He tells us in 1 Corinthians 11:23–31:

> For I received from the Lord that which I also delivered to you, that the Lord Jesus in the night in which He was betrayed took bread; and when He had given thanks, He broke it and said, "This is My body, which is for you; do this in remembrance of Me." In the same way He took the cup also after supper, saying, "This cup is the new covenant in My blood; do this, as often as you drink it, in remembrance of Me." For as often as you eat this bread and drink the cup, you proclaim the Lord's death until He comes. Therefore whoever eats the bread or drinks the cup of the Lord in an unworthy manner, shall be guilty of the body and the blood of the Lord. But a man must examine himself, and in so doing he is to eat of the bread and drink of the cup. For he who eats and drinks, eats and drinks judgment to himself if he does not judge the body rightly. For this reason many among you are weak and sick, and a number sleep. But if we judged ourselves rightly, we would not be judged.

Here, then, are two witnesses to the institution of the Lord's Supper. Are we obligated, by the words themselves, to understand this in the way the Roman Church teaches? First, we must recognize the function of symbolic language in Scripture. We have already seen the use of it by our Lord in John 6. Some Roman apologists quickly assert that it would be highly improbable that the Lord Jesus, on such a serious and vital occasion as this, would risk being misunderstood through the use of "non-literal" language. Yet, it is on the very same night that Jesus gives the discourse to the disciples that is found in John 15, wherein He says, "I am the vine, you are the branches." No one asserts that He was being absurdly literal here. I don't know of any religious groups that teach that Jesus literally became a vine with branches by making this statement. Unless someone wishes to argue that the content and message of John 15 is unimportant, the fact that the Lord was willing to use symbolic language at this time—and that He expected His disciples to understand it in that way—derails the objection to the Lord's use of symbols.

The texts themselves provide further basis for the symbolic interpretation of the words of the Lord. Both Matthew and Paul record the fact that the blood of which the Lord Jesus speaks is the "blood of the covenant" of the "new testament (covenant) in My blood." The Scriptures are unanimous in saying that the blood of the New Covenant is the blood of the Cross. Also, the Bible plainly teaches in Hebrews 9 and 10 that the sacrifice of Christ on the Cross was a one-time, never to be repeated, complete and perfect action. There is simply no reason at all to assume that these words carry any other meaning than to communicate the representation of the blood of Christ soon to be shed at Calvary. These Apostles taught that it was the blood of Christ alone that is the basis of the New Covenant.

Furthermore, we see that even after the supposed "consecration," the Lord, and Paul after Him, continue to refer to the elements as bread and wine, not as the body or blood of Christ! When Jesus refers to the cup, He says, "I will not drink again of this *fruit of the vine* from now on until that day when I drink it new with you in My Father's kingdom" (Matthew 26:29). One can picture the Lord Jesus, still holding the cup, and referring to it as He speaks. But what does He say? Does He say it is literally blood? No, He says it is the fruit of the vine. And then He says He will not drink of it again until He would drink it with the disciples in His Father's kingdom. Does this mean that Jesus will still be transubstantiating wine into His blood in the kingdom of God? We are looking at the text very closely, very literally, but that is what is demanded by the Roman position. If we are forced to take "this is My blood" as literally as the Roman Catholic Church insists, we must point out the contradictions and errors that come as a result of this method of interpretation.

Paul, too, after the blessing refers to the bread not as the body of Christ but as bread. The verse reads: "As often as you eat the bread and drink the cup" (1 Corinthians 11:26). It does not say that we eat the body of Christ or drink His blood. When the person eats and drinks unworthily, it is said that he is eating bread and drinking of the cup. Each time it is bread and wine, not body and blood.

But what of his comments immediately thereafter, where he speaks of not "discerning" or "recognizing" the body of the Lord? Does this require us to believe that the bread and the wine are actually the body and blood of the Lord? Only if we believe that a symbol is meaningless and trite. If we do not, but accept the seriousness of the Lord's Supper, without jumping to extreme literalism we can see how the behavior of the people in Corinth was a sin against the institution and purpose of the Supper of Christ. Participation in the Supper is meant to be a memorial (not a sacrifice) of the death of Christ, not the carefree and impious party it had become at Corinth. In that light, a person's misunderstanding of the Supper would be a serious sin, as Paul explains. But to take this to mean that the bread and the wine are literally the body and blood of Christ in the Roman sense is to go beyond the meaning of the text.

We must remember that the use of figures or symbols is widespread in Scripture. In nearly every other instance, the Roman interpretation recognizes the symbol and does not ask for strict literalism. A symbolic understanding of Jesus' words, "This is My body" does not in any way reduce the importance of the Supper. If we do as the Lord commanded, calling to mind His broken body and shed blood and thankfully confessing our complete reliance on the atoning work of Jesus Christ, we are showing the greatest demonstration of the fruit of His death until He comes. Each time we break the bread and partake of the fruit of the vine, we are showing the unity that is ours in the only place that Christian unity can be found—the Lord Jesus Christ. We are acknowledging that all Christians everywhere owe all that they are or ever will be to the work of Christ at Calvary. We look back to the Cross, for it is there that our redemption was accomplished. It is there that we received a full and complete remission for our sins. We do not look at another sacrifice or a "re-presentation" of the sacrifice of Christ. There is no need for this. It is a memorial supper, as the Lord said. We remember what has happened. But by remembering we do not cause the past to happen again.

Therefore, the plain meaning of the words of Christ must be that which *the disciples themselves would have understood at the time*. They have just celebrated the Passover, itself incredibly rich in symbolism. Each of the items on the table was to the Jewish people a symbol of something, a reminder of their escape from Egypt by the hand of God. They were already thinking symbolically. So when Jesus takes bread and breaks it and says, "This is My body," no one in the room thought that He had just changed the bread into the same body that stood before them. And when He said the wine was His blood, He explained that it was the blood of the covenant, which they would have understood against the background of the blood of the sacrifice that had been sprinkled upon the people to ratify the covenant long, long ago. The blood of the covenant was blood from a sacrificial victim, not a living person. Knowing this, the meaning of Christ's words are clear: His blood, shed on Calvary, is the blood of the New Covenant. But since Christ had not yet died at the time of the Last Supper, it is impossible for this to actually be the blood of the New Covenant!

Clearly, then, Christ is using the wine as a symbol of the blood of the New Covenant and the bread as a symbol of His broken body. They have to be symbols, since the reality of the crucifixion had not yet taken place! Christ's body was not yet broken, yet He breaks the bread as a symbol of the breaking of His body; His blood is not yet shed, yet He speaks of it as shed. All of this was pointing forward to the Cross. The supper finds its substance, its fulfillment, in the Cross and in nothing else. It looks to that one sacrifice and reminds us that it was there and there alone that our redemption was accomplished.

Is Christ's Death Effective?

Let us move to Hebrews 9 and 10 as a response to the idea that the Mass, as a propitiatory sacrifice, has finite value. Rome teaches that believers can approach this "re-presentation" of the sacrifice of Christ a thousand times or more in their life and still die "impure," needing yet to undergo the suffering of atonement in Purgatory before being able to enter into the presence of God.

Just as Paul is the primary expositor of the doctrine of justification, the writer to the Hebrews is foremost in explaining and expounding on the Atonement of Christ.[11] Throughout his epistle he demonstrates the superiority of Christ to all that had come before, and in chapters 9 and 10 the superiority of the New Covenant over the Old—the sacrifice of Christ over those of the priests before the altar. He points out that Christ entered into the Holy Place "once for all,"[12] not by the blood of bulls and goats but by His own blood, "having obtained eternal redemption" (9:12). Christ's sacrifice, unlike the sacrifices of old, is able to cleanse the consciences of those for whom it is made (9:14). The writer continues to contrast the Old and the New, and we read toward the end of the chapter (verses 24 through 28):

> For Christ did not enter a holy place made with hands, a mere copy of the true one, but into heaven itself, now to appear in the presence of God for us; nor was it that He would offer Himself often, as the high priest enters the holy place year by year with blood not his own. Otherwise, He would have needed to suffer often since the foundation of the world; but now once at the consummation of the ages He has been manifested to put away sin by the sacrifice of Himself. And inasmuch as it is appointed for men to die once and after this comes judgment, so Christ also, having been offered once to bear the sins of many, will appear a second time for salvation without reference to sin, to those who eagerly await Him.

Christ entered into the true Holy Place, heaven itself, to appear in the presence of the Father for us. Because of the perfection of His work He does not need to offer his sacrifice repeatedly, as did the old high priest who entered the Holy of Holies once each year with "blood that is not his own."

Christ did not need to "suffer often." His one act of suffering is sufficient, since He was able to "put away sin by the sacrifice of Himself." The old sacrifices could not put away sin and therefore had to be repeated. Repetition demonstrates insufficiency. But Christ, "having been offered *once* to bear the sins of many," demonstrates the total sufficiency of His work by its *singularity* and *completeness*. To emphasize this, the writer goes on to say in chapter 10, verses 1 through 4:

> For the Law, since it has only a shadow of the good things to come and not the very form of things, can never, by the same sacrifices which they offer continually year by year, make perfect those who draw near. Otherwise, would they not have ceased to be offered, because the worshipers, having once been cleansed, would no longer have had consciousness of sins? But in those sacrifices there is a reminder of sins year by year. For it is impossible for the blood of bulls and goats to take away sins.

How is a person who draws near to be made perfect? Those who approached God through the old sacrifices were not perfected by them. In fact, the sacrifices only served to remind the people of their sins. The repeated offering of the sacrifice on the Day of Atonement told them, every year, of their imperfection.[13] There must be some other remedy for sin, and that remedy is found in the perfect sacrifice—the Lamb of God, who does not simply cover over the sins of His people but bears them away.

The imperfection of the old sacrifices is highlighted by their being repeated over and over again. If they had been effective, they would have stopped being offered. If they had accomplished their goal, they would have ended. But since they went on and on they witness to their own inadequacy and insufficiency.

What, then, is the opposite of this? That if a sacrifice is sufficient, adequate, and proper, it will accomplish its goal *and will not be offered over and over again*. This is how Christ's sacrifice is strikingly superior to those of the Old Covenant. Verses 5 through 8 reiterate this point, and verse 9 concludes that Christ takes away the first covenant "in order to establish the second," that being the New Covenant in His blood. This New Covenant is perfect and flawless, unlike the first (8:7–13). It is this "will" or "covenant" we read about in verses 10 through 14:

> By this will we have been sanctified through the offering of the body of Jesus Christ once for all. And every priest stands daily ministering and offering time after time the same sacri-

fices, which can never take away sins; but He, having offered one sacrifice for sins for all time, SAT DOWN AT THE RIGHT HAND OF GOD, waiting from that time onward UNTIL HIS ENEMIES BE MADE A FOOTSTOOL FOR HIS FEET. For by one offering He has perfected for all time those who are sanctified.

The contrast could not be stated in any stronger terms. The high priest offered sacrifices that could "never take away sins." He stood in the Holy Place, never sitting down, never resting, because his work was never completed. The offerings he made were inadequate to perfect those for whom he made them. But Christ's sacrifice accomplishes its goal. He does not stand, repeatedly offering His work. His work of atonement is completed. Instead, He is seated, His work finished, the one offering needed to perfect for all time. There is no need for repetition or for "re-presentation," as the writer points out in verse 18: "Now where there is forgiveness of these things, there is no longer any offering for sin." If an offering is still being made, forgiveness remains incomplete. If the offerings cease, forgiveness is a reality.

The relevance of this passage to the Roman Catholic doctrine of the Mass as a "propitiatory sacrifice" is clear. Rome insists that the Mass is the *very same sacrifice* as that of Calvary, differing only in manner (bloody versus unbloody). Yet it is admitted that the *effect* of the Mass is limited, and that a person can draw near to the Mass over and over again and still die "impure." According to their doctrine, it is quite possible for a person to attend Mass every day of his life, commit a mortal sin the hour before his death, and be lost for eternity, despite having approached the Mass as a sacrifice thousands of times. The Roman Catholic response would be that such a person is unlikely to commit such a serious sin because so much grace had already been given him through attendance at so many Masses. The fact remains that God's grace is said to be channeled through the Sacraments, especially through the Mass. Yet *that grace cannot accomplish its goal outside of the cooperation of the person drawing near to worship*, and so the possibility of being lost for eternity remains.

The repetitive nature of the Mass stands in stark contrast to the completedness of the Cross.[14] As the writer to the Hebrews said, if such a sacrifice as what is presented in the Mass were sufficient, wouldn't the persons drawing near be cleansed and have no more need of the offering? But the fact that they must come back over and over again shows that this sacrifice of the Mass has more in common with the old sacrifices of the Old Covenant than it does with the sacrifice of Jesus Christ on Calvary.

But what about Protestant churches? Don't we also celebrate the Lord's Supper repeatedly? We do, but as a *memorial*, a wondrous time in which we *proclaim the Lord's death*, not *"re-present"* the Lord's death as a sacrifice. The propitiation for our sins has already been accomplished in *one* sacrifice, not in the "re-presentation" of that sacrifice in an "unbloody" fashion on an altar at the command of a priest.

The inability of the Mass to fully cleanse those who draw near serves as an excellent backdrop to our next subject, which takes us past the door of death into the concept of Purgatory.

12

THE DIVINE WAITING ROOM

F. X. Shouppe recounts one of many stories that has given form to the popular conception of the Roman Catholic doctrine of Purgatory:

> In the year 1589, in the monastery of St. Mary of the Angels, in Florence, died a Religious who was much esteemed by her sisters in religion, but who soon appeared to St. Magdalen de Pazzi to implore her assistance in the rigorous Purgatory to which she was condemned. The saint was in prayer before the Blessed Sacrament when she perceived the deceased kneeling in the middle of the church in an attitude of profound adoration. She had around her a mantle of flames that seemed to consume her, but a white robe that covered her body protected her in part from the action of the fire. Greatly astonished, Magdalen desired to know what this signified, and she was answered that this soul suffered thus for having had little devotion toward the August Sacrament of the Altar. Notwithstanding the rules and holy customs of her Order, she had communicated but rarely, and then with indifference. It was for this reason Divine Justice had condemned her to come every day to adore the Blessed Sacrament, and to submit to the torture of fire at the feet of Jesus Christ. Nevertheless, in reward for her virginal purity, represented by the white robe, her Divine Spouse had greatly mitigated her sufferings.
>
> Such was the revelation which God made to His servant. She was deeply touched, and made every effort to assist the poor soul by all the suffrages in her power. She often related this ap-

parition, and made use of it to exhort her spiritual daughters to zeal for Holy Communion.

The concept of Purgatory seen in such a story has a long history in Roman Catholic theology. In most places in the world today, this viewpoint remains the norm. But in the United States and in other Western countries, these concepts are less than popular. Seeking to make this concept more attractive to those in their cultures, Roman Catholic apologists have come up with different ways of discussing current teaching of the Roman Catholic Church. There are some *attractive* presentations of the doctrine of Purgatory today. The idea of an "anteroom to heaven" where "self-love is turned to love for God" and we are "consumed with the all-encompassing love of God" does not carry with it the more popular notions of what Purgatory is like.

More than one Protestant has found his objections vanishing after his first exposure to what *seems* like a rather logical belief. Once a person has accepted the idea that one can be justified but not fully cleansed, that there are different kinds of sins—mortal and venial—and that there are "temporal punishments" for these sins that we must expiate by our deeds of penance and our sufferings, Purgatory becomes a logical belief. How else could it be? Nothing imperfect can enter into heaven; therefore, since we are not perfected in justification, there must be some process whereby that perfection can take place and some time for it to happen. And therefore we have Purgatory.

I would strongly assert that none of the preceding concepts are in harmony with the Scriptures' teaching on what it means to be justified, what it means to be forgiven, and what it means to be cleansed. Instead of addressing topics again that we have already discussed, I would like to point out some problems with the doctrine of Purgatory itself and demonstrate why it is one of the *clearest* examples of how the official and unquestionable dogma of Rome violates the Gospel message.

Purgatory

The *Catechism of the Catholic Church* says of Purgatory:

1030 All who die in God's grace and friendship, but still imperfectly purified, are indeed assured of their eternal salvation;

but after death they undergo purification, so as to achieve the holiness necessary to enter the joy of heaven.

1031 The Church gives the name *Purgatory* to this final purification of the elect, which is entirely different from the punishment of the damned. The Church formulated her doctrine of faith on Purgatory especially at the Councils of Florence and Trent.

Since the *Catechism* only devotes three paragraphs to this topic and refers us to Florence and Trent for an explanation of the "doctrine of faith," it is necessary to see what the Roman Church said in earlier days.

> Council of Florence (1439): DS (1304) [*De novissimis*] It has likewise defined, that, if those truly penitent have departed in the love of God, before they have made satisfaction by worthy fruits of penance for sins of commission and omission, the souls of these are cleansed after death by purgatorial punishments; and so that they may be released from punishments of this kind, the suffrages of the living faithful are of advantage to them, namely, the sacrifices of Masses, prayers, and almsgiving, and other works of piety, which are customarily performed by the faithful for other faithful according to the institutions of the Church.
>
> Council of Trent (1563): DS (1820) Since the Catholic Church, instructed by the Holy Spirit, in conformity with the sacred writings and the ancient tradition of the Fathers in sacred councils, and very recently in this ecumenical Synod, has taught that there is a purgatory, and that the souls detained there are assisted by the suffrages of the faithful, and especially by the acceptable sacrifice of the altar, the holy Synod commands the bishops that they insist that the sound doctrine of purgatory, which has been transmitted by the holy Fathers and holy Councils, be believed by the faithful of Christ, be maintained, taught, and everywhere preached.[2]

I would like to put off the discussion of how the souls in Purgatory are "helped" by almsgiving and so on until later. For now I want to focus on the idea that a person can be *justified*, a believer in Jesus Christ, trusting solely in Him and His work, and yet die *impure* and have to undergo punishment before entering into God's presence.

That seems to me to be the central issue here. I think John Hardon summed the doctrine up as well as it can be:

> The reason of faith is that nothing defiled can enter heaven, and therefore anyone less than perfect must first be purified before he can be admitted to the vision of God. In more concrete terms, which have been carved out of centuries of the Church's reflection on revelation, there exists purgatory, in which the souls of the just who die with the stains of sins are cleansed by expiation before they are admitted to heaven. They can be helped, however, by the intercession of the faithful on earth.
>
> Who are the souls of the just? They are those that leave the body in the state of sanctifying grace and are therefore destined by right to enter heavenly glory. Their particular judgment was favorable, although conditional. They must first be cleansed before they can see the face of God. The condition is always fulfilled.
>
> When we speak of "stains of sins," the expression is consciously ambivalent. It first means the temporal punishment due to venial or mortal sins already forgiven as to guilt but not fully remitted as to penalty when a person dies. It may also mean the venial sins themselves, not forgiven as to guilt or punishment before death.[3]

In discussing the sacrifice of the Mass, the Council of Trent said,

> Wherefore, according to the tradition of the Apostles, it [the Mass] is rightly offered not only for the sins, punishments, satisfactions, and other necessities of the faithful who are living, but also for those departed in Christ but not yet fully purified.[4]

That last line haunts me. If I am "in Christ," I am purified *in Him*. He is my holiness, my sanctification, *my all* (1 Corinthians 1:30–31). I am a new creature in Him (2 Corinthians 5:17), and my sins have been taken away by His all-sufficient atonement (Colossians 2:13–15; 1 Peter 2:24). Yet Roman Catholic writers speak of the "suffering of atonement" (referred to as *satispassio*) that I need to undergo in order to eventually be able to stand in the presence of God. Note the words of Ludwig Ott:

> The remission of the venial sins which are not yet remitted, occurs . . . as it does in this life, by an act of contrition deriving

from charity and performed with the help of grace. This act of contrition, which is presumably awakened immediately after entry into the purifying fire, does not, however, effect the abrogation or the diminution of the punishment for sins, since in the other world there is no longer any possibility of merit.

The temporal punishments for sins are atoned for in the purifying fire by the so-called suffering of atonement (satispassio), that is, by the willing bearing of the expiatory punishments imposed by God.[5]

What is the "suffering of atonement"? Is not Christ's suffering sufficient for those who are His? Suppose I undergo this "suffering of atonement" in Purgatory and thereby atone for the temporal punishments of my sins. Will I not then, upon entering into the presence of God, stand before Him clothed in the righteousness of Christ and my own righteousness, which I worked out through my own sufferings? How can my glory and honor be solely given to Christ when in fact at least some of my righteousness comes about through my own suffering?

The argument is often made that Rome insists that all opportunities of receiving merit and expiating sin come from the grace of God and the merit of Christ, but I have never found any Roman Catholic source that indicates that the "suffering of atonement" in Purgatory is at all related to the work or merit of Christ. It is not Christ's merit that is being applied to me when I suffer in Purgatory. This is a means of expiation totally outside of the work of Christ at the Cross. And, seemingly, if a person does not willingly bear the expiatory punishments imposed by God in Purgatory, that person will never enter into heaven. Once again we see why the Reformers insisted on all those "solas." They recognized that while Rome would often insist on the truth about how people are made right with God, they would also just as quickly compromise that truth by adding some human tradition or invention, thus destroying the purity of the Gospel.

The Treasury of Merit and Indulgences

In concluding his review of the medieval doctrine of indulgences, Dr. Philip Schaff wrote,

The traffic in ecclesiastical places and the forgiveness of sins constitutes the very last scene of medieval Church history. On the eve of the Reformation, we have the spectacle of the pope solemnly renewing the claim to have rule over both spheres, civil and ecclesiastical, and to hold in his hand the salvation of all mankind, yea, and actually supporting the extravagant luxuries of his worldly court with moneys drawn from the trade in sacred things. How deep-seated the pernicious principle had become was made manifest in the bull which Leo issues, November 9, 1518, a full year after the nailing of the Theses on the church door at Wittenberg, in which all were threatened with excommunication who failed to preach and believe that the pope had the right to grant indulgences.[6]

No Roman Catholic doctrine more clearly illustrates the difference between the biblical and the Roman teachings on salvation than the doctrine of indulgences. While in our previous discussion we have focused primarily on justification, here we touch on a topic that provides us with another angle from which to view the Roman Catholic concept of salvation. The view is, to say the least, striking. Those who believe the Roman Catholic Church is "saying the same thing but in different words" must deal honestly with the issue of indulgences and their continued affirmation by the Roman Catholic Church.

A common misconception is that the practice of indulgences by the Roman Catholic Church ended centuries ago. Let's look briefly at what modern-day Rome says about this subject. I quote from *Indulgentiarum Doctrina*, the Apostolic Constitution on the Revision of Indulgences, a post-Vatican II document, dated January 1, 1967. This document is referenced no less than seven times, and quoted six times, in the chapters on the topic in the new *Catechism*,[7] demonstrating that this doctrine remains in force in the most modern expositions of Roman Catholic teaching.

We first note that *Indulgentiarum Doctrina* insists that the belief in Purgatory and the expiation of sins therein, the concept of penitential expiation, and the belief in the *thesaurus meritorum*, the "treasury of merit," have always been in the Church. From these beliefs, it is said, the concept of indulgences is derived.

Listen carefully to some quotations from this document. The concept of sin that underlies the doctrine of indulgences is important:

Sins must be expiated. This may be done on this earth through the sorrows, miseries, and trials of this life and, above all, through death. Otherwise the expiation must be made in the next life through fire and torments or purifying punishments. . . . The reasons for their imposition are that our souls need to be purified.[8]

Purgatory then enters the discussion in these words:

The doctrine of purgatory clearly demonstrates that even when the guilt of sin has been taken away, punishment for it or the consequences of it may remain to be expiated or cleansed. They often are. In fact, in purgatory the souls of those "who died in the charity of God and truly repentant, but who had not made satisfaction with adequate penance for their sins and omissions" are cleansed after death with punishments designed to purge away their debt.[9]

This refers us once again to the concept of *satispassio*, the suffering of atonement, which we noted above. The document goes on to refer to the saints who "have carried their crosses to make expiation for their own sins and the sins of others."

The next teaching that must be understood is the *treasury of the church*, also known as the "treasury of merit." *Indulgentiarum Doctrina* says of the treasury:

On the contrary the "treasury of the Church" is the infinite value, which can never be exhausted, which Christ's merits have before God. . . . This treasury includes as well the prayers and good works of the Blessed Virgin Mary. They are truly immense, unfathomable, and even pristine in their value before God. In the treasury, too, are the prayers and good works of all the saints, all those who have followed in the footsteps of Christ the Lord and by his grace have made their lives holy and carried out the mission the Father entrusted to them. In this way they attained their own salvation and at the same time cooperated in saving their brothers in the unity of the Mystical Body.

The "treasury of merit" is a concept that developed long after the time of the Apostles and eventually became a source of great corruption in the Roman Catholic Church. The concept is that Christ had "excess merit"—beyond that required to bring about the salvation of humankind. Consequently, this excess merit goes into the treasury and is available through the Church to be given to those in need of it. It is important to realize that it is not *only* Christ's merit that is in the treasury. Mary, likewise, had more "merit" than was required for her salvation; therefore, her excess merit goes into the *same* treasury, adding to the superabundance of Christ's merit. But this is not all. The saints also had more merit than they personally needed to enter into heaven, so their excess merit is placed in the treasury along with that of Christ and Mary. The treasury of merit presents a *mixture* of the merit of Christ, that of the Virgin Mary, and of the saints. As the document puts it, "The merits of the Blessed Mother of God and of all the elect . . . are known to add further to this treasure."[10]

An indulgence, then, could be likened to a "withdrawal" of a portion of this merit and the application of it to the "account" of the person obtaining the indulgence. *Indulgentiarum Doctrina*, quoting from the Papal bull of Boniface VIII, says,

> For "God's only-begotten Son . . . has won a treasure for the militant Church . . . he has entrusted it to blessed Peter, the keybearer of heaven, and to his successors who are Christ's vicars on earth, so that they may distribute it to the faithful for their salvation."[11]

It should not be forgotten that Rome claims that the treasury of merit, from which these indulgences allegedly are derived, is under the control of the Roman hierarchy. The document quoted above plainly states,

> In addition, we ought not to forget that when they try to gain indulgences the faithful submit with docility to the lawful pastors of the Church. Above all, they acknowledge the authority of the successor of Blessed Peter, the keybearer of heaven.[12]

The document goes on to lay great weight upon the value of indulgences and goes so far as to say,

> The beneficial institution of indulgences therefore does its part in bringing it about that the Church might be presented to Christ without spot or wrinkle but holy and without blemish,

excellently united with Christ in the supernatural bond of charity.[13]

Here the purification of the Church herself is connected with the
practice of indulgences! The document even cites Ephesians 5:27 at
this point, which reads,

> . . . that He might present to Himself the church in all her
> glory, having no spot or wrinkle or any such thing; but that she
> would be holy and blameless.

Unfortunately, the infallible Church seems to have missed the context of this passage, which is provided by the preceding verses:

> Husbands, love your wives, just as Christ also loved the
> church and gave Himself up for her, so that He might sanctify
> her, having cleansed her by the washing of water with the word.

Nothing could possibly be further from the thinking of the Apostle
Paul than the idea that the Church is purified by the application of
the intermingled "merits" of Christ, Mary, and the saints. The purification and sanctification of the Church is the work of Christ *alone*
by His grace *alone*. Jesus Christ is more than capable of accomplish-
ing this task without the "excess merits" of anyone. Furthermore, as
we shall see, there is nothing in Sacred Scripture that hints at the
idea that Christ has decided to mix His merit with that of His re-
deemed in order to sanctify the Church through the means of indulgences. *The ramifications of this belief must be considered by anyone
who would identify Rome's official teaching as consistent with biblical
standards.*

It has been my experience that some, upon first encountering
such startling statements as those quoted above, have trouble rec-
onciling this view with the rather "Protestantized" presentations of
many of the more popular Roman Catholic speakers today. One finds
many in American Roman Catholicism downplaying doctrines such
as indulgences, and for obvious reasons. Indeed, in a recent national
radio debate I raised this issue on the air because I believe it is extremely relevant to the entire doctrine of salvation. My opponent, a
convert to Catholicism, took great exception, noting during a break
that this is a "nonissue." But it is difficult to dismiss this as a nonissue
when the Roman Catholic Church—in the official teaching of the

Magisterium—makes statements such as these:

> In fact, in granting an indulgence the Church uses its power as minister of Christ's Redemption. It not only prays. It intervenes with its authority to dispense to the faithful, provided they have the right dispositions, the treasury of satisfaction which Christ and the saints won for the remission of temporal punishments.[14]
>
> Moreover, the religious practice of indulgences arouses again confidence and hope that we can be fully reconciled with the Father.[15]

According to Rome, indulgences are meant to arouse hope that we can be reconciled to the Father. Believers are reconciled to the Father by the work of Jesus Christ *alone!* Even more, Paul taught that we *have been* reconciled:

> For if while we were enemies we were reconciled to God through the death of His Son, much more, having been reconciled, we shall be saved by His life. And not only this, but we also exult in God through our Lord Jesus Christ, through whom we have now received the reconciliation (Romans 5:10–11; *see also* 2 Corinthians 5:18–20).

We are completely reconciled by Christ's death. Can an indulgence made up of the mixed merits of Christ, Mary, and the saints add something to the firm assurance that Christ's death alone is sufficient to reconcile me to the Father? Instead, the addition of human action or merit to that perfect work of Christ is again seen to be the norm in Roman Catholic theology. There *was* a reason why the Reformers emphasized the *solas.*

But even here—in the granting of indulgences—the idea of human works and certain dispositions takes center stage. *Indulgentiarum Doctrina* states,

> To gain indulgences the work prescribed must be done. But that is not all. The faithful must have the dispositions that are necessary. These are that they must love God, hate sin, trust in Christ's merits, *and believe firmly in the great help they obtain from the Communion of Saints* (emphasis added).[16]

The document goes on to establish rules dictating how these indulgences can be gained, which include such items as this:

> A plenary indulgence, applicable only to the dead, can be gained in all churches and public oratories (and in semi-public oratories by those who have the right to use them) on November 2.[17]

Here we have, quite honestly and without unnecessary offense, the grace of God doled out bit by bit on particular days and through particular works of man.[18] The historical abuse of this doctrine is well known,[19] and the role it played in bringing about the Reformation is documented throughout the history of the period. We need to make sure that it is clearly understood that this is *still* Roman Catholic doctrine, that it is *still* the official teaching of the Vatican itself. Note these words:

> Supported by these truths, holy Mother Church again recommends the practice of indulgences to the faithful. . . . The Church recommends its faithful not to abandon or neglect the holy traditions of those who have gone before.[20]

The Bible and Purgatory

In the attempt to find biblical substantiation for the concept of Purgatory, two primary passages are put forward: Matthew 12:32 and 1 Corinthians 3:10–15. In Matthew, we read the Lord saying,

> Whoever speaks a word against the Son of Man, it shall be forgiven him; but whoever speaks against the Holy Spirit, it shall not be forgiven him, either in this age or in the age to come.

The Lord Jesus is speaking of the "unpardonable sin" of blasphemy against the Holy Spirit. We immediately note the same rule of interpretation we highlighted in our discussion of justification: beware of "tangential references." The topic in this passage is not Purgatory, so to be relevant any alleged reference to it must find support throughout the rest of inspired Scripture.

The Roman Catholic interpreter looks at this passage and says, "See, it is possible to have sins forgiven in the age to come, just as Jesus said. This gives some support to the doctrine of Purgatory."

Aside from the oft-repeated truth that sin is either forgiven in Christ Jesus or it is not forgiven at all, does the Roman Church have a solid position here?

The pastor of the Church at Geneva, John Calvin, long ago replied to the Roman Catholic interpretation of this passage:

> When the Lord, they say, makes known that the "sin against the Holy Spirit is not to be forgiven either in this age or in the age to come" . . . he hints at the same time that there is forgiveness of certain sins in the world to come. But who cannot see that the Lord is there speaking of the guilt of sin? But if this is so, what has it to do with their purgatory. Since, in their opinion, punishment of sins is undergone in purgatory, why do they deny that their guilt is remitted in the present life? . . . When the Lord willed to cut off all hope of pardon for such shameful wickedness, he did not consider it enough to say that it would never be forgiven; but in order to emphasize it even more, he used a division by which he embraced the judgment that the conscience of every man experiences in this life and the final judgment that will be given openly at the resurrection. It is as if he said: "Beware of malicious rebellion as of present ruin. For he who would purposely try to extinguish the proffered light of the Spirit will attain pardon neither in this life, which is given to sinners for their conversion, nor in the Last Day, on which the lambs will be separated from the goats by the angels of God and the Kingdom of Heaven will be cleansed of all offenses."[21]

Christ emphasizes the impossibility of forgiveness for this blasphemy, not the concept that there is forgiveness for sin in the age to come. The "age to come" for the Jewish person referred to the final age, the "Day of Yahweh." So to say that there would be no forgiveness for that sin in that age to come is the same as saying "it is unforgivable, period!" This is clearly the understanding of the biblical writers, for when we consult the parallel passage in Mark 3:29 we find the following:

> . . . but whoever blasphemes against the Holy Spirit never has forgiveness, but is guilty of an eternal sin.

What in Matthew is rendered "nor in the age to come" is rendered in Mark as "an eternal sin" that "never has forgiveness."

More popular are these words of Paul to the Corinthians found in 1 Corinthians 3:10–15:

> According to the grace of God which was given to me, like a wise master builder I laid a foundation, and another is building on it. But each man must be careful how he builds on it. For no man can lay a foundation other than the one which is laid, which is Jesus Christ. Now if any man builds on the foundation with gold, silver, precious stones, wood, hay, straw, each man's work will become evident; for the day will show it because it is to be revealed with fire, and the fire itself will test the quality of each man's work. If any man's work which he has built on it remains, he will receive a reward. If any man's work is burned up, he will suffer loss; but he himself will be saved, yet so as through fire.

The Roman Catholic view sees in these words a reference to Purgatory, believing that the concepts of judgment, loss, and reward support the concept of a cleansing after death. Yet when we allow the passage to speak for itself, we find almost nothing that supports the concept of Purgatory. The mention of fire seems to be about the only common concept between this judgment of believers and the Roman doctrine of Purgatory (even though modern Catholic writers are quick to point out that the Roman Church has never dogmatically affirmed that there is a literal fire in Purgatory).

What is judged is the type of works the Christian has done. Sins and their punishments are not even mentioned. It is *works* that are judged and put through the fire, yet Rome teaches that it is the person who must suffer in order to be purified from the "temporal punishments" of sin. The point of the text is that if a person's works withstand the judgment, the person receives a reward. If not, the person suffers loss—not punishment—yet is saved, "but as through fire." The passage does not say the person goes through fire, is punished, or suffers to make atonement for sin. It simply says that the Christian's works are judged for their own merit, and if those works are found to be made of wood, hay, and straw, the works will be burned up and the person will receive no reward.

For the Christian, the idea of not being able to present to his Lord works that were done for the proper motivation, works that were built with gold, silver, and precious stones, is a terrifying one indeed.

It is no light matter to stand before the judgment throne of Christ! Yet we must strongly affirm that this judgment is not a judgment relative to sin but to works and rewards. The believer has already been judged with reference to sin in Christ Jesus and has passed out of death into life, never to come into judgment for sin again (John 5:24). The believer's sins were judged in Christ Jesus. The remaining judgment is not about salvation but about reward. These verses have nothing to do with Purgatory or with suffering to make atonement for sins or their punishments.

The Bible and Indulgences

We do not find anywhere in Scripture or in the writings of the early Fathers any mention of a belief in indulgences.[22] Indeed, the Scriptures and the writings of the early Fathers give us no indication of the concept of the treasury of merit or of indulgences. Rome is again found teaching a concept that—like the idea of Papal Infallibility or the Bodily Assumption of Mary—is a doctrine without any basis in Scripture and no basis in anything that can even remotely or honestly be called "Apostolic tradition." But most importantly, we find that the doctrine of indulgences and its related concepts of merit, expiation of sins by suffering, etc., stands firmly against the Gospel of God's free grace in Christ. Paul taught:

> But God demonstrates His own love toward us, in that while we were yet sinners, Christ died for us. Much more then, having now been justified by His blood, we shall be saved from the wrath of God through Him. For if while we were enemies we were reconciled to God through the death of His Son, much more, having been reconciled, we shall be saved by His life. And not only this, but we also exult in God through our Lord Jesus Christ, through whom we have now received the reconciliation (Romans 5:8–11).

Here the Scriptures teach that we are justified by *His* blood, not by anyone or anything else. We are *saved* from the wrath of God *through Him*, not through the mediation or merit of Mary, the saints, or our own suffering. We already *have been reconciled*; we are not in the process of *being* reconciled. Indulgences have no meaning in a relationship where reconciliation has already taken place. If I am reconciled with God, why would I need a "transfer of merit" from a treasury of merit? What is more, we have received the reconciliation in *One*, Jesus Christ, and in Him *alone* (another *sola*).

Paul taught elsewhere concerning Christ that it was He "whom God displayed publicly as a propitiation in His blood through faith" (Romans 3:25). Where, then, do we ever hear of our making expiation for sins or having propitiatory power? Propitiation is a stronger term than mere expiation. While expiation speaks of the forgiveness of sins, propitiation speaks of that *as well as* the turning away of God's wrath. The believer who has faith in Christ is reconciled by His death and has received the propitiation for his or her sins. No punishments remain in such a relationship. The believer has peace, for the relationship is made whole and right. A relationship in which punishments remain to be exacted is not the relationship that is described in Scripture regarding believers and Christ.

> Therefore, He had to be made like His brethren in all things, so that He might become a merciful and faithful high priest in things pertaining to God, to make propitiation for the sins of the people (Hebrews 2:17).

The question that must be asked is this: did Christ or did He not make propitiation for the sins of the people of God? And if in fact He did, why do I need to *add to that work* such concepts as indulgences, merits, or the "suffering of atonement"?

> But Jesus, on the other hand, because He continues forever, holds His priesthood permanently. Therefore He is able also to save forever those who draw near to God through Him, since He always lives to make intercession for them (Hebrews 7:24–25).

If Christ is able to save *forever* (some translations render it, "to the uttermost") those who come unto God by Him (not by any other means), how can the Roman Catholic Church say that I must make expiation for my own sins, both on earth as well as in Purgatory? The same writer to the Hebrews said later, "For by one offering He has perfected for all time those who are sanctified" (Hebrews 10:14). Are believers "perfected for all time," yet they still need to expiate sins, endure punishments, and undergo the suffering of atonement, making indulgences helpful and necessary? Surely not!

Someone will surely say, "But doesn't the Bible speak of God chastening His children?" Yes, it certainly does. Note the Epistle to the Hebrews again:

> "FOR THOSE WHOM THE LORD LOVES HE DISCIPLINES, AND HE SCOURGES EVERY SON WHOM HE RECEIVES." It is for discipline that you endure; God deals with you as with sons; for what son is there whom his father does not discipline? But if you are without discipline, of which all have become partakers, then you are illegitimate children and not sons (Hebrews 12:6–8).

Does this passage and others like it teach us that God is leveling legal *punishment* for our sins, even after we have been justified by the death of Christ? Are we to believe what we read in *Indulgentiarum Doctrina*: "God's holiness and justice inflict them"?[23] Is it God's holiness and justice that bring the chastening of Hebrews 12, or is it His love and Fatherhood?

The difference between the Roman Catholic concept and the biblical one is just this: while Rome teaches that God's justice and holiness bring judgment to bear upon our sins, the Bible teaches that God's justice and holiness brought judgment to bear upon Jesus Christ *in the place of* sinners. The chastening that believers experience is not demanded by justice, because justice was fully satisfied in the perfect Substitute, Jesus Christ. God chastens us as a Father, conforming us to the image of His beloved Son, not as a Judge exacting justice from us.

The Gospel of Jesus Christ presents a Perfect, All-Sufficient Savior who endured the wrath of God in the place of His people. To Him is due all glory, honor, and praise, for He alone is Savior. Indulgences detract from the honor and glory of Christ, and therefore must be repudiated by any person whose heart burns with love for the Lord and Savior Jesus Christ.

13

WHEN *SOLA SCRIPTURA* IS REJECTED

In our discussion of *sola scriptura*, we noted the claim on the part of some modern Roman Catholic apologists that all of God's revelation is either explicitly *or implicitly* found in *both* Scripture and tradition. This more modern viewpoint is to be distinguished from the older and more popular view that says that *part* of God's revelation is in Scripture, and *part* in tradition.[1] We further noted that in reality the Roman Catholic position is not so much an argument for "Scripture and tradition" as it is an argument for "Scripture and the Church," with the emphasis on "Church." Since Rome claims the ability to define and interpret tradition without external guidelines, it is plain to see that such a stand is nothing more than an argument in favor of the Scripture as interpreted by the Roman Catholic Church.

When Roman Catholic teachers indicate that all of their beliefs are at least *implicitly* contained in the Bible, what do they mean? How clearly can we see these "implicit" doctrines? Could we see them without wearing the glasses provided by "tradition" as defined by Rome?

In this chapter I wish to provide three examples of what happens when *sola scriptura* is rejected. The first is drawn from an article found in the December 1991 *This Rock* magazine, the publication of the Catholic apologetics organization *Catholic Answers*. Here Patrick Madrid, then vice-president of *Catholic Answers*, provides us with an article titled "Ark of the New Covenant." In the article, Mr. Madrid attempts to provide a biblical basis for the doctrine of the Immaculate Conception. Since Mr. Madrid has publicly affirmed his belief in the "material sufficiency" of Scripture, it should be educational to see what kind of biblical argumentation goes into finding such "implicit" beliefs in the Bible. The second example will be taken from the Roman Catholic definitions of worship and veneration, and how these definitions are applied to the saints and Mary. And finally, we will note some prayers that are common in Roman Catholic piety, and see how far removed they are from the biblical testimony.

A Biblical Basis for the Immaculate Conception?

The article begins with the story of a witnessing encounter between Mr. Madrid and a Calvary Chapel pastor. Starting on the very cover of the magazine, we read, "His face stiffened, and his eyes narrowed to slits. Until now the Calvary Chapel pastor had been calm as he 'shared the gospel' with me, but when I mentioned my belief in Mary's Immaculate Conception, his attitude changed." A little later Mr. Madrid continues,

> After we'd examined the biblical evidence for the doctrine, the anti-Marianism he'd shown became muted, but it was clear that, at least emotionally if not biblically, Mary was a stumbling block for him. Like most Christians (Catholic and Protestant) the minister was unaware of the biblical support for the Church's teaching on the Immaculate Conception. But sometimes even knowledge of these passages isn't enough. Many former Evangelicals who have converted to the Catholic Church relate how hard it was for them to put aside prejudices and embrace Marian doctrines even after they'd thoroughly satisfied themselves through prayer and Scripture study that such teachings were indeed biblical.

Before providing what the "Bible has to say in favor of the Catholic position" regarding Mary's Immaculate Conception, Mr. Madrid takes the time to review some common objections to the doctrine from the Protestant perspective. He asserts that Mary was indeed saved from sin, but in a "different and more glorious way than the rest of us are." The merits of Christ were applied to her in an anticipatory way prior to her birth, he says, so that she was born without sin. By citing the examples of babies who are aborted or people born with mental deficiencies, Mr. Madrid thinks to show that Paul's universal statements of sinfulness (Romans 3 and 5) allow for exceptions.[2] It is true that the Bible does not explicitly say that Mary sinned. But it also doesn't explicitly give the names of all who have sinned. It doesn't need to. I think the reason that it does not address Mary's situation is quite simple—neither Luke nor any other biblical writer had any notion of the Immaculate Conception, so it does not enter into their writings. Mr. Madrid should be aware of the danger of this kind of exegesis. He is an expert on Mormonism, and must realize that there is also no explicit statement that "Jesus is not the spirit-brother of Lucifer" (a Mormon belief that he and I would both reject). Patrick Madrid has to resort to "interpretive methods" that leave the door open for any kind of teaching—whether Mormon, Jehovah's Witness, Moonie, or any other.

In introducing the biblical evidence for the Immaculate Conception, Mr. Madrid says the following:

> Now let's consider what the Bible has to say in favor of the Catholic position. It's important to recognize that neither the words "Immaculate Conception" nor the precise formula adopted by the Church to enunciate this truth are found in the Bible. This doesn't mean the doctrine isn't biblical, only that the truth of the Immaculate Conception, like the truths of the Trinity and Jesus' hypostatic union (that Jesus was incarnated as God and man, possessing completely and simultaneously two natures, divine and human, in one divine person), is mentioned either in other words or only indirectly.

Madrid makes a good point. One does not need to find the phrase "Immaculate Conception" in the Bible for it to be biblical any more than one has to find the term "Trinity" in the Bible for it to be biblical. We agree on this point. However, knowing that Madrid, like myself, works extensively with Mormons, and that he is familiar with Jehovah's Witnesses as well, I am certain that he is aware that the depth and breadth of biblical evidence for both the Trinity and the hypostatic union far outweighs that of the Immaculate Conception. Layer after layer of biblical data can be presented, in context, for the Trinity—one could fill an entire book with evidence of monotheism, the existence of the three Persons, and the equality of those Persons (the three foundations of the doctrine of the Trinity). One could do a linguistic study, for example, and show how *theotetos*,[3] that is, "deity," in Colossians 2:9, clearly demonstrates that Jesus is God in human flesh. One could examine John's usage of *ego eimi*,[4] "I Am," and see how this, too, shows the deity of Christ. One can note the many instances of "triadic formulae" throughout the New Testament, where the Father, Son, and Spirit are placed together in divine settings (Ephesians 4:4–5; 2 Corinthians 13:14). Given that Madrid parallels the Immaculate Conception with the Trinity and the hypostatic union, then, do we find him presenting the same kind of biblical evidence for the doctrine? No, we do not. Instead, he compiles the specifically exegetical material into one short paragraph of fifteen lines. Here it is:

> Look first at two passages in Luke 1. In verse 28, the angel Gabriel greets Mary as "*kecharitomene*" ("full of grace" or "highly favored"). This is a recognition of her sinless state. In verse 42 Elizabeth greets Mary as "blessed among women." The original import of this phrase is lost in English translation. Since neither the Hebrew nor Aramaic languages have superlatives (best, highest, tallest, holiest), a speaker of those languages would have say [sic], "You are tall among men" or "You are wealthy among men" to mean "You are the tallest" or "You are the wealthiest." Elizabeth's words mean Mary was the holiest of all women.

That is the entirety of the specific, exegetical evidence of the doctrine, according to Madrid. Yes, he goes on to present many "typological" attempts (material that depends on types or symbols rather than direct assertion or teaching) to find Mary in various Old Testament stories. (We shall examine them below.) But with reference to specific, direct teaching, this is all that he offers in defense of the interpretation. By this evidence the Immaculate Conception does not qualify to be included in the Trinity/hypostatic union category of biblical teachings—those not mentioned directly by name but are taught conceptually. The documentation is paltry when compared to the direct evidence for these.

Let us look more closely at Madrid's interpretation and begin with the first assertion. Luke 1:28 says,

> And coming in, he said to her, "Greetings, favored one! The Lord *is* with you."

Madrid's sole comment on this passage is, "This is a recognition of her sinless state." How does he know this? He doesn't say. But the head of *Catholic Answers*, Karl Keating, provides a fuller discussion in his book *Catholicism and Fundamentalism*. In speaking of the Greek term "*kecharitomene*" he alleges:

> The newer translations leave out something the Greek conveys, something the older translation conveys, which is that this grace (and the core of the word *kecharitomene* is *charis*, after all) is at once permanent and of a singular kind. The Greek indicates a perfection of grace. A perfection must be perfect not only intensively, but extensively. The grace Mary enjoyed must not only have been as "full" or strong or complete as possible at any given time, but it must have extended over the whole of her life, from conception. That is, she must have been in a state of sanctifying grace from the first moment of her existence to have been called "full of grace" or to have been filled with divine favor in a singular way. This is just what the doctrine of the Immaculate Conception holds. . . .[5]

Here Keating stretches the bounds of serious exegetical integrity past the breaking point. This can be seen by examining the term in question, the perfect passive participle "*kecharitomene*."[6] Does the term carry within it an entire doctrine unknown in the rest of the New Testament and unheard of by the first three centuries of the Christian Church? Or are modern Roman Catholic interpreters reading into this term a tremendous amount of material that was never intended by Luke?

First, let's look at the root meaning of "*kecharitomene*," the Greek word "*caritoo*."[7] Bauer's *A Greek-English Lexicon of the New Testament and Other Early Christian Literature* defines the usage of "*caritoo*" at Luke 1:28, "favored one (in the sight of God)."[8] No lexical source that we have found gives as a meaning of *caritoo* "sinlessness." The term refers to favor—in the case of Luke 1:28, divine favor, that is, God's grace. The only other occurrence of *caritoo* is in Ephesians 1:6, ". . . to the praise of the glory of His grace, which he freely bestowed (*caritoo*) on us in the Beloved." If the bare term *caritoo* means "sinlessness," then it follows that the elect of God throughout their lives have been sinless as well.

However, if we look at Mr. Keating's presentation, it seems clear that he is basing his interpretation not primarily on the root meaning of the word *caritoo*, but on the form it takes in Luke 1:28, the perfect passive participle, "*kecharitomene*." Note that Keating alleges that the "Greek indicates a perfection of grace." He seems to be playing on the perfect tense of the participle. But as anyone trained in Greek is aware, there is no way to jump from the perfect tense of a participle to the idea that the Greek "indicates a perfection of grace." Greek participles derive their time element from the main verb of the sentence.[9] The main emphasis of a participle is found in its *aspect*, a present participle providing the idea of *continuing action*, the aorist *undefined action*, and the perfect *completed action with abiding results to the present.*

What are we to do with the perfect tense of the participle, then? We might take it as an intensive perfect, one that emphatically states that something *is*,[10] but most likely it is simply emphasizing the certainty of the favor given, just as the perfect passive participle emphasizes the completedness of the action in Matthew 25:34 ("Come, *you who are blessed* by my Father . . ."); 1 Thessalonians 1:4 ("knowing, brethren *beloved* by God . . ."); and 2 Thessalonians 2:13 ("But we should always give thanks to God for you, brethren *beloved* by the Lord . . ."). No one would argue that in Matthew 25:34, Jesus means to tell us that the righteous have a "perfection of blessedness that indicates that they had this perfection throughout their life, for a perfection must be perfect not only intensively, but extensively" (to borrow from Mr. Keating's presentation). The application of Keating's thoughts to any of the above passages results in untenable conclusions.

Thus, it is obvious that when Keating says that the Greek indicates that Mary "must have been in a state of sanctifying grace from the first moment of her existence to have been called 'full of grace' or to have been filled with divine favor in a singular way," he is, in fact, not deriving this from the Greek at all but from his own theology, which he then reads back into the text. There is nothing in the Greek to support the interpretation put forward by Keating and Madrid. The angel addressed Mary as "highly favored," for, as he himself said, "Do not be afraid, Mary; for you have found favor with God" (Luke 1:30).

The second passage cited by Madrid is found in Luke 1:42, which reads,

> And she cried out with a loud voice and said, "Blessed *are* you among women, and blessed *is* the fruit of your womb!"

Madrid is quite correct to point out that Hebrew and Aramaic do not have superlative forms, and that the phrase "blessed among women"[11] should be translated as a superlative. I would suggest something like, "you are most blessed of all women." However, as is often the case, truth can be used in a sleight-of-hand trick, and that is what we have here. While the discussion of the superlative force is true, Madrid slips in an unwarranted conclusion, right on the heels of his proper discussion of the superlative force of the passage. Note that he concludes his paragraph with the sentence, "Elizabeth's words mean Mary was the holiest of all women." To substantiate such a statement, Madrid would have to prove to us that "*eulogeo*"[12] does not actually mean "blessed" here (as all lexical sources say it does) but actually means "holy." Instead, Madrid makes the bald assertion and leaves it at that—without any explanation.

Do Elizabeth's words tell us that Mary was the holiest of all women? A simple reading of the passage does not indicate that idea. There is nothing in the word "blessed" that speaks of sinlessness or holiness. If Madrid attempts to use the form of the term to come up with the idea of the Immaculate Conception, does it follow that all the righteous in Matthew 25:34 were immaculately conceived as well? The same term, after all, is used of them. Of course that would be an incorrect understanding, but it is the only logical conclusion open to the Roman apologist.

Types of Mary

Patrick Madrid's article did not end with the paragraph cited earlier. Instead, a whole section is dedicated to the discussion of "types" of Mary in the Old Testament. In order to provide a sense of the interpretation a Roman Catholic must utilize to find "biblical evidence" for the Immaculate Conception, we provide the first example from Madrid's article:

> Mary's Immaculate Conception is foreshadowed in Genesis 1, where God creates the universe in an immaculate state, free from any blemish or stain or sin or imperfection. This is borne out by the repeated mention in Genesis 1 of God beholding his

creations and saying they were "very good." Out of pristine matter the Lord created Adam, the first immaculately created human being, forming him from the "womb" of the Earth. The immaculate elements from which the first Adam received his substance foreshadowed the immaculate mother from whom the second Adam (Romans 5:14) took his human substance.

This is a rather unusual interpretation. Mary foreshadowed in creation? There is no emphasis in the original Hebrew text on the "immaculate" elements of the earth, or on the idea that Adam was formed in the "womb" of the immaculate earth. Don't misunderstand, I have no problem with the types that are directly presented to us in Scripture—Paul uses such an allegory in Galatians 4:21–31. But I also realize that there is no end to the types that one can find in Scripture, nor any controls on how far you can take such an interpretive method.

An examination of the types Madrid presents shows us the danger of this kind of interpretation. Forced by lack of direct evidence to rely on this lesser source of information, Madrid points to Genesis 3:15 and the "proto-evangelon":

> And I will put enmity between you and the woman, and between your seed and her seed; He shall bruise you on the head, and you shall bruise him on the heel.

After identifying the "woman" as Mary, Madrid says,

> If Mary was not completely sinless this prophecy becomes untenable. Why is that? The passage points to Mary's Immaculate Conception because it mentions a complete enmity between the woman and Satan. Such enmity would have been impossible if Mary were tainted by sin, original or actual (see 2 Corinthians 6:14).

Does this passage even address a "complete enmity" between the woman and Satan? On what basis can Mr. Madrid insert into this passage the concept of Immaculate Conception? Since there is enmity between believers and the world, does that make all believers sinless? Does the fact that we still have sin in our lives mean that no enmity exists at all? This interpretation is fraught with difficulties.

The greatest effort in typological interpretation by Madrid comes in his attempt to parallel the Ark of the Covenant and Mary. The first parallel he draws has to do with the fact that God took such great pains to make sure the Ark was properly constructed. He says,

> God wanted the ark to be as perfect and unblemished as humanly possible so it would be worthy of the honor of bearing the written Word of God. How much more so would God want Mary, the ark of the new covenant, to be perfect and unblemished since she would carry within her womb the Word of God in flesh.

While this may seem reasonable to those who already accept this doctrine, we can easily point out absurdities to which the parallel can be pushed. For example, must Mary have been stolen by God's enemies for a time, so that she could be brought back to the people of God with great rejoicing (2 Samuel 6:14–15)? Who was Mary's Uzzah (2 Samuel 6:3–8)? Madrid draws a further parallel between the three months the ark was with Obededom and the three months Mary was with Elizabeth. What, then, is the parallel with David's action of sacrificing a bull and a fattened calf when those who were carrying the ark had taken six steps (2 Samuel 6:13)? Madrid feels free to pick and choose those aspects of Mary's life he wishes to parallel in the Ark and those which he does not—there are no rules in this kind of interpretation, and it can lead to almost any conclusion. He seems to recognize at least some of this, for he says,

> Granted, none of these verses "proves" Mary's Immaculate Conception, but they all point to it. After all, the Bible nowhere says Mary committed any sin or languished under original sin. As far as explicit statements are concerned, the Bible is silent on most of the issue, yet all the biblical evidence supports the Catholic teaching.

We are glad to see that he recognizes that all that has come before does not "prove" the Immaculate Conception. The doctrine is believable only if we believe the Roman Catholic Church is infallible and wields an authority that does not need Scriptural basis.

We can see clearly what happens when one accepts the "Scripture and the Church" concept of authority. Madrid claims all Roman Catholic teachings are found at least implicitly in Scripture. What that means, in light of the preceding examination, is that we can use the most questionable forms of exegesis, import meanings into words and grammatical forms that result in exegetical chaos, and find types and shadows to "discover" *barely* discernible "implicit" reference to such doctrines as the Immaculate Conception, the Bodily Assumption, or Papal Infallibility. This method of hermeneutics is clearly a formula ripe for abuse, and history shows us—from indulgences to the veneration of Mary—that such abuse is an ever present reality.

Worship, *Dulia*, *Latria*

The conversation takes place almost daily between the informed Roman Catholic and the less-than-informed Protestant:

Protestant: It appears to me that the Roman Catholic Church allows for the worship of saints. Isn't that idolatry?

Catholic: Oh, I see you haven't really studied our Church. We don't worship saints, or even Mary—we worship God and God alone.

Protestant: Then what are you doing bowing down before a statue of Mary or some other saint?

Catholic: You need to understand the difference between the worship we give to God, which we call *latria*, and the veneration given to saints, which we call *dulia*. *Latria* is not *dulia*, and since we reserve *latria*, the highest form of worship, only for God, and never give it to the saints, then we obviously are not worshiping the saints.

If the Protestant still has his wits about him, he might respond, "I don't know much about *latria* or *dulia*, but I do know this: when you bow down before a statue and say prayers and light candles, no matter what you call it, I call it worship."

The veneration of saints is an integral part of Roman Catholic life and practice. Anyone who has visited a Roman Catholic Church knows that images are a prominent aspect of Catholic worship. This phenomena is widespread—wherever Roman Catholicism is, you will find the veneration of saints, and in particular, of Mary. While Catholicism outside of the United States may be better known for its strong attachment to the saints, even within the United States there is still a great tendency toward this activity.

Protestants from the time of the Reformation on have charged that the veneration of saints is in reality nothing more than idolatry. Though no one believes that Rome teaches that the saints are actually gods of the same kind as God the Father or Jesus Christ, it is true that the saints are "venerated" in a religious context, which, biblically speaking, is worship. They are not only honored in a way that Protestants feel is condemned in Scripture, but the fact that Roman Catholics are inclined to pray to a saint and ask for that individual's intercession is also seen as being antibiblical. The Bible strongly condemns communication with the dead. It does not matter if those who have died were good or bad, saintly or evil—it forthrightly forbids communication between the living and the dead. The only communication allowed in Scripture with the spiritual realm is that which originates with people in prayer to God and Him alone. Prayer is an act of worship, and we are to worship God only.

In the face of such accusations, Rome has developed over the years an intricate system of doctrinal distinctions that allows the Roman Catholic to say "worship is due to God alone" and yet continue to pray to Mary and the saints and bow down before statues while reciting the Rosary. It is not our purpose here to go into the whole subject of *hagiolatry*, the worship or veneration of saints. Rather, by examining the teaching that has come forth from the Roman Church on this subject, particularly on the definition of worship itself, we demonstrate what happens when the Bible is no longer held as the sole rule of faith.

When the Reformers began charging the Roman hierarchy with fostering idolatry in the worship of saints, the Church responded with the definitions that had been worked out in the Scholastic period centuries before. These different terms are still used today. Nothing has changed.

The first term to be examined is *latria*. *Latria*, according to Roman Catholic authority John Hardon, is,

> The veneration due to God alone for his supreme excellence and to show people's complete submission to him. It is essentially adoration. As absolute *latria*, it is given only to God, as the Trinity, or one of the Divine Persons, Christ as God and as man, the Sacred Heart of Jesus, and the Holy Eucharist. Representations of God as images connected with the Divinity may receive relative *latria*, which is given not to the symbol but to the Godhead, whom it signifies.[13]

Latria, then, is in Catholic theology the highest form of worship. It is reserved for God and God alone. We should note as well that the term itself comes from the Greek, where it is found in the noun form, *latreia*,[14] as well as the verbal form, both of which appear in the text of the New Testament.

Saints are not given *latria*, according to Rome. This would be doing just what the Protestants say Catholics are doing—worshiping the saints. What, then, are Catholics doing when they "venerate" the saints?

Saints are rendered *dulia*. What is *dulia*? Robert Broderick defines it as follows:

> Dulia is the special worship, generally called veneration, given to the angels and saints because as friends of God they share in His excellence.[15]

Dulia is differentiated from *latria*, though, according to Broderick, both are forms of worship.[16] *Latria* is a "higher form" of worship than *dulia*. Therefore, when the Bible speaks of worshiping God alone, this refers to *latria*. We are, however, allowed to give *dulia* to others.

Hyperdulia is the highest form of *dulia* and is to be given to Mary alone. Broderick says,

> Hyperdulia is the veneration proper to the Blessed Mother alone; it is the highest form of veneration short of adoration.[17]

Giving *hyperdulia* to Mary is as close as the Catholic can come to giving something akin to *latria*. But by their definition, Catholics insist a distinction remains between the two forms of worship. So Mary and the saints are venerated but not worshiped in the same way as God is worshiped.

Hardon sums up the Roman Catholic position well. He defines veneration as,

> Honor paid to the saints who, by their intercession and example and in their possession of God, minister to human sanctification, helping the faithful grow in Christian virtue. Venerating the saints does not detract from the glory given to God, since whatever good they possess is a gift from his bounty. They reflect the divine perfections, and their supernatural qualities result from the graces Christ merited for them by the Cross.[18]

Hardon claims that the veneration of saints does not detract from the glory given to God, for whatever good the saints possess is theirs in view of the merits of Christ. We definitely agree with the last of that statement—any good that any person has is the result of the mercy and grace of God. But the *source* of that good—Christ—makes veneration of any person living or dead no less wrong. Hardon also agrues the Roman Catholic view that the veneration of saints, though in a sense properly called worship, is not in fact idolatry, since their highest worship, *latria*, is reserved for God alone. Because God receives something unique (*latria*), we are to believe that the religious veneration given to the saints (*dulia*) is then acceptable in God's sight. The Roman Catholic Church deflects all charges of idolatry, then, by the differentiation of the two terms *latria* and *dulia*.[19]

Service and Worship in Scripture

Is there a basis for this differentiation? Does this distinction between these two Greek terms provide a defense against the citation of the commandment of Exodus 20:5, "You shall not worship them or serve them; for I, the LORD your God, am a jealous God"?

John Calvin responded to the Roman Catholic claims in the heat of the battle for the Reformation. While his speech today strikes us as "politically incorrect," he speaks the truth regarding this vital issue:

> In fact, the distinction between *latria* and *dulia*, as they called them, was invented in order that divine honors might seem to be transferred with impunity to angels and the dead. For it is obvious that the honor the papists give to the saints really does not differ from the honoring of God. Indeed, they worship both God and the saints indiscriminately, except that, when they are pressed, they wriggle out with the excuse that they keep unimpaired for God what is due him because they leave *latria* to him. But since the thing itself, not the word, is in question, who can permit them to make light of this most important of all matters? But—to pass over this also—their distinction in the end boils down to this: they render honor [*cultus*] to God alone, but undergo servitude [*servitium*] for the others. For λατρεία among the Greeks means the same thing as *cultus* among the Latins; δουλεία properly signifies *servitus*; and yet in

210 / THE ROMAN CATHOLIC CONTROVERSY

Scripture this distinction is sometimes blurred. But suppose we concede it to be unvarying. Then we must inquire what both words mean; δουλεία is servitude; λατρεία, honor. Now no one doubts that it is greater to be enslaved than to honor. For it would very often be hard for you to be enslaved to one whom you are not unwilling to honor. Thus it would be unequal dealing to assign to the saints what is greater and leave to God what is lesser. Yet many of the old writers used this distinction. What, then, if all perceive that it is not only inept but entirely worthless?[20]

Calvin's point is clear: if we allow the distinction to stand, then the saints receive what is higher in value than what God receives. To serve someone is certainly more important than to give honor to someone. Even Calvin did not allow the distinction itself to stand, for the claimed differences between *latria* and *dulia* evaporate under an examination of biblical usage and meaning. We can so clearly illustrate our point: Is biblical usage and meaning the most important factor, or does Roman tradition take the supreme position?

Earlier we cited the passage from Exodus 20:5. Previously to this, God had commanded that the people were to have no other God before Him. Then Yahweh prohibited His people from having any part with idols. They were to have no images of anything in heaven above or in the earth beneath. This would surely include images of God, the Trinity, or any of the saints. He says that "You shall not worship them or serve them" (Exodus 20:5). The term translated "worship" is the Hebrew term *avad*.[21] The most common translation of the term is "to serve." However, in religious contexts, the term is frequently translated as "worship." There is no difficulty in understanding the meaning of the term that brings about the two translations of "serve" and "worship." The difficulty lies in our own English language, not in the original Hebrew. The simple fact of the matter is that *avad* means both to serve and to worship. Both concepts are tied up in the one term, and one cannot separate the two, especially in a religious context.

When the translators of the Greek Septuagint (the Greek translation of the Hebrew Old Testament) rendered *avad* into Greek, they did so by using a couple of different terms. Most important to our purposes here is the fact that both *dulia* and *latria*, in their verbal and substantival forms, are used to translate the one term *avad*.

Clearly the Septuagint translators recognized the fact that *avad* meant *both* to worship and to serve, to give *latria* and to give *dulia*.

When we come to the New Testament, we find that both terms are used with similar frequency in both their noun and verb forms. We also discover that there is absolutely no distinction made between them relevant to religious worship. As an example, we note Paul's words in Galatians 4:8:

> However at that time, when you did not know God, you were slaves to those which by nature are no gods.

But when you did not know God, you served,[22] or were slaves to, those which by nature are not gods. Paul is speaking of the former idolatry of the Galatians. They served (*dulia*) idols, those which by nature are not gods at all. Are we to assume, then, on the basis of the Roman definitions, that since they only *served* these idols that they were then free from the charge of idolatry, since they didn't give *latria* as well? Of course not! Their service of these idols was wrong whether the term *latria* or *dulia* was used. In fact, in the Latin Vulgate, both *duleuo* (to serve) and *latreuo* (to worship) are rendered by the same term, *servio*.[23] No matter how the defender of Rome tries, no basis can possibly be found in Scripture for the distinction of *latria* and *dulia*.

Certainly there are examples of people reverencing and honoring other people in Scripture. But the biblical injunction is that in any and all religious contexts this activity is strictly forbidden. When Cornelius bowed before Peter, Peter told him to stand because he was just a man (Acts 10:25–26). When John tried to bow down before the angelic messenger (Revelation 19:10; 22:8–9), he was rebuked and told to worship only God. And today, when a man or a woman bows down before a statue of Mary or Peter or John or the Angel Michael and says a prayer or lights a candle, that person, despite the fact that they may have been taught from childhood that this was right and honorable and good, is engaging in veneration within an inarguably religious context. That person, therefore, is doing exactly what Exodus 20:5 forbids.

The Exaltation of Mary

What is the final result of the rejection of *sola scriptura*? There are many, but one that is striking is the Roman Catholic teaching on the person of the Virgin Mary, the Lord's mother. Many Protestants are unaware of the exalted position assigned to Mary in Roman Catholic theology, and even more so in Roman Catholic piety. Roman Catholic apologists often say that some of the more extravagant claims made about Mary are not part of the "official" teaching, and therefore Rome should not be held accountable for such things. Nevertheless, since Rome has the ecclesiastical power to *end* this kind of devotion—and yet does not exercise this power but instead adopts an attitude that *fosters* this devotion—how can she escape such a responsibility?

We will not enter into a full discussion of this topic.[24] Instead, I wish only to provide the following citations for those who may not realize just how far a system can go without the restraint of the constant reforming power of the Scriptures as a guide and boundary. The citations will speak for themselves. We comment only on the first, a prayer to Mary that is quite common in Roman Catholic piety:

> O Mother of Perpetual Help, thou art the dispenser of all the goods which God grants to us miserable sinners, and for this reason he has made thee so powerful, so rich, and so bountiful, that thou mayest help us in our misery. Thou art the advocate of the most wretched and abandoned sinners who have recourse to thee. Come then, to my help, dearest Mother, for I recommend myself to thee. In thy hands I place my eternal salvation and to thee do I entrust my soul. Count me among thy most devoted servants; take me under thy protection, and it is enough for me. For, if thou protect me, dear Mother, I fear nothing; not from my sins, because thou wilt obtain for me the pardon of them; nor from the devils, because thou art more powerful than all hell together; nor even from Jesus, my Judge himself, because by one prayer from thee he will be appeased. But one thing I fear, that in the hour of temptation I may neglect to call on thee and thus perish miserably. Obtain for me, then, the pardon of my sins, love for Jesus, final perseverance, and the grace always to have recourse to thee, O Mother of Perpetual Help.[25]

Please note the final words of this prayer. The person praying expresses confidence in Mary so that he or she no longer fears three things. First, he no longer fear his sins, because she, Mary, will obtain pardon for him. Secondly, there is no more fear of devils, because Mary is more powerful than all hell together. But finally, the third thing from which this person desires protection is none other than the Lord Jesus himself. A common thread will be found in many of the citations below: a fear of the Savior. Note this quotation as a quick example:

> "There is no doubt," [St. Bernard] adds, "that Jesus Christ is the only mediator of justice between men and God; that, by virtue of his own merits and promises, he will and can obtain us pardon and divine favors; but because men acknowledge and fear the divine Majesty, which is in him as God, for this reason it was necessary to assign us another advocate, to whom we might have recourse with less fear and more confidence, and this advocate is Mary, than whom we cannot find one more powerful with his divine majesty, or one more merciful toward ourselves." The saint says, "Christ is a faithful and powerful Mediator between God and men, but in him men fear the majesty of God. A mediator, then, was needed with the mediator himself; nor could a more fitting one be found than Mary."[26]

Do people really pray these prayers and believe this? A few years ago I debated Gerry Matatics, a former Protestant, now a convert to Roman Catholicism. We discussed Mary and the saints on a radio station in Boston. At one point I quoted the above prayer, to which Mr. Matatics responded with grave seriousness and intense emotion, "I can only hope that someday you, too, Mr. White, will pray that prayer."

What have the Popes said about Mary? Pope Leo XIII in an encyclical (September 22, 1891) said of Mary's mediation:

> With equal truth may it be also affirmed that, by the will of God, Mary is the intermediary through whom is distributed unto us this immense treasure of mercies gathered by God, for mercy and truth were created by Jesus Christ. Thus as no man goeth to the Father but by the Son, so no man goeth to Christ but by His Mother.

Likewise, elsewhere in the same encyclical we read,

> Mary is this glorious intermediary; she is the mighty Mother of the Almighty; but—what is still sweeter—she is gentle, extreme in tenderness, of a limitless lovingkindness. As such God gave her to us. Having chosen her for the Mother of His only

begotten Son, He taught her all a mother's feeling that breathes nothing but pardon and love. Such Christ desired she should be, for He consented to be subject to Mary and to obey her as a son a mother. Such He proclaimed her from the cross when he entrusted to her care and love the whole of the race of man in the person of His disciple John. Such, finally, she proves herself by her courage in gathering in the maternal duties towards us all. . . . And this circumstance, which assuredly is to be attributed to the Divine action and direction upon men, rather than to the wisdom and efforts of individuals, strengthens and consoles Our heart, filling Us with great hope for the ultimate and most glorious triumph of the Church under the auspices of Mary. . . . How grateful and magnificent a spectacle to see in the cities and towns and villages, on land and sea—wherever the Catholic faith has penetrated—many hundreds of thousands of pious people uniting their praises and prayers with one voice and heart at every moment of the day, saluting Mary, invoking Mary, hoping everything through Mary. Through her may all the faithful strive to obtain from her Divine Son that the nations plunged in error may return to the Christian teaching and precepts, in which is the foundation of the public safety and the source of peace and true happiness.

The same Pope said in another encyclical (September 8, 1892),

When we have recourse to Mary in prayer, we are having recourse to the Mother of mercy, who is so well disposed toward us that, whatever the necessity that presses upon us, especially in attaining eternal life, she is instantly at our side of her own accord, even though she has not been invoked. She dispenses grace with a generous hand from that treasure with which from the beginning she was divinely endowed in fullest abundance that she might be worthy to be the Mother of God. By the fullness of grace which confers on her the most illustrious of her many titles, the Blessed Virgin is infinitely superior to all the hierarchies of men and angels, the one creature who is closest of all to Christ. "It is a great thing in any saint to have grace sufficient for the salvation of many souls; but to have enough to suffice for the salvation of everybody in the world is the greatest of all; and this is found in Christ and in the Blessed Virgin."

And two years later (September 8, 1894), Leo XIII said,

Moreover, it was before the eyes of Mary that was to be finished the Divine Sacrifice for which she had borne and brought up the Victim. As we contemplate Him in the last and most piteous of those Mysteries, there stood by the Cross of Jesus His Mother, who, in a miracle of charity, so that she might receive us as her sons, offered generously to Divine Justice her own Son, and died in her heart with Him, stabbed with the sword of sorrow.[27]

Pope Pius X says in an encyclical dated February 2, 1904,

We are then, it will be seen, very far from attributing to the Mother of God a productive power of grace—a power which belongs to God alone. Yet, since Mary carries it over all in holiness and union with Jesus Christ, and has been associated by Jesus Christ in the work of redemption, she merits for us "*de congruo*," in the language of theologians, what Jesus Christ merits for us "*de condigno*," and she is the supreme Minister of the distribution of graces. Jesus "sitteth on the right hand of the majesty on high" (Hebrews i. b.). Mary sitteth at the right hand of her Son—a refuge so secure and a help so trusty against all dangers that we have nothing to fear or to despair of under her guidance, her patronage, her protection.

Pope Pius XII added in his encyclical of October 11, 1954,

Certainly, in the full and strict meaning of the term, only Jesus Christ, the God-Man, is King; but Mary, too, as Mother of the divine Christ, as His associate in the redemption, in his struggle with His enemies and His final victory over them, has a share, though in a limited and analogous way, in His royal dignity. For from her union with Christ she attains a radiant eminence transcending that of any other creature; from her union with Christ she receives the royal right to dispose of the treasures of the Divine Redeemer's Kingdom; from her union with Christ finally is derived the inexhaustible efficacy of her maternal intercession before the Son and His Father.

And John Paul II, in his recent encyclical, *Veritatis Splendor*, said,

"Mary is the Mother of Mercy because it is to her that Jesus entrusts his Church and all humanity." From these Papal decrees, the reader can see that Papal documents are *full* of such references to Mary.[28]

It cannot be said that the leadership of the Roman Catholic Church has distanced itself in any way from the strongest assertions of devotion to Mary.

But what of more popular sources? The single most widely read work on Mary is that of St. Alphonsus Ligouri, *The Glories of Mary*. Let us look at a few citations from this work:

> Mary not only assists her beloved servants at death and encourages them, but she herself accompanies them to the tribunal-seat of God.[29]

> With reason does an ancient writer call her "the only hope of sinners," for by her help alone can we hope for the remission of sins.[30]

> He falls and is lost who has not recourse to Mary.[31]

> But now, if God is angry with a sinner, and Mary takes him under her protection, she withholds the avenging arm of her Son, and saves him. "And so," continues the same saint, "no one can be found more fit for this office than Mary, who seizes the sword of divine justice with her own hands to prevent it from falling upon and punishing the sinner."[32]

> St. Anselm, to increase our confidence, adds, that "when we have recourse to this divine Mother, not only we may be sure of her protection, but that often we shall be heard more quickly, and be thus preserved, if we have recourse to Mary and call on her holy name, than we should be if we called on the name of Jesus our Saviour," and the reason he gives for it is, "that to Jesus as a judge, it belongs also to punish; but mercy alone belongs to the Blessed Virgin as a patroness." Meaning, that we more easily find salvation by having recourse to the Mother than by going to the Son.[33]

> And shall we scruple to ask her to save us, when "the way of salvation is open to none otherwise than through Mary"?[34]

> [St. Peter Damian] addresses her in these words: "All power is given to thee in heaven and on earth, and nothing is impossible to thee who canst raise those who are in despair to the hope of salvation."[35]

> "At the command of Mary all obey—even God." St. Bernardine fears not to utter this sentence, meaning, indeed, to say

that God grants the prayers of Mary as if they were commands. . . . Since the Mother, then, should have the same power as the Son, rightly has Jesus, who is omnipotent, made Mary also omnipotent; though, of course, it is always true that where the Son is omnipotent by nature, the Mother is only so by grace.[36]

"Be comforted then, O you who fear," will I say with St. Thomas of Villanova: "Breathe freely and take courage, O wretched sinners; this great Virgin, who is the Mother of your God and judge, is also the advocate of the whole human race; fit for this office, for she can do what she wills with God; most wise, for she knows all the means of appeasing him; universal, for she welcomes all, and refuses to defend no one."[37]

[Prayer of St. Ephraim:] O Immaculate Virgin, we are under thy protection . . . we beseech thee to prevent thy beloved Son, who is irritated by our sins, from abandoning us to the power of the devil.[38]

The holy Church herself attributes to the merits of Mary's faith the destruction of all heresies: "Rejoice, O Virgin Mary, for thou alone hast destroyed all heresies throughout the world."[39]

In conclusion, we note the words of Karl Keating from as recently as 1988:

Second, Mary is the Mediatrix of all graces because of her intercession for us in heaven. What this means is that no grace accrues to us without her intercession. We are not to suppose that we are obliged to ask for all graces through her or that her intercession is intrinsically necessary for the application of graces. Instead, through God's will, grace is not conferred on anyone without Mary's cooperation.

True, scriptural proofs for this are lacking. Theologians refer to a mystical interpretation of John 19:26 ("Woman behold thy son, son behold thy mother"), an interpretation that sees John as the representative of the human race, Mary thus becoming the spiritual mother. They note the doctrine is reasonable because it is fitting.

This is little consolation to fundamentalists, of course, who see little fitting about it and who put little stock in speculative theology and even less in mystical theology. As a practical matter, this kind of doctrine is one of the last accepted by someone approaching the Church, particularly someone coming to the

Church from fundamentalism, *and it is accepted, ultimately, on the authority of the Church rather than on the authority of clear scriptural references* (emphasis added).[40]

We can certainly agree with that final statement: such doctrines as this do indeed lack Scriptural proofs, and will be accepted not on the basis of the Bible but on the basis of the claims to authority of the Roman Catholic Church. Surely we can see here with perfect clarity the truth of what we said before: one either accepts *sola scriptura*, or one embraces *sola Roma*.

14

SOLA GRATIA

J. I. Packer, in his fine introductory essay to James Buchanan's work *The Doctrine of Justification*, wrote,

> Martin Luther described the doctrine of justification by faith as *articulus stantis vel cadentis ecclesiae*—the article of faith that decides whether the church is standing or falling. By this he meant that when this doctrine is understood, believed, and preached, as it was in New Testament times, the church stands in the grace of God and is alive; but where it is neglected, overlaid, or denied, as it was in mediaeval Catholicism, the church falls from grace and its life drains away, leaving it in a state of darkness and death. The reason why the Reformation happened, and Protestant churches came into being, was that Luther and his fellow Reformers believed completely in this respect that no faithful Christian could with a good conscience continue within her ranks.[1]

And so we have to ask ourselves a question: has Rome changed her doctrine of justification since the days of the Reformation? How do we—according to the Rome of today—find peace with God? As Packer says, the Reformers believed that when the truth of justification by faith is "neglected, overlaid, or denied," the Church enters into a state of darkness and death. Has Rome, since then, renounced those teachings that the Reformers *rightly* saw as being denials of justification by grace through faith *alone*?

No matter how hard we try to find some means of answering such a question in the affirmative, we simply cannot do so without stretching the truth. Do we find Roman Catholics who affirm *sola gratia* and *sola fide*? Yes, thanks be to God, we do, but we have to question how firmly these folks are planted in the soil that is Roman Catholicism. We might point out that there is truth in the saying "Words mean something," and if a person holds to a theology directly contrary to the official and dogmatic definitions provided by *any* religious group, what value is there in their allegiance to that group? For example, if a person calls himself a Christian and yet denies that Jesus rose from the dead, what value can be put on their claim? They may use the term "Christian," but to deny that Jesus rose from the dead separates them from what the term *means*. It becomes a meaningless symbol.

In the same way, we encounter many today who are willing to affirm—in some fashion or aspect—justification by faith *without* the addition of works of merit, etc. They nevertheless cling to the name Roman Catholic. We are thankful that these people have been blessed with the knowledge of God's truth, but individual beliefs do not define the official position of a religious faith. Rome's *official* teachings continue to deny justification by faith *alone*, and when other teachings are allowed into the discussion—such as the Mass and Purgatory—there are *fundamental* and *basic* differences between Protestants and Roman Catholics on the central issue of the Gospel itself. If a person wishes to deny or in some other way remove himself from the authority of these *official* statements, we can only applaud him. But at the same time we have to wonder why such a person wishes to maintain the *name* Roman Catholic while denying the *substance* of its faith.

What About Peace With God?

We come then to the "big question." How shall we respond to the information we have here presented? I believe Christians committed to God's truth must think long and hard on the issues presented by Rome: such things as the Sacraments, the state of grace, the Mass as a propitiatory sacrifice, Purgatory, merit, and indulgences. Should we share the Gospel with those who claim to already know it?

While we are thankful God's grace surpasses even the most stubborn human barriers, we must also begin with basic truths and face the obvious conclusions. Rome's official gospel is not the Apostle Paul's Gospel. Paul would have never recognized the treasury of merit, indulgences, purgatorial cleansing, etc. Nor would he have understood the concept of the Mass as a propitiatory sacrifice. His doctrine of justification differs in a marked way from that taught by the Vatican today. Can we seriously think that while Paul responded strongly to the addition of circumcision to the Gospel in his letter to the Galatians, he would have overlooked the teaching that we can merit eternal life by works done in a state of grace, or that we can draw near to the death of Christ a thousand times and yet die in an impure state? Can we really think he would have viewed as a matter of "freedom" the teaching that men can undergo the "suffering of atonement" in Purgatory to merit release from temporal punishment of their sins? Listen to Paul's words in Galatians 5:1: "It was for *freedom* that Christ set us free; therefore keep standing firm and do not be subject again to a yoke of slavery" (emphasis added).

I conclude that the *official* teachings of Rome have compromised the Gospel through both addition and subtraction. Not only are the central places of grace and faith replaced with a human-centered concept, but additions are made that likewise violate the spirit of the Gospel of grace. Does the Roman Catholic gospel save? I do not believe it can.

Does it follow that all Roman Catholics are lost? Not unless we believe that all Roman Catholics walk in lock-step with the official teachings of the Vatican. I am thankful there are those who know the freedom of grace even while maintaining a relationship with a Church that does not give place to that freedom in its official teachings.

What of evangelism? Because Paul said he wished to evangelize even the *believers* at Rome (Romans 1:15), I agree that *all people*, including those who claim religious faith, should be the objects of evangelism. Many Protestants are in need of evangelism. I can't think of anyone who does not need to be reminded on a regular basis of the supremacy and free gift of God's grace. Any person who is *without* hope needs to hear about Christ. Any person who holds to a *false* hope needs to hear the message of the Cross. And I believe that even if a person has been baptized—Roman Catholic, Protestant, or otherwise—and has not been touched by the Spirit of God, regenerated, and made a child of God by faith in Christ Jesus, he or she needs to hear the message, "Repent and believe the Gospel." At that point, labels are not relevant.

But what of the person who is actively involved in Roman Catholicism and claims faith? Some would say, "Keep your message to yourself." But consider with me: What if a person says, "I have entrusted my salvation to Mary, the Mother of God"? Can I hold my tongue when Mary herself would be the first to warn such a person that she is incapable of doing anything for his or her salvation?

What if I meet a person on his way to Mass who speaks of his desire to have the proper attitude and intentions so that the maximum amount of benefit can be derived from this "sacrifice"? Would the writer to the Hebrews remain silent at this point for the sake of "unity"? Or should I speak to such a person of the completedness and sufficiency of Christ's work?

And what if I meet a person going to confession who believes he is at enmity with God due to a mortal sin? Should I allow him to believe that a sacramental act will remove only the eternal punishment of that mortal sin, but that he will need to work off temporal punishments by performing certain penances? Should I not speak to this person of the peace of God that comes through having a perfect Savior who carried *all* of our sins in His body upon the cross?

As religiously incorrect as it may be, I cannot keep quiet. The stakes are too high. If I truly love others, I will do what I can to direct them toward the Gospel, even if it results in conflict. What if I preach the Gospel to a person who is already converted? If a person has truly embraced Christ by faith, that person will hear my heart and my word and will say a hearty "amen." But if he does not know the peace that comes from being justified by God's grace through faith, I may become a messenger of life to him.

But What About ECT?

The now well-known document *Evangelicals and Catholics Together* makes many statements on a theological, factual, or historical basis with which I would take issue. But while entire books have been written about the issues raised by this document, there is really only one statement that needs to be examined:

> We affirm together that we are justified by grace through faith because of Christ.[2]

Everything else in the document, to me, is insignificant beside this statement. We can only ask: "What does this mean?" In light of what we have seen concerning the major tenets of our faith, what does it mean to say that both sides in this dispute affirm that "we are justified by grace through faith because of Christ"? Can unity be created by simply going back to the "least common denominator"? The sharp reader will immediately notice that the above statement is, from the Protestant perspective, missing a very important word. We rejoice and are thankful that justification, grace, faith, and Christ are there.[3]

But what is missing? The term "alone." Faith *alone*. *Sola fide*. We have seen that there *is* a valid reason for making sure we understand that faith—true, saving faith—is *alone* the instrument of justification. Yet it is not in the document. That is because Rome cannot affirm its truth. In fact, she anathematized its addition long ago.

Evangelicals and Catholics Together seeks to provide a common ground for united social action by Roman Catholics and Protestants. Everyone can agree that we live in a decadent society and that all who share a common morality have a special bond on that level. But I have to ask: What is the greatest power available to Christians? Is it a "moral consensus," or is it as Paul says of the Gospel, "It is the power of God for salvation to everyone who believes"? (Romans 1:16). What is to be gained, then, by trading our greatest source of power—a power that can change our very hearts—for political unity? I am not saying this was the motivation of the signers of *ECT*. I know neither their hearts nor their intentions. But the document compromises the very heart of the biblical doctrine of justification by obviously leaving out the one word that *would* provide a basis for unity between us. Its ambiguity, I fear, is purposeful. While the ability to compromise may be of great benefit in the political world, those who continue to stubbornly believe that God has revealed His truth and His Gospel see the spiritual damage compromise on this point will bring.

Sola Gratia, Soli Deo Gloria

The Christian Gospel is the message of grace. To a world deluged in a tidal wave of sin, the Christian presents a message of hope based not on what we can do for ourselves, but on what God has done for us through Jesus Christ. And to hearts longing for peace, the Gospel brings peace in its fullness. Lasting peace. Perfect peace. Peace purchased on Calvary's tree and sealed by the Holy Spirit.

Sola Gratia means "grace alone." God's grace is sufficient to bring about the salvation of His people. It needs no additions, no help along the way. God is powerful to save. And because of this, the believer can heartily agree with the second phrase, *Soli Deo Gloria*, "to God alone be the glory." God gets all the glory, for God has brought salvation to us. God did not simply make the plan available. God fully accomplished it and applies it by His Spirit. He alone receives honor for what He has done.

And it is because of this that I have peace with God. My salvation is His work, and He has pledged to finish that work (Ephesians 1:14). I have peace today not because of my outer circumstances, my religious works, or anything else. I have peace with God because of Christ and Christ alone. I am accepted in Him. That is the Gospel of grace, and it is that Gospel I long to see all my brothers and sisters embrace, to His glory.

BIBLIOGRAPHY

Aland, Kurt, and Barbara Aland. *The Text of the New Testament.* Grand Rapids: Eerdmans, 1987.

Alford, Dean. *The New Testament for English Readers.* Grand Rapids: Baker, 1983.

Armstrong, John, ed. *Roman Catholicism.* Chicago: Moody Press, 1994.

Bauckham, Richard J. *2 Peter* in the *Word Biblical Commentary.* Waco, Texas: Word Books, 1983.

Bauer, Arndt, Gingrich, and Danker. *A Greek-English Lexicon of the New Testament and Other Early Christian Literature,* 2nd ed. Chicago: The University of Chicago Press: 1979.

Beckwith, Roger. *The Old Testament Canon of the New Testament Church.* Grand Rapids: Eerdmans, 1985.

Broderick, Robert. *The Catholic Encyclopedia.* Huntington, Ind.: Our Sunday Visitor, 1976.

Bruner, Frederick Dale. *Matthew: A Commentary.* Dallas: Word, Inc., 1990.

Buchanan, James. *The Doctrine of Justification.* Edinburgh: The Banner of Truth Trust, 1984.

Butler, B. C. *The Church and Infallibility: A Reply to the Abridged "Salmon."* New York: Sheed and Ward, 1954.

Caragounis, Chrys. *Peter and the Rock.* New York: Walter de Gruyter, 1990.

Catechism of the Catholic Church. New Hope, Kentucky: Urbi et Orbi Communications, 1994.

Cathcart, William. *The Papal System.* Watertown, WI: Baptist Heritage Press, 1989.

Colson, Charles, and Richard John Neuhaus. *Evangelicals and Catholics Together: Toward a Common Mission.* Dallas: Word, Inc., 1995.

Cranfield, C. E. B. *Commentary on Romans* in *The International Critical Commentary.* Edinburgh: T & T Clark, 1975.

Cullmann, Oscar. *The Christology of the New Testament.* London, 1959.

Dana, H. E., and J. R. Mantey. *A Manual Grammar of the Greek New Testament.* New York: The MacMillan Co., 1955.

Denzinger, Henry. *The Sources of Catholic Dogma.* St. Louis: B. Herder Book Co., 1957.

Geisler, Norman, and Ralph MacKenzie. *Roman Catholics and Evangelicals: Agreements and Differences.* Grand Rapids: Baker, 1995.

Gibbons, John Cardinal. *The Faith of Our Fathers.* Rockford, Ill.: TAN Books and Publishers, 1980.

Gundry, Robert H. *A Survey of the New Testament.* Grand Rapids: Zondervan, 1981.

———. *Matthew: A Commentary on His Literary and Theological Art.* Grand Rapids: Eerdmans, 1982.

Hahn, Scott and Kimberly. *Rome Sweet Home: Our Journey to Catholicism.* San Francisco: Ignatius Press, 1993.

Hardon, John S. J. *The Catholic Catechism.* New York: Doubleday & Co., Inc., 1975.

Hardon, John. *Pocket Catholic Dictionary.* Garden City, N.Y.: Image Books, 1985.

Hendrickson, William. *New Testament Commentary: The Gospel of Matthew.* Grand Rapids: Baker, 1973.

Hodge, Charles. *Systematic Theology.* Grand Rapids: Eerdmans, 1986.

Jerome Biblical Commentary. Englewood Cliffs, N.J.: Prentice-Hall, Inc., 1968.

Kauffman, Timothy. *Quite Contrary.* Huntsville, Ala.: White Horse Publications, 1994.

Keating, Karl. *Catholicism and Fundamentalism: The Attack on "Romanism" by "Bible Christians."* San Francisco: Ignatius Press, 1988.

Kistler, Don, ed. *A Spectacle Unto God: The Life and Death of Christopher Love.* Morgan, Pa.: Soli Deo Gloria Publications, 1994.

———, ed. *Justification by Faith Alone.* Morgan, Pa.: Soli Deo Gloria Publications, 1995.

———, ed. *Sola Scriptura! The Protestant Position on the Bible.* Morgan, Pa.: Soli Deo Gloria Publications, 1995.

Kittel, Gerhard, and Geoffrey Bromiley, eds. *Theological Dictionary of the New Testament.* Grand Rapids: Eerdmans, 1964. S.v. "πέτρα" by Oscar Cullmann.

———. *Theological Dictionary of the New Testament.* Grand Rapids: Eerdmans, 1964. S.v. "εἰρήνη" by Werner Foerster.

———. *Theological Dictionary of the New Testament.* Grand Rapids: Eerdmans, 1964. S.v. "δικαιόω" by Gottlob Schrenk.

Lightfoot, J. B. *Saint Paul's Epistles to the Colossians and to Philemon.* Grand Rapids: Zondervan, 1978.

Ligouri, St. Alphonsus. *The Glories of Mary*. Brooklyn: Redemptorist Fathers, 1931.

Louw, Johannes P., and Eugena A. Nida. *Greek-English Lexicon of the New Testament Based on Semantic Domains*. United Bible Societies: 1988.

Madrid, Patrick, ed. *Surprised by Truth*. San Diego: Basilica Press, 1994.

McCarthy, James. *The Gospel According to Rome*. Eugene, Ore.: Harvest House Publishers, 1995.

Metzger, Bruce Manning. *A Textual Commentary on the Greek New Testament*. New York: United Bible Societies, 1975.

Miller, Elliot, and Kenneth Samples. *The Cult of the Virgin*. Grand Rapids: Baker, 1992.

Murray, John. *Redemption Accomplished and Applied*. Grand Rapids: Eerdmans, 1955.

New Catholic Encyclopedia. Washington, D.C.: The Catholic University of America, 1967.

Newman, John Henry Cardinal. *An Essay on the Development of Christian Doctrine*. Notre Dame, Ind.: University of Notre Dame Press, 1989.

Nicoll, W. Robertson. *The Expositor's Greek Testament*. Grand Rapids: Eerdmans, 1983.

Ott, Ludwig. *Fundamentals of Catholic Dogma*. Rockford, Ill.: TAN Books and Publishers, 1974.

Premm, Matthias. *Dogmatic Theology for the Laity*. Rockford, Ill.: TAN Books and Publishers, 1977.

Reinecker, Fritz, and Cleon Rogers. *Linguistic Key to the Greek New Testament*. Grand Rapids: Zondervan, 1982.

Salmon, George. *The Infallibility of the Church*. Grand Rapids: Baker, 1959.

Schaff, Philip, ed. *A Select Library of Nicene and Post-Nicene Fathers of the Christian Church*. Second Series, Grand Rapids: Eerdmans, 1983.

———. *History of the Christian Church*. Grand Rapids: Eerdmans, 1985.

Shouppe, F. X. *Purgatory: Explained by the Lives and Legends of the Saints*. Rockford, Ill.: TAN Books and Publishers, 1986.

Sproul, R. C. *Faith Alone*. Grand Rapids: Baker, 1995.

The Canons and Decrees of the Council of Trent, trans. H. J. Schroeder, O.P. Rockford: Ill.: TAN Books and Publishers, 1978.

The Companion to the Catechism of the Catholic Church: A Compendium of Texts Referred to in the Catechism of the Catholic Church. San Franscisco: Ignatius Press, 1994.

The Documents of Vatican II. New York: Crossroad, 1966.

The Expositor's Bible Commentary. Grand Rapids: Zondervan, 1984.

The International Standard Bible Encyclopedia. Grand Rapids: Eerdmans, 1956.

Trench, Richard. *Synonyms of the New Testament*. Grand Rapids: Eerdmans, 1983 .

Van Til, Cornelius. *The Defense of the Faith*. Phillipsburg, N.J.: Presbyterian and Reformed Publishing Company, 1967.

Vine, W. E. *An Expository Dictionary of New Testament Words*. Old Tappan, N.J.: Fleming H. Revell Company, 1966.

Waldron, Samuel. *A Modern Exposition of the 1689 Baptist Confession of Faith*. Durham, England: Evangelical Press, 1995.

Warfield, B. B. *The Inspiration and Authority of the Bible*. Philipsburg, N.J.: Presbyterian and Reformed Publishing Co., 1948.

Webster, William. *Peter and the Rock*. Battle Ground, Wash.: Christian Resources, 1996.

————. *Roman Catholicism at the Bar of History*. Banner of Truth, 1995.

White, James. *Drawn by the Father*. Southbridge, Mass.: Crowne Publications, 1991.

Zins, Robert. *Romanism*. Huntsville, Ala.: White Horse Publications, 1995.

NOTES

Preface

1. See, for example, Patrick Madrid, "The White Man's Burden" in *This Rock* magazine (October 1993), pp. 11–16.
2. The Roman Catholic/Protestant debate has been marked by vitriol and anger. It is easier to understand how at the time of the Reformation such feelings were so rampant: one could literally be killed for one's beliefs. But many today invest just as much anger and hatred into the topic, and, I believe, to no avail. Once someone attacks you, it becomes easier for you to respond in kind. And in the process, the great truths that are at stake are lost in the resulting smoke and confusion. I have sought to avoid playing the insult game, despite being the object of the opprobrium of many defenders of Roman Catholicism.

Chapter 1

1. Charles Colson and Richard John Neuhaus, *Evangelicals and Catholics Together: Toward a Common Mission* (Dallas: Word, Inc., 1995), p. 18.
2. *The King James Only Controversy* (Minneapolis: Bethany House Publishers, 1995).
3. I recognize from the start the fact that both terms "Roman Catholic" and "Protestant" have tremendously wide usages in our world today. I further recognize that in many ways the liberal Protestant, like the liberal Roman Catholic, is further removed from me on issues of truth, revelation, and the like than the conservative Roman Catholic. In this work I will focus upon the believing, orthodox Roman Catholic: the individual who takes the teachings of the Pope and the Vatican seriously, and believes those teachings to have divine approval.

4. Another element that makes the discussion of the essentials difficult is that Catholicism in the United States often exhibits a much wider spectrum of belief than it does in primarily Catholic nations, such as Italy, Spain, Mexico, or Brazil. This "freedom" results in many differing opinions as to what Rome actually does teach on the central doctrines of the faith. One will find "Bible-believing" priests in the United States who are open about their commitment to beliefs that would be almost nonexistent among Italian or Spanish Roman Catholics.

Chapter 2

1. In today's atmosphere it needs to be noted that this skill has always been considered important for ministers, and for good reason, because the Bible lays out as part of a minister's responsibilities the task of "refuting" those who contradict his sound teaching and doctrine (Titus 1:9). Don Kistler, writing about the life and death of Christopher Love, a British minister, noted the role of such education in the life of a minister:

> The undergraduate would study logic for four terms and then dispute twice before being granted his degree. On Mondays, Tuesdays, Wednesdays, and Fridays at 9:00 A.M., he would attend the college lecture in rhetoric, and at 1:00 P.M. those same days he would attend the college lecture in Greek. Students were additionally required to "declaim" in Latin or Greek on alternate Saturdays.
>
> Debating was a primary means of preparing a young student to be a divine. These disputations had originally developed centuries earlier as a means of resolving questions that could not be agreed upon even by the most learned authorities (*A Spectacle Unto God: The Life and Death of Christopher Love* [Morgan, Pa.: Soli Deo Gloria Publications, 1994], pp. 20–21).

2. I hasten to exempt from this statement those members of the Anabaptist Movement who refused to take up arms in any situation, including situations motivated by religious differences. Men like Conrad Grebel, Balthasar Hübmaier, and Michael Sattler cannot be charged with the misdeeds of the magisterial Reformers and the hierarchy of the Roman Catholic Church.

Chapter 3

1. It should be noted that the terms "justification" and "righteousness," along with their related verbal forms, "to justify" and "to make righteous," do not refer to *different* things. They are simply two English

terms used to translate a single Greek term (δικαιοσύνη, δικαιόω).

2. This is necessitated by the grammar of the Greek. We here have an aorist passive participle, δικαιωθέντες. Two items should be noted in this word. First, it is passive in voice, pointing us away from ourselves and toward God as the source of our justification. Second, the aorist participle's action refers to a period *prior to* the action of the main verb. Hence, the participle looks back upon our justification as an action in the past, and on the basis of that past action speaks of our having peace with God now.

3. Some Roman Catholic apologists point to the fact that a textual variant exists at this point in the underlying Greek texts. The two readings found are the indicative ἔχομεν and the subjunctive ἔχωμεν. The difference between the two readings would be "we have peace with God" (indicative) and "let us have peace with God" (hortatory subjunctive). I believe the indicative is the only logical reading, and numerous textual scholars agree. Note the following sources:

> Though the indicative *ἔχομεν* is a good deal less strongly attested than the subjunctive *ἔχωμεν*, it is almost certainly to be preferred on the ground of intrinsic probability. It is clear from v. 1. Of that, Paul regards the believer's peace with God as a fact. It would therefore be inconsistent for him to say here "let us obtain peace" (Paul would hardly think of peace with God as something to be obtained by human endeavor). If the subjunctive is read, we must understand it in some sense as "let us enjoy the peace we have" or "let us guard the peace we have" (cf., e.g., Origen, Chrysostom). But this is not free from objection; for it would surely be strange for Paul, in such a carefully argued writing as this, to exhort his readers to enjoy or to guard a peace he has not yet explicitly shown to be possessed by them. While it is of course true that considerations such as have just been mentioned could easily have led to the substitution of the indicative for the subjunctive, a deliberate alteration in the opposite direction would also be understandable, since a copyist might well have felt that, after so much doctrinal statement, an element of exhortation was called for. But, since the difference in pronunciation between *o* and *ω* was slight, a change in either direction could easily occur, whenever in the transmission of the text dictation was employed (cf. the textual variations in, e.g., 6:2; 14:19; 1 Corinthians 15:49). (C.E.B. Cranfield, *Commentary on Romans* in *The International Critical Commentary* [Edinburgh: T & T Clark, 1975], p. 257).

> The context of vv. 1–11 suggests ἔχομεν. The better attestation of ἔχωμεν is offset by the fact that in Romans 14:19 there

is better attestation of the impossible indicative διώκομεν instead of the conjunctive, which alone is possible. In manuscript tradition there is an uncontrollable vacillation between the indicative and conjunctive. Of the first person plural. (Werner Foerster in the *Theological Dictionary of the New Testament*, Gerhard Kittel, ed. [Grand Rapids: Eerdmans, 1964], II: 416).

Although the subjunctive ἔχωμεν . . . has far better external support than the indicative ἔχομεν . . . a majority of the Committee judged that internal evidence must here take precedence. Because in this passage it appears that Paul is not exhorting but stating facts ("peace" is the possession of those who have been justified), only the indicative is consonant with the apostle's argument. (Bruce Manning Metzger, *A Textual Commentary on the Greek New Testament* [New York: United Bible Societies, 1975], p. 511).

It should be noted that in the above citations the authors refer to "better attestation" in the sense of superior manuscripts, not superior numbers. This explains why the Hodges-Farstad *The Greek New Testament According to the Majority Text* as well as the *Textus Receptus* read the indicative rather than the subjunctive. And should it be argued that this is merely a Protestant attempt to get around a troubling passage, the Roman Catholic *Jerome Biblical Commentary* (Englewood Cliffs, N.J.: Prentice-Hall, Inc., 1968) II: 305, says of this same variant, "The present indicative *echomen* ("we have" [peace]) is preferred by modern commentators to the present subjunctive *echōmen* ("let us have"), which, though better attested, is an obvious scribal correction."

4. Ludwig Ott, *Fundamentals of Catholic Dogma* (Rockford, Ill.: TAN Books and Publishers, 1974), p. 262.
5. *Catechism of the Catholic Church*, 2010.

Chapter 4

1. Fourth Session, *Decree Concerning the Canonical Scriptures.*
2. Note as well that this passage from Vatican II asserts that the Church alone has the authority to interpret *both* the written Word of God (the Scriptures) *and* the "unwritten" Word of God, that is, the traditions. Rome claims that only she is able to interpret *both* forms of revelation, which means that she alone is responsible for not only defining but interpreting the "traditions" upon which she bases so much of her modern theology. Obviously, there is no external means of checking her authority, as she not only defines what tradition is, she tells us what it means.

3. Karl Keating, *Catholicism and Fundamentalism* (San Francisco: Ignatius Press, 1988), p. 127.

4. Keating's valiant attempt to avoid the circular reasoning of this position (as found on pp. 123–127 of *Catholicism and Fundamentalism*) by positing a "spiral" argument does not work. It begins with taking the Bible simply as history (the Bible never claims to be simply history), and from this concluding that Jesus was who He claimed to be. While the Bible's testimony to the historical reality of the death and Resurrection is a valid argument, people will not be convinced that Jesus is truly God merely on this basis. Such a conviction is spiritually borne. From the claims of Christ, Keating notes that:

> Christ founded a Church with the rudiments of all we see in the Catholic Church today—papacy, hierarchy, priesthood, sacraments, teaching authority, and, as a consequence of the last, infallibility. . . . We thus have taken purely historical material and concluded that there exists a Church, which is the Catholic Church, divinely protected against teaching error. Now we are at the last part of the argument. That Church tells us the Bible is inspired, and we can take the Church's word for it precisely because the Church is infallible.

The Bible does record that Christ founded the Church, but the Bible does not mention anything about a Papacy, gives us only elders and deacons, no priests, two ordinances (the Lord's Supper and Baptism), and a teaching authority that, after the days of the Apostles, is completely derivative from Scripture (2 Timothy 3:16–17). Obviously, Keating's argument is not historical at all. It begs the question and assumes what it is designed to prove. It is a circular argument.

5. John Hardon defines the term "Magisterium" as "The Church's teaching authority, vested in the bishops, as successors of the Apostles, under the Roman Pontiff, as successor of St. Peter. Also vested in the Pope, as Vicar of Christ and visible head of the Catholic Church" (*Pocket Catholic Dictionary* [Garden City, New York: Image Books, 1985], pp. 237–238). Roman Catholics differentiate between the "ordinary Magisterium," referring to the normal teaching office of the church, and the "extraordinary Magisterium," which refers to special occasions wherein the Pope or ecumenical councils make definitions or decisions that are binding upon all the faithful, and are therefore infallible.

6. Of course, the exact same phenomenon is to be found among American Catholics. And while one does find more unanimity of opinion in locations were Catholicism reigns supreme, there remain very serious, very major differences of opinion that are not done away with by the existence of the Magisterium. We will note some of these differences in later chapters.

7. "Magisterial authority"=the teaching authority of the hierarchy of the Roman Catholic Church.

8. We should note that even when the Apostles were teaching in the early Church there were schisms and heresies. Part of the assumption of Roman apologists who offer "certainty" based upon Roman tradition is the idea that if one has access to the oral preaching and traditions of the Apostles, one will have certainty and therefore unity of belief in the Church. Yet even the New Testament reveals that this is not the case.

9. The same desire likewise lies behind many of those who have moved toward the various Orthodox churches as well.

10. Note that the Jehovah's Witnesses make the exact same claim, only in reference to their own hierarchy. When faced with biblical evidence for the Trinity, the Witness is told, "Trust Brooklyn!"

11. We will discuss some of these changes in later chapters.

12. See the discussion of 2 Peter 1:20 in the following chapter.

13. Some have argued that unless you have an infallible means of interpreting the Scriptures (i.e., the teaching Magisterium of the Church), you cannot teach with authority. This is illustrated in a conversation reported by a convert to Roman Catholicism, Tim Staples, in a book edited by Patrick Madrid, *Surprised by Truth* (San Diego: Basilica Press, 1994), p. 218. The Roman Catholic asks Staples if he believes his interpretations of Scripture are infallible. Staples responds that he does not. The Roman Catholic replies:

> "If that is so," he countered, "how can your interpretations of Scripture be binding upon the consciences of the members of your congregation? If you have no guarantee that your interpretations are correct, why should they trust you? And if your interpretations are purely human in nature and origin, aren't they then merely traditions of men? Jesus condemned tradtions [sic] of men that nullify the Word of God. If it's possible, as you admit, that your interpretations may be wrong—you have no infallible way of knowing for sure—then it's possible that they are nullifying the Word of God."

Staples is unable to respond to this argument. Yet, in light of what we have seen, the response is plain. First, the Roman Catholic has no infallible way of knowing Rome is in fact the authority she claims to be. Secondly, he also has no way of infallibly interpreting the interpretations of the infallible interpreter! As soon as Rome puts an interpretation into writing (and she has infallibly interpreted only a handful of biblical passages to begin with), you then have to interpret that interpretation, and as is readily proven, Roman Catholic theologians often disagree about what was meant by this Council or that dogmatic decree. Thirdly, a congregation's trust in their pastor should be based upon his fidelity to the Word of God and his willingness to work hard at his task of preaching and teaching it, not on some supposed infallibility on the part of the pastor! Fourth, the preaching of the pastor is authoritative and binding upon the consciences of Christians when it is in line with the Apostolic witness of truth, recorded for us in Scripture. The Spirit applies that preached Word to our hearts and confirms it in our spirits. And finally, the last line should well be applied to Rome itself, for, as we shall see in the next chapter, it is *Rome* that has no means of correcting her own errors, and hence ends up nullifying the Word of God by her traditions.

Chapter 5

1. Basil of Caesarea, *Letter CLXXXIX* as found in Schaff and Wace, *A Select Library of Nicene and Post-Nicene Fathers of the Christian Church*, Second Series (Grand Rapids: Eerdmans, 1983), p. 229.
2. It does not follow that every man who confesses the ultimacy of Scripture will exhibit perfect application of this truth in his life or doctrine. I would say Basil, for example, at times allowed his traditions to override the testimony of Scripture. It is a lifelong process for *all* believers to be constantly examining their beliefs and seeking conformity with the truth of the Bible.
3. Karl Keating, *Catholicism and Fundamentalism: The Attack on "Romanism" by "Bible Christians"* (San Francisco: Ignatius Press, 1988), p. 136.
4. The reference to 2 Timothy 2:2 will be dealt with below. We might note that if Mr. Keating feels John 21:25 disqualifies the Bible from being the complete rule of faith, it likewise disqualifies Roman Catholic "tradition," for certainly Roman Catholic tradition does not provide us with the exhaustive details of Jesus' ministry, either.
5. The great Reformer of Geneva, John Calvin, had a clear grasp of the issue:

   > This, then, is the difference. Our opponents (speaking of the Roman Catholic Church) locate the authority of the Church outside God's Word, that is, outside of Scripture and Scripture alone. But we insist that it be attached to the Word and to not allow it to be separated from it. And what wonder if Christ's bride and pupil be subject to her spouse and teacher so that she pays constant and careful attention to His words. For this is the arrangement of a well-governed house. The wife obeys the husband's authority. This is the plan of a well-ordered school, that there the teaching of the schoolmaster alone should be heard. For this reason the Church should not be wise

of itself, should not devise anything of itself but should set the limit of its own wisdom where Christ has made an end of speaking. In this way the Church will distrust all the devisings of its own reason. But in those things where it rests upon God's Word the Church will not waiver with any distrust or doubting but will repose in great assurance and firm constancy (*Institutes of the Christian Religion,* IV:8:13).

6. Some Roman Catholic apologists argue that this involves a "massive paradigm shift," and insist that the Protestant provide biblical evidence of this "shift." Yet, the Roman Catholic Church admits that Scriptural revelation ended with the death of the Apostles, and hence admits as part of her own theology the same "massive paradigm shift" that we are asked to prove!

7. We will discuss the details of the different Roman Catholic understandings of tradition below.

8. Samuel Waldron in *A Modern Exposition of the 1689 Baptist Confession of* Faith (Durham, England: Evangelical Press, 1995) rightly points out that this is not a claim to "omni-sufficiency." When one claims that something is sufficient, the obvious question that must be asked is, "Sufficient for what?" Waldron rightly says on pp. 43–44,

> What, then, is the purpose for which the Scriptures are sufficient? The sufficiency of the Scriptures is nothing more nor less than their sufficiency to achieve the purposes of redemptive revelation. Surely this is clear from the qualifying statement of the Confession: 'all things necessary for his own glory, man's salvation, faith and life'. . . . The sufficiency of the Bible means its sole sufficiency. It is sufficient to achieve the purposes of redemptive revelation without being supplemented by new revelations (claimed by some Anabaptists and others) or by traditions of men (like those extrabiblical traditions claimed by the Roman Catholic Church).

9. This is a common misrepresentation found in many Roman Catholic writings. Note, for example, Patrick Madrid's statement concerning *sola scriptura* in a debate on this subject:

> He says that I can't refute the Greek translations. Well, of course! I didn't bring a Greek library with me tonight. I didn't bring all sorts of linguistic apparatuses to throw at you to try to build my case based on what this scholar or that scholar might say. I brought the Bible. I believe in going by what God's Word says. And Mr. White's position, you have to remember, is he wants to have it both ways. He's telling you on one hand, Scripture's sufficient. Well that means that Scripture is perspicuous (slapping hands together), that you can look at it and see

what it means. And that you can tell what the Bible means. Mr. White is then saying, well, not in this case. Because in this case you need Greek lexicons, and you need this scholar to prove what this word means, and that scholar to prove what that means. If Mr. White is going to be consistent he has to argue for the perspicuity of Scripture. If it's sufficient formally for all doctrine it must be able to on the face of it tell us what it means. I don't believe Mr. White can prove that, especially in the area of baptismal regeneration.

In a later article in *This Rock* magazine (October 1993), p. 15, Mr. Madrid expanded on this claim and insisted that *if* the Bible is sufficient, then there should be no doctrinal disputes among those who read it!

> For *sola scriptura* to be true, Scripture must be sufficient to settle all doctrinal disputes and quandaries. But it's not sufficient to settle *this* dispute or others which cause the fragmentation and confusion within Protestantism. White failed (or refused) to grasp the implications of this fact.

We will discuss the idea that if the Bible is sufficient, then there should not be any doctrinal disagreements later in this chapter.

10. Paul quotes Luke's writings with the standard introduction of "for the Scriptures say..." (1 Timothy 5:18, quoting Luke 10:7), and Peter refers to Paul's writings as "Scripture" in 2 Peter 3:16. Hence, the same principles referred to here that apply to the Old Testament would hold true for the New as well.

11. Paul's words are explicit and unmistakable. He refers to the "holy writings" as those which are *able* (Greek: τὰ δυνάμενά) to make Timothy wise unto salvation. This is an explicit assertion of an *ability* on the part of the Scriptures themselves. I emphasize this because some Roman apologists reject the idea that the Scriptures can be spoken of as being "able" to anything at all, but that they are instead inanimate and hence incapable of "action." Yet the Scripture's testimony to itself is that it is "living and active" (Hebrews 4:12).

12. Greek: θεόπνευστος.

13. B. B. Warfield, *The Inspiration and Authority of the Bible* (Philipsburg, N.J.: Presbyterian and Reformed Publishing Company, 1948), p. 296.

14. Another passage that directly asserts the same truths about the Scripture is found in the writings of Peter, specifically, 2 Peter 1:20–21:

> Knowing this first of all, that no Scriptural prophecy ever came about by the prophet's own personal interpretation (or explanation), for no prophecy ever was borne by the will of man; rather, while being carried along by the Holy Spirit, men spoke from God.

A word of explanation is necessary in regard to the above translation. This text is frequently used by Roman Catholics to insist that Scripture is of no "private interpretation," the point being that one must have the Roman hierarchy to interpret the text—the individual is incapable of such a momentous task. But this is not the point of Peter at all. The text, taken as a whole, makes it clear that the concern of Peter is not with "interpretation" of the text but rather with the origin and resultant surety of the text. Immediately before, Peter refers to his experience of hearing the voice of the Father speak to the Son on the Mount of Transfiguration (Matthew 17). But despite this personal experience, Peter insists that we have the "more sure" word of prophecy. Why is this written revelation more "sure" than his own personal experience? Because of the nature of that revelation. He exhorts his readers to "know this first," that no prophecy ever came about by the prophet's own interpretation. The term "the prophet" is not in the Greek text, but is to be understood. Why? First, in explaining himself in the next verse, Peter will say that "no prophecy was ever 'borne' of the will of man" (the term "borne" to be understood as the past participle of "bear," to carry). Rather, men spoke from God as they were "borne" along by the Holy Spirit (Peter purposefully using the same term in different forms to contrast human origin with the divine origin of Scripture). Secondly, the term translated "private interpretation" is the Greek term ἐπιλύσεως (epiluseous). One lexical source says of the term, ἐπιλύσις releasing, solving, explaining, interpreting. The word almost comes to mean 'inspiration'." This follows right in line with the context, for it would refer to the origin of the prophetic word, not to its interpretation. Hence the text is consistent with itself in indicating the following things:

First, that the prophetic word, clearly understood to be Scripture itself, does not have its origin in the human will. As Paul indicated in 2 Timothy 3:16, the origin of Scripture is divine.

Secondly, the men who gave to us Sacred Scripture were "carried along" or "borne along" by the Holy Spirit of God. They were not driven by simply human desires and emotions, but were carried by the Holy Spirit, directed by Him.

Thirdly, what these men spoke as they were being borne along by the Holy Spirit they "spoke from God." They did not simply speak about God, or in reference to God, but what they spoke was *from* God! Here again is the divine origin of Scripture, for what is from God according to Peter is God-breathed according to Paul—simply two different ways of saying the same thing. For a fuller discussion of the translation of this passage, including a useful bibliography, see Richard J. Bauckham, *2 Peter* in the *Word Biblical Commentary* (Waco, Texas:

Word Books, 1983), pp. 228–235.

15. Greek: ἄρτιος, which is related in its root to the second term we will examine, the verb which is translated "fully equipped," ἐξαρτίζω.

16. W. E. Vine, *An Expository Dictionary of New Testament Words* (Old Tappan, N. J.: Fleming H. Revell Co., 1966), p. 220.

17. Bauer, Arndt, Gingrich, and Danker, *A Greek-English Lexicon of the New Testament and Other Early Christian Literature*, 2nd ed. (Chicago: The University of Chicago Press: 1979), p. 110.

18. Johannes P. Louw and Eugene A. Nida, *Greek-English Lexicon of the New Testament Based on Semantic Domains* (United Bible Societies: 1988), 1:679–680. The great Greek scholar Richard Trench, in his *Synonyms of the New Testament* (Grand Rapids: Eerdmans, 1983), p. 77, said with reference to this term,

> If we ask ourselves under what special aspects completeness is contemplated in ἄρτιος, it would be safe to answer that it is not as the presence only of all the parts which are necessary for that completeness, but involves further the adaptation and aptitude of these parts for the ends which they were designed to serve. The man of God, St. Paul would say, should be furnished and accomplished with all which is necessary for the carrying out of the work to which he is appointed (p. 77).

19. The term is ἐξαρτίζω, here in the perfect passive participial form. Vine tells us that in 2 Timothy it means to "fit out," that is, "to furnish completely" (p. 219). Bauer, Arndt, and Gingrich express this with the term "equip" (p. 273).

20. Louw and Nida, p. 680. Fritz Reinecker and Cleon Rogers in their helpful work, *Linguistic Key to the Greek New Testament*, speak of both ἄρτιος and ἐξαρτίζω. Here we find the following:

> ἄρτιος, fit, complete, capable, *sufficient*; i.e., able to meet all demands ... ἐξαρτίζω, completely outfitted, fully furnished, fully equipped, fully supplied.

21. When presenting this biblical truth in a debate on *sola scriptura* I once asked my Roman Catholic opponent, "Sir, do you not believe that it is a good work to pray to Mary? Yet the Scriptures nowhere teach this. Do you not believe that it is good to believe and teach that Mary was bodily assumed into heaven? Yet the Bible does not teach this. Do you not believe that the man of God should teach that the Pope in Rome is infallible in his teaching office? Yet the Scriptures know nothing of such a concept." The point is plain: the Bible claims to be sufficient resource of the man of God in doing *every good work*. Another objection raised, however, is that Paul elsewhere speaks of doing "good works." For example, in 2 Timothy 2:21 Paul speaks of the man of God cleansing himself so that he can be a vessel of honor, useful to the Master,

"prepared for every good work" (εἰς πᾶν ἔργον ἀγαθὸν ἡτοιμασμένον). Does it not follow then, some would suggest, that cleansing of the ways is another "item" next to Scripture that is necessary for the equipping of the man of God?

The problem here lies in the confusion of the *source* of the man of God's ability to engage in the work of the ministry in the Church (which is the topic of 3:14–17), and the subject of *sanctification in the person's life*, discussed in 2 Timothy 2:21. Note closely Paul's words: "If a man cleanses himself from the latter, he will be an instrument for noble purposes," literally, a vessel unto honor. Note Paul is addressing personal behavior here, as is made plain in the next phrase, "made holy," that is, sanctified. We are talking about the process of sanctification in the life of the man of God, but we are not talking about the source from which he draws so as to teach, reprove, rebuke, etc. Paul goes on, "useful to the Master and prepared to do any good work." The term "prepared" is not *artios* or *exartizo* (as in 2 Timothy 3:16). It is a term that differs markedly in its semantic domain and meaning: ἑτοιμάζω (*hetoimazo*), which specifically speaks of making preparations, of becoming prepared and ready. This is right in line with the context: Paul is talking about a man purifying himself, denying godlessness and walking in a godly fashion. This is just what *hetoimazo* refers to. But in chapter 3 he speaks of sufficiency and capability because he is not talking about something the man himself does, but of the perfection of the source from which the man of God draws: the God-breathed Scriptures.

22. For a historical defense of *sola scriptura*, see my article in *Sola Scriptura! The Protestant Position on the Bible*, Don Kistler, ed., (Morgan, Pa.: Soli Deo Gloria Publications, 1995), pp. 29–64.

Chapter 6

1. In the edition of the documents of Vatican II edited by Walter Abbott, S.J., a very enlightening footnote appears at this point that reads, "This careful formula was one of the last additions to the text, made at the Pope's request. It does not exclude the opinion that all revelation is in some way, though perhaps obscurely, contained in Scripture. But this may not suffice for certitude, and in fact the Church always understands and interprets Scripture in the light of her continuous tradition" (*The Documents of Vatican II* [New York: Crossroad, 1966], p. 117.

2. The new *Catholic Catechism* specifically interprets this passage in section 85 in these words: "This means that the task of interpretation has been entrusted to the bishops in communion with the successor of Peter, the Bishop of Rome."

3. Should one be tempted to think that this situation has somehow changed over the years, the recent (November 24, 1995) comments of Pope John Paul II to the staff of the Congregation for the Doctrine of the Faith should set the record straight. We read,

> In the Encyclicals *Veritatis splendor* and *Evangelium vitae,* as well as in the Apostolic Letter *Ordinatio sacerdotalis,* I wished once again to set forth the constant doctrine of the Church's faith with an act confirming truths which are clearly witnessed to by Scripture, the apostolic Tradition, and the unanimous teaching of the Pastors. These declarations, by virtue of the authority handed down to the Successor of Peter to "confirm the brethren" (Luke 22:32), thus express the common certitude present in the life and teaching of the Church.
>
> It therefore seems urgently necessary to recover the authentic concept of authority, not only from the formal juridicial standpoint, but more profoundly, as a means of guaranteeing, safeguarding, and guiding the Christian community in fidelity to and continuity with Tradition, to make it possible for believers to be in contact with the preaching of the Apostles and with the source of the Christian reality itself.

The entire speech is most enlightening and can be found in English translation in the January 1996 edition of *Inside the Vatican.*

4. It should be noted that quite often when we encounter the use of the term "tradition" in the writings of the early Fathers of the Christian faith, they are referring to this kind of "disciplinary, liturgical, or devotional" traditions. Despite this, many Roman Catholic apologists will cite such passages as being supportive of the broader Roman concept of tradition, in contradiction to their own Church's *Catechism.*

5. Not only do Roman Catholic theologians take differing views, but on an apologetic level the defenders of Rome, too, take different views, sometimes at the same time! This often leads to tremendous amounts of confusion, especially on the part of those who are honestly trying to work through a difficult issue. For example, Karl Keating wrote the following regarding the role of Scripture and tradition in his book *Catholicism and Fundamentalism* (San Francisco: Ignatius Press, 1988), p. 151:

> It is true that Catholics do not think revelation ended with what is in the New Testament. They believe, though, that it ended with the death of the last apostle. The part of revelation that was not committed to writing—the part that is outside of the New Testament and is the oral teaching that is the basis of Tradition—*that* part of revelation Catholics also accept, and in this they follow the apostle Paul's injunction: "Stand firm, then,

242 / THE ROMAN CATHOLIC CONTROVERSY

> brethren, and hold by the traditions you have learned, in word or in writing, from us" (2 Thessalonians 2:14 [Douay-Rheims]).

This is plainly the *partim-partim* view, with two separate sources of divine revelation, the Scriptures and the separate, external oral traditions. This is plainly not the "material sufficiency" viewpoint that asserts that everything is in Scripture and everything is in tradition. However, a few years later Mr. Keating's own magazine, *This Rock*, promoted the *other* viewpoint in an article by James Akin. Mr. Akin took this writer to task for "failing to grasp" the "material sufficiency" argument, saying that "many Protestants attempt to prove their doctrine by asserting the material sufficiency of Scripture. That is a move that does no good because a Catholic can agree with material sufficiency" (*This Rock* [October 1993], p. 15). While the Roman Catholic claim to "material sufficiency" is in reality a rather empty one, the fact remains that Mr. Akin is saying it does no good to prove that the position taken by Mr. Keating is in error and is untenable! This use of "whichever argument is best for this situation" is a common problem in Protestant/Catholic dialogues.

6. *New Catholic Encyclopedia* (1967) Vol. 14, p. 228.

7. For an example of how vague the term "implicitly" can be, see Chapter 13 in the discussion of the Immaculate Conception.

8. A tremendous example of this is found in the use of the phrase *prima scriptura* by former evangelical turned Roman Catholic apologist Scott Hahn.

9. Keating, *Catholicism and Fundamentalism*, pp. 142–153.

Chapter 7

1. Scott and Kimberly Hahn, *Rome Sweet Home: Our Journey to Catholicism* (San Francisco: Ignatius Press, 1993), pp. 51–52. It is difficult to overlook the fact that if this story represents the actual events, Scott Hahn obviously never took the time to look closely at the foundations of his own beliefs while in seminary, or as a professor. We note as well the fact that the student's response is hardly telling against a proper and meaningful interpretation of both Matthew 15 (no, Jesus wasn't condemning all tradition: He was, however, saying that all tradition is subject to the higher authority of Scripture, which is the importance of Matthew 15 in this instance) and 2 Timothy 3:16–17 (the passage says that all Scripture, because it is God-breathed, is *able* to thoroughly equip the man of God for *every* good work). Hahn's admission that he was not even familiar with 2 Thessalonians 2:15 and its relevance to Roman claims only proves that, in light of his having already abandoned justification by faith alone, he was ripe for conversion to a sys-

tem that substitutes its own authority for that of the Bible.

2. Hahn refers here to the twin pillars of *sola scriptura* and *sola fide*, "faith alone."

3. Dr. Gerstner responded to Hahn in an article titled "Rome NOT Home" in *Justification by Faith Alone* (Morgan, Pa.: Soli Deo Gloria Publications, 1995), pp. 166–185.

4. See "The Bible Made Me Do It" in *Surprised by Truth* (San Diego: Basilica Press, 1994), pp. 211–240.

5. Ibid., pp. 30, 50, 66, 119, 138, 215, 250, 264.

6. A Roman Catholic priest made famous by his stand on the issue of there being no salvation outside of the Roman Catholic faith.

7. See Cornelius Van Til, *The Defense of the Faith*, (Phillipsburg, N.J.: Presbyterian and Reformed Publishing Company, 1967), pp. 56–57.

8. Karl Keating, *Catholicism and Fundamentalism*, p. 145.

9. The debate over the differences between the Protestant and Roman Catholic canons is beyond the scope of this work. The reader is directed to the work of Norman Geisler and Ralph MacKenzie, *Roman Catholics and Evangelicals: Agreements and Differences* (Grand Rapids: Baker, 1995), pp. 157–175, as well as Roger Beckwith, *The Old Testament Canon of the New Testament Church* (Grand Rapids: Eerdmans, 1985), for in-depth information on that topic. See as well the White vs. Matatics Debate at Boston College (April 1993) for a Protestant/Catholic discussion of the issue.

10. Likewise two Roman Catholic apologists, Tim Staples and Clayton Bower Jr., when discussing this topic on a Roman Catholic radio program, said the following:

> So actually the Catholic Church—and, if you've heard me speak before, this kind of knocks some Protestants off of their seat—but the Catholic Church technically is not a Bible-based Church. The Bible is a Church-based book. And that's what has to be remembered. The Church came first, was around for a generation or two before the New Testament was even completed, and it's the book that came out of the Church, not the Church out of the Bible. So ultimately I have to say that I believe that Jesus Christ said, "Thou art Peter and on this rock I build my church, and unto thee I give the keys of the kingdom of heaven, and the gates of hell shall not prevail against it." Christ promised that that institution, the Church, which He deliberately founded, would not fail. The gates of hell wouldn't prevail against it. Sadly, the basic premise of the Reformers of the sixteenth century—Reformers is probably a misnomer, but anyway, the Reformationists—was that, in fact, it did fail, that the Church had to be reconstituted, and the only thing left to

go by was this book that was left behind (St. Joseph Catholic Radio Presents, program of January 6, 1996).

This statement is most revealing. First, it presents the common kind of "apologetic" that is being presented to Roman Catholics today. Secondly, the viewpoint it presents on the relationship of the Scripture and the Church is rather striking. Unfortunately, the statement also engages in obvious equivocation. Two terms, the Bible and the New Testament, are used interchangeably, though it is obvious that the two terms are *not* synonymous. It is common to hear controversialists confusing the two terms in stating the claim that "the Church came *before* the Bible." No, the Scriptures preexisted the Church, obviously, in that the Old Testament *was* the Bible of the New Testament Church. The New Testament is filled with citations of the Old with the fully authoritative introduction, "It is written" or "Scripture says." The Church was *never* without Scripture. The Church was founded in the *midst* of the giving of revelation. The Old Testament revelation preceded the Church, the New Testament revelation followed after. The Church never pretended to be the "mother" of the Old Testament, nor did she view herself as the origin or source of the New.

11. One might well point out that this view of the canon is "higher" than the Roman viewpoint, as it asserts a canon that is infallible and divine in nature, depending upon no human authority, and is beyond, in reality, the disputes that have plagued Rome's attempts to canonize the apocryphal books. Along those same lines, the Roman concept of canon is surface-level. They do not (since the days of Sixtus, anyway) claim to know the *complete* canon, i.e., down to the very text. They may say Matthew is canonical, but they can't say if Matthew 18:11 is canonical (Matthew 18:11 involves a textual variation). Protestants, on the other hand, continue to delve into lower, textual criticism because of our belief that what is θεόπνευστος is canonical, hence, we must continue to strive to have the best text God makes available to us.

12. This was the answer given by Clayton Bower to a caller on the St. Joseph Radio Presents program of January 6, 1996. The caller, a convert back to Roman Catholicism from Lutheranism, had encountered some of my debate tapes and asked the *exact* same question of Bower, even to the point of using 2 Chronicles and Isaiah. Bower's response was most revealing, for he admitted that the Jews did *not* have an infallible authority on the issue of the canon. The caller seemed surprised and said, "Even though they had the seat of Moses?" (a reference to Matthew 23:1) to which Bower responded, "Yes." From that perspective, then, there could be no argument that an infallible authority is needed *today* if the Lord Jesus could hold men responsible for the teaching of the Scriptures *then*.

13. Those holding the more traditional *partim-partim* position use this verse with great frequency. They argue that the oral tradition spoken of here is identical with the oral tradition their position presents as being necessary to have *all* of God's special revelation. In this view these traditions would contain inspired material *other than* that which is found in the Scriptures. This inspired material comes from the Apostles and has been handed down through the Church over the course of the centuries, guarded and kept pure by the power of the episcopate. Those holding the newer "material sufficiency" viewpoint also cite the verse, though with less force. Since their position does not assert the existence of developed, revelational truths that differ in substance from that which is found in Scripture, the specific application of this verse to their position is unclear. If they say that this oral tradition amounts to a body of uninspired (yet infallible) *interpretations* of Scripture, the passage provides them little assistance, as Paul is obviously not talking about such a concept here. What is more, are we to believe Paul provided separate uninspired yet infallible "interpretations" of his own writings along with the writings themselves? Or was he providing such interpretations of others? Given the fact that the New Testament was still being written at this point, it is illogical to suggest that such oral interpretations of previously written canonical documents is in view here.
14. Greek: στήκετε.
15. The two Greek terms Paul uses are terms that refer to such a process of handing on a tradition, those terms being παραλαμβάνω and παραδίδωμι.
16. Tertullian, *De Præscriptione Hæreticorum* (*The Prescription Against Heretics*), p. 25.
17. Robert Gundry, *Matthew: A Commentary on His Literary and Theological Art* (Grand Rapids: Eerdmans, 1982), pp. 454–455.

Chapter 8

1. While an examination of the historical data that is opposed to modern Roman Catholic claims would be most useful, space does not allow it. The reader is strongly encouraged to read the fine presentations available on this topic. *See* William Webster, *The Church of Rome at the Bar of History* (Banner of Truth, 1995) as well as his fuller work on Matthew 16:18 titled *Peter and the Rock* (Battle Ground, Wash.: Christian Resources, 1996); George Salmon, *The Infallibility of the Church* (Grand Rapids: Baker, 1959), and the relevant sections of Philipp Schaff's *History of the Christian Church* (Grand Rapids: Eerdmans, 1985).
2. Section 100.

3. John Cardinal Gibbons, *The Faith of Our Fathers* (Rockford, Ill.: TAN Books and Publishers, 1980), p. 78.

4. We recognize that the position that the Papacy was in fact founded directly by Jesus Christ, in the sense that it was functioning from the days of Peter onward, is not held by all Roman Catholics today. While this is certainly the position that has been held historically by Rome, and is plainly the assertion of Vatican I, modern apologists have realized that there are deep problems with this perspective. Therefore, we recognize that there are Roman Catholics who would not assert that we can find the Papacy functioning in the New Testament, for, as John Henry Cardinal Newman said in his book, *An Essay on the Development of Christian Doctrine* (Notre Dame, Ind.: University of Notre Dame Press, 1989),

> While Apostles were on earth, there was the display neither of Bishop nor Pope; their power had no prominence, as being exercised by Apostles. In course of time, first the power of the Bishop displayed itself, and then the power of the Pope (p. 149).

5. The early tradition of the Church associates Peter with Rome throughout. Anyone going solely on the basis of the reports of the Fathers must conclude Peter was in Rome, at the very least at his death. But Rome has yet to seriously deal with the many biblical and chronological problems that face the assertion that Peter was there for any long period of time *functioning* as the bishop of the church in that city.

6. James says, "Hear me!" using the imperative mode of the verb ἀκούω, ἀκούσατέ μου. He is also the only one who gives a judgment, as seen in verse 19, "I judge," in the Greek, ἐγὼ κρίνω, which is variously translated as "it is my judgment" (NASB), "my sentence is" (KJV), and "I have reached the decision" (NRSV). The other use of κρίνω in Acts is in chapter 7, verse 7, where God *judges* the nation that enslaves Israel.

7. As cited by George Salmon, *The Infallibility of the Church*, pp. 345–346, (B. C. Butler, *The Church and Infallibility: A Reply to the Abridged "Salmon"* [New York: Sheed and Ward, 1954], pp. 190–191) can only point to another reference in Cyril (Migne, *Patrologiæ Græcæ*, lxxii: 424) that refers not to John 21, but Matthew 16, which says the Lord appointed Peter "shepherd." Of course He did: just as He appointed the rest of the Apostles.

8. Greek: στηρίζειν is used four times in Acts.

9. *The Expositor's Greek Testament* (Grand Rapids: Eerdmans, 1983), 1:11.

10. *The International Standard Bible Encyclopedia* (Grand Rapids: Eerdmans, 1956), 3:2010.

11. *The Expositor's Bible Commentary* (Grand Rapids: Zondervan, 1984), 8:11–12.
12. *A Survey of the New Testament* (Grand Rapids: Zondervan, 1981), p. 82.
13. *The Text of the New Testament* (Grand Rapids: Eerdmans, 1987), p. 52.
14. If you are convinced that Jesus would have been speaking Aramaic at the time of this discussion, I would like to suggest for your reading the recent work of Chrys Caragounis, available in English translation under the title *Peter and the Rock* (New York: Walter de Gruyter, 1990). Caragounis provides compelling documentation against the theory that we have here in Matthew 16 a repetition of the Aramaic term *Kepha*, demonstrating that the evidence would more likely favor the use of the Aramaic term *minrah* for the phrase, "upon this rock I will build my church." In any case, the fact is plain that any supposed re-creation of a supposed Aramaic original is merely supposition, and cannot in any way be taken as conclusive in any argument. The Gospel of Matthew with which we have to work is written in Greek, not in Aramaic. Since Roman Catholics claim that the Church decides the canon, and since the Gospel of Matthew that Rome accepts as canonical is the *Greek* version of Matthew (no other being known), why should we need to appeal to some other unknown, unexaminable gospel to establish the Roman position?
15. Now it is true that there are many Protestant interpreters who identify Peter as the rock in Matthew 16. For example, Dr. William Hendrickson (*New Testament Commentary: The Gospel of Matthew*, [Grand Rapids: Baker, 1973], p. 645) follows this course. However, he and the other Protestant interpreters that might be cited are quick to reject any Papal pretensions that are placed upon this passage. Dr. Hendrickson presented three views that, he said, "must be rejected," one view that is to be appreciated, and the one that he takes himself. The second view presented that "must be rejected" is that "This passage . . . proves that Peter was the first Pope." He then quotes the same passage from Cardinal Gibbon's book *The Faith of our Fathers* that I cited at the beginning of this chapter, and responds to it as follows: "The passage does not support any such bestowal of well-nigh absolute authority on a mere man or on his successors."

    Similarly we find Dean Alford identifying Peter as the rock, but following this with the statement:

> We may certainly exclaim with Bengel, "All this may be said with safety; for what has this to do with Rome?" Nothing can be further from any legitimate interpretation of this promise, than the idea of a perpetual primacy in the successors of Peter; the very notion of succession is precluded by the form of the

comparison, which concerns the person, and *him only*, so far as it involves that direct promise. In its other and general sense, as applying to all those living stones (Peter's own expression for members of Christ's Church) of whom the Church should be built, it implies, as Origen excellently comments on it, saying, that all this must be understood as said not only to Peter, as in the letter of the Gospel, but to every one who is such as Peter here showed himself, as the spirit of the Gospel teaches us (*The New Testament for English Readers*, [Grand Rapids: Baker, 1983], Vol. I, p. 119.)

Protestant interpreters who see Peter as the rock are clear in denying the Roman interpretation of the passage, insisting instead that this passage must be taken *historically*. Cullmann in the *Theological Dictionary of the New Testament* (Grand Rapids: Eerdmans, 1964) Vol. I, p. 99, follows other Protestants in saying Peter is this, "only and not otherwise than as the Simon whom Christ has taken in hand," that is, the *elected* Peter. They emphasize, as Dr. Frederick Dale Bruner in his work, *Matthew: A Commentary*, (Dallas: Word, Inc., 1990),

> . . . the uniqueness, the historical once-for-allness, of Peter's commission as rock. The text does *not* say "on this rock *and on his successors* I will build my church." *Solus Petrus*. To take this text *literally* is to honor Peter only. Peter was given the first place by Jesus as the one who first confessed Jesus Christ the divine Son, and so Peter is made the first rock of the church. For the church *is* "built upon the foundation of the apostles [like Peter] and prophets, Jesus Christ himself being the cornerstone" (Ephesians 2:20) (2:575).

These Protestants' identification of Peter as the rock is of little assistance to the Roman position, for the fulfillment of Peter's commission, as they see it, is directly *contradictory* to the Roman concept; that is, they see Peter using the keys in a *declaratory* manner in preaching the Gospel first to the Jews and then to the Gentiles. No basis is admitted by these interpreters for an *office* of Pope in this passage.

16. Greek: δώσω, future of δίδωμι.
17. Note a comparison of the words of the Lord Jesus in Matthew 16:19 and 18:18. The only differences are due to the use of the singular in 16:19 and the plural in 18:18; the root words are identical:

> Matthew 16:19: ὃ ἐὰν δήσῃς ἐπὶ τῆς γῆς ἔσται δεδεμένον ἐν τοῖς οὐρανοῖς, καὶ ὃ ἐὰν λύσῃς ἐπὶ τῆς γῆς ἔσται λελυμένον ἐν τοῖς οὐρανοῖς.
> Matthew 18:18: ὅσα ἐὰν δήσητε ἐπὶ τῆς γῆς ἔσται δεδεμένα ἐν οὐρανῷ, καὶ ὅσα ἐὰν λύσητε ἐπὶ τῆς γῆς ἔσται λελ-

υμένα ἐν οὐρανῷ.

18. I comment briefly on the novel attempt by Roman Catholic apologists to apply Isaiah 22 and the key to the house of David to Peter himself in Matthew 16. Such an attempted connection is logically necessary for the Roman position, for there must be some effort made to establish succession in this passage, for Matthew's words make no mention of it. Yet, upon what basis do we identify the *keys* (plural, Greek: κλεῖδας) of the kingdom of heaven, which are associated plainly with the preaching of the Gospel of Jesus Christ, with the *key* (singular, Greek: κλεῖν as cited in Rev. 3:7; some LXX manuscripts have "glory" instead of "key," while other manuscripts have the singular form of the term "key" κλεῖδαν. The Hebrew of Isaiah 22:22, מַפְתֵּחַ is singular as well) of the house of David, which is Messianic in nature? And should we not instead accept the interpretation given by the Lord Jesus himself, when he cites Isaiah 22:22 of *himself* in Revelation 3:7, "And to the angel of the church in Philadelphia write: He who is holy, who is true, who has the key of David, who opens and no one will shut, and who shuts and no one opens, says this." Jesus has, present tense (Greek: ὁ ἔχων), the key of David. He does not say that He gives this key to anyone else. Indeed, when we look at how the Lord introduces himself in each of these letters, the descriptions set Him apart from all creatures. Should we not then reject such an obvious attempt at exegesis, and instead stay with the plain meaning of Scripture? I am unaware of a single Father of the Christian faith in the first 700 years of the Christian era who ever connected Isaiah 22:22 with Matthew 16, and then applied this to Peter's supposed successors.

19. Salmon, *The Infallibility of the Church*, pp. 343–344.

20. Webster provides a wonderfully complete survey of the patristic interpretation of the passage in *Peter and the Rock* (Battle Ground, Wash.: Christian Resources, 1996).

21. Ibid., p. 337.

22. Butler in his response to Salmon attempted to defuse this difficult reality by citing the work of Fr. Joseph Crehan. Crehan gave as those in favor of Peter as the rock, 16; in favor of the apostolic college, 6; in favor of Peter's faith, 17, and in favor of Christ, 4. This still adds up to 27 out of 43 (62.8%) giving a "perverse" opinion on the passage. Crehan's most intriguing attempt to explain *why* this is, found in Butler's footnote (pp. 190–191), is most instructive with reference to the lengths to which some will go to attempt to keep modern Roman statements "true."

23. Salmon, p. 335.

24. As cited by Schaff, 3:306.

25. In fact, I might note in passing that Dr. Fröhlich (in Pelikan, 3:47 as

cited by Bruner, *Matthew: A Commentary*, 2:575) said, "The most aston-
ishing fact is that in the entire Middle Ages, in contrast with the po-
lemical literature of the period, specifically exegetical literature universally made the equation 'rock-Christ' not 'rock-Peter.' I am inclined
to agree with William Cathcart in his work, *The Papal System* (Watertown, Wis.: Baptist Heritage Press, 1989) who wrote with reference to
the patristic interpretation of the rock as Christ,

> The same view of this Scripture was taken by other leading
> Fathers of the Church. And, outside of Rome, for the first five
> centuries of our era, no Christian Father of any note dreamt
> that this saying gave Peter the sovereignty of the Church (p.
> 77).

26. Charles Hodge, *Systematic Theology* (Grand Rapids: Eerdmans, 1986),
    I:130, 150.
27. One could number Pope John Paul II in this group, for he said just
    recently to the staff of the Congregation for the Doctrine of the Faith
    (English translation taken from "Inside the Vatican" (January 1996), p.
    13):

> It is not possible, however, to overlook one of the decisive
> aspects that lies at the base of the malaise and uneasiness in
> certain parts of the ecclesiastical world: it is a question of the
> way authority is conceived. In the case of the Magisterium, au-
> thority is not exercised only when the charism of infallibility is
> invoked; its exercise has a wider field, which is required by the
> appropriate defense of the revealed deposit.
>
> For a community based on shared adherence to the Word
> of God and on the resulting certainty of living in the truth, *au-
> thority for determining the content to be believed and professed is
> something that cannot be renounced* (emphasis added). . . . How-
> ever, this does not entitle one to hold that the pronouncements
> and doctrinal decisions of the Magisterium call for irrevocable
> assent only when it states them in a solemn judgment or defin-
> itive act, and that, consequently, in all other cases one need only
> consider the arguments or reasons employed.

28. The literature on this subject is vast. Almost any unbiased historical
    work on the history of the Church will provide the reader with more
    than sufficient data illustrating the errors of Popes of the past. I note
    the following areas to direct the reader toward useful information. I
    cannot do anything more than list these topics, knowing full well that
    Roman Catholic apologists have developed explanations for them—
    explanations that I strongly encourage the reader to examine, for I am
    confident that the reader will find them wanting. But I simply note the
    examples of Liberiûs, bishop of Rome, who signed the Arianized Sir-

mium Creed; of Pope Honorius, the monothelite who was anathematized by Councils and Popes as a heretic for centuries; of the condemnation by Popes of Galileo and his theories concerning the movement of the planets, etc.; and of Pope Sixtus and his "infallible" *Vulgate* version of the Bible (which ended up being anything but infallible). These examples were all raised by those Roman Catholic delegates at Vatican I who opposed the definition of infallibility. But by various means the supporters of the doctrine silenced them, and the doctrine was promulgated despite their protests.

Chapter 9

1. John Hardon, *Pocket Catholic Dictionary* (New York: Image Books, 1985), p. 449.
2. Ibid., p. 271.
3. Council of Trent, Sixth Session, 4.
4. Ludwig Ott, *Fundamentals of Catholic Dogma* (Rockford, Ill.: TAN Books and Publishers, 1974), p. 433.
5. Ibid. *See also*, Denzinger, p. 899.
6. Denzinger, p. 693. The phrase "of different kinds" refers to different kinds of punishment than Purgatory, which were mentioned immediately preceding this sentence.
7. Council of Trent, Fourteenth Session, 8.
8. Ott, *Fundamentals of Catholic Dogma*, p. 434.
9. Council of Trent, Sixth Session, Canon 30.
10. Matthias Premm, *Dogmatic Theology for the Laity* (Rockford, Ill.: TAN Books and Publishers, 1977), pp. 262–263.
11. John O'Brien, *The Faith of Millions* (Huntington, Ind.: Our Sunday Visitor, Inc., 1974), pp. 142–143.
12. The Council of Vienne (1311–1312) said regarding baptism, "Besides, one baptism, which regenerates all who are baptized in Christ must be faithfully confessed by all just as 'one God and one faith' [Ephesians 4:5], which celebrated in water in the name of the Father and of the Son and of the Holy Spirit we believe to be commonly the perfect remedy for salvation for adults as for children." *See* Denzinger, 482.
13. Ott, p. 416.
14. The canons attached to the decrees of Trent are most illuminating, and the following are important for the person who wishes to really determine if Rome anathematized mere misunderstandings, or, in many cases, the actual teachings of the Reformers. Below we reproduce the more important canons that are not cited elsewhere in the body of this text:

> Canon 4: If anyone says that man's free will moved and

aroused by God, by assenting to God's call and action, in no way cooperates toward disposing and preparing itself to obtain the grace of justification, that it cannot refuse its assent if it wishes, but that, as something inanimate, it does nothing whatever and is merely passive, let him be anathema.

Canon 5: If anyone says that after the sin of Adam man's free will was lost and destroyed, or that it is a thing only in name, indeed a name without a reality, a fiction introduced into the Church by Satan, let him be anathema.

Canon 9: If anyone says that the sinner is justified by faith alone, meaning that nothing else is required to cooperate in order to obtain the grace of justification, and that it is not in any way necessary that he be prepared and disposed by the action of his own will, let him be anathema.

Canon 12: If anyone says that justifying faith is nothing else than confidence in divine mercy, which remits sins for Christ's sake, or that it is this confidence alone that justifies us, let him be anathema.

Canon 14: If anyone says that man is absolved from his sins and justified because he firmly believes that he is absolved and justified, or that no one is truly justified except him who believes himself justified, and that by his faith alone absolution and justification are effected, let him be anathema.

Canon 15: If anyone says that a man who is born again and justified is bound *ex fide* to believe that he is certainly in the number of the predestined, let him be anathema.

Canon 17: If anyone says that the grace of justification is shared by those only who are predestined to life, but that all others who are called are called indeed but receive not grace, as if they are by divine power predestined to evil, let him be anathema.

Canon 33: If anyone says that the Catholic doctrine of justification as set forth by the holy Council in the present decree, derogates in some respect from the glory of God or the merits of our Lord Jesus Christ, and does not rather illustrate the truth of our faith and no less the glory of God and of Christ Jesus, let him be anathema.

15. Indeed, in summing up the matter, it is claimed that a person cannot be justified without accepting the definitions just put forward by the Council.
16. Ludwig Ott, *Fundamentals of Catholic Dogma*, p. 262.
17. Sixth Session, Chapter VIII.
18. Sixth Session, Chapter XIV.

19. Ibid.
20. Ott, *Fundamentals of Catholic Dogma*, p. 264. *See also* pp. 267–268.
21. Karl Keating, *Catholicism and Fundamentalism* (San Francisco: Ignatius Press, 1988), pp. 167–168.
22. The new *Catechism* puts it this way: **2011** "The charity of Christ is the source in us of all our merits before God."
23. If you think this is merely a matter of splitting hairs, stop now and consider the words of Paul in Romans 11:6: "But if it is by grace, it is no longer on the basis of works, otherwise grace is no longer grace."
24. The Tiber River flows through Rome itself, forming a natural barrier to the west of the city.
25. Denzinger, 423.
26. Denzinger, 1647.
27. Another example from Leo XIII is found in his encyclical *Annum Ingressi Sumus*.
28. Denzinger, 430.
29. Denzinger, 469.
30. Denzinger, 714.
31. Vatican II, *Decree on Ecumenism*, 4.
32. Vatican II, *Lumen Gentium*, 16.
33. Ibid., 14.
34. Ibid.
35. The *current* dogmatic teaching is best illustrated in the letter of F. Cardinal Marchetti-Selvaggiani for the Congregation for the Doctrine of the Faith to the Archbishop of Boston, James Cushing. This letter can be found in *The Companion to the Catechism of the Catholic Church: A Compendium of Texts Referred to in the Catechism of the Catholic Church* (San Francisco: Ignatius Press, 1994), pp. 360–362.

Chapter 10

1. John Murray rightly noted the main reasons why the topic of justification does not command the attention of people in the modern world the way it did in the past:

> And we all are all wrong with him because we have all sinned and come short of the glory of God. Far too frequently we fail to entertain the gravity of this fact. Hence the reality of our sin and the reality of the wrath of God upon us for our sin do not come into our reckoning. This is the reason why the grand article of justification does not ring the bells in the innermost depths of our spirit. And this is the reason why the gospel of justification is to such an extent a meaningless sound in the world and in the church of the twentieth century. We are

not imbued with the profound sense of the reality of God, of his majesty and holiness. And sin, if reckoned with at all, is little more than a misfortune or maladjustment (*Redemption Accomplished and Applied* [Grand Rapids: Eerdmans, 1955], p. 117).

2. Many fine expositions of this topic exist. The reader is directed to the relevant sections of John Calvin's *Institutes of the Christian Religion*, as well as more modern works such as James Buchanan's *The Doctrine of Justification* (Edinburgh: Banner of Truth Trust, 1984), Don Kistler, ed., *Justification by Faith Alone* (Morgan, Pa.: Soli Deo Gloria Publications, 1995), R. C. Sproul, *Faith Alone* (Grand Rapids: Baker, 1995), and those works by Hodge, Warfield, and Murray cited in the endnotes.

3. Chapter 11, sections 1–3.

4. Question 33.

5. The opposite of saving faith is dead faith as described by the Apostle James in James 2:14ff. The kind of faith that James is attacking is a faith that does not result in works. Yet, this is not saving faith, and when Protestants speak of "*sola fide*," faith alone, we are speaking of *saving faith alone*, not *dead faith alone*. The faith Paul spoke of in Ephesians 2 and in Titus 3 always resulted in good works. So, James and Paul are not using the word "faith" in the same way. For Paul, "faith" is saving faith, the very gift of the sovereign God, given in regeneration. James, on the other hand, is talking about faith that is, as he said, dead—faith that does not result in works. We agree that saving faith will not be alone, and hence we are not asserting that salvation can come by such dead faith.

6. As B. B. Warfield put it, "The saving power of faith resides thus not in itself, but in the Almighty Saviour on whom it rests. . . . It is not, strictly speaking, even faith in Christ that saves, but Christ that saves through faith." "The Biblical Doctrine of Faith" in *The Works of Benjamin B. Warfield* (Grand Rapids: Baker, 1981), II;504.

7. The Greek is striking. The "one who works" in verse 4 is τῷ ἐργαζομένῳ. The "one who does not work" is the direct negation of the same phrase, τῷ μὴ ἐργαζομένῳ, literally, "the not working one," followed by the adversative use of δὲ, introducing the opposite of "working," that being "believing." No stronger contrast could be drawn.

8. The law functions to show us our sin and failure, and this forces us to look for a Savior. The law then becomes our "tutor" or "schoolmaster," teaching us of our sin and directing us to the Savior, Christ Jesus (Galatians 3:24). The law does not attempt to justify us, for it cannot do so, nor, Paul argues, was it ever intended to do so. Faith in the promise always *preceded* the law. The function of the law is fulfilled when, upon examining God's holy will that is revealed therein, we see our own sin

in the light of God's transcendent holiness, and know thereby our utter helplessness and guilt. Convicted of our sin, and understanding the impossibility of our "bypassing" the holy standards of the law through any kind of works we might do, we flee to God's mercy that is shown so completely in the person of Jesus Christ. The law does not justify, but it directs us to Christ.

9. What is the righteousness of Christ? Charles Hodge wrote,

> By the righteousness of Christ is meant all he became, did, and suffered to satisfy the demands of divine justice, and merit for his people the forgiveness of sin and the gift of eternal life. The righteousness of Christ is commonly represented as including his active and passive obedience (Hodge, *Systematic Theology*, III:142).

The righteousness of Christ, then, includes the entire work of Christ in redeeming sinners by His substitutionary death (this would be the "passive" element of His obedience) *as well as* His "active," perfect, and complete obedience to the entire law of God. Of course, the division of "active" and "passive" obedience is not strictly biblical, in that the Bible does not use these terms. We are not talking about two *different things* when we speak of Christ's righteousness; we are identifying instead a "positive" and "negative" aspect, an "active" and "passive" obedience on His part. In reality, we are struggling to use human language to describe the breadth and depth of the work of the Lord Jesus—no small task indeed!

10. See the discussion of this concept in Chapter 12.

11. Ironically, Clement of Rome (A.D. 95), listed as one of the early Popes in traditional lists, spoke quite differently. Note his words:

> They all therefore were glorified and magnified, not through themselves or their own works or the righteous doing which they wrought, but through His will. And so we, having been called through His will in Christ Jesus, are not justified through ourselves or through our own wisdom or understanding or piety or works which we wrought in holiness of heart, but through faith, whereby the Almighty God justified all men that have been from the beginning; to whom be the glory for ever and ever. Amen (Clement of Rome, 32).

12. See the discussion of the Mass in Chapter 11.

13. Hebrew: צדקה.

14. Gottlob Schrenk notes in *The Theological Dictionary of the New Testament* (Grand Rapids: Eerdmans, 1964), II:212:

> In the LXX δικαιοῦν (corresponding to צדק) is a forensic term. Yet it does not have a predominant negative connotation

("to condemn") as in Greek but is constantly used in the positive sense of "to pronounce righteous," "to justify," "to vindicate." . . . The forensic element is even stronger in the LXX than the Massoretic text.

15. Protestant theologians have identified a twofold nature to justification. John Murray used the terms "constitutive" and "declarative" to describe this situation.

> Justification is therefore a constitutive act whereby the righteousness of Christ is imputed to our account and we are accordingly accepted as righteous in God's sight. . . . Justification is both a declarative and a constitutive act of God's free grace (John Murray, *Redemption Accomplished and Applied*, p. 124).

The "constitutive" element is the positive *imputation* of Christ's righteousness to the believer, and this is the grounds, then, of the "declarative" element, that being the declaration of the righteousness of the believer. It should be noted that the imputation of Christ's righteousness is taken in the same sense as it is in the New Testament—as a legal imputation, not a subjective one.

16. Hebrew: חשב.

17. Greek: λογίζομαι.

18. The imputation of the righteousness of Christ is the action of the merciful Father who sees the accomplishment of His Son in behalf of His people as sufficient and complete. John Murray commented,

> When we think of such an act of grace on God's part, we have the answer to our question: how can God justify the ungodly? The righteousness of Christ is the righteousness of his perfect obedience, a righteousness undefiled and undefilable, a righteousness which not only warrants the justification of the ungodly but one that necessarily elicits and constrains such justification. God cannot but accept into his favour those who are invested with the righteousness of his own Son (John Murray, *Redemption Accomplished and Applied*, p.124).

And Charles Hodge, in his *Systematic Theology* (Grand Rapids: Eerdmans, 1986), III:145, further asserts,

> So when righteousness is imputed to the believer, he does not thereby become subjectively righteous. If the righteousness be adequate, and if the imputation be made on adequate grounds and by competent authority, the person to whom the imputation is made has the right to be treated as righteous. And, therefore, in the forensic, although not in the moral or subjective sense, the imputation of the righteousness of Christ does make the sinner righteous. That is, it gives him a right to

the full pardon of all his sins and a claim in justice to eternal life.

19. Karl Keating, *Catholicism and Fundamentalism* (San Francisco: Ignatius Press, 1988), pp. 167–168.
20. Used by permission.

Chapter 11

1. John O'Brien, *The Faith of Millions* (Huntington, Ill.: Our Sunday Visitor Inc., 1974), pp. 255–256.
2. Paragraphs 1987 through 1995.
3. Paragraphs 1322 through 1419.
4. Paragraph 1364.
5. We do not enter into the entire discussion of the Aristotelian distinction of accident and substance, etc.
6. See paragraph 1366 of the *Catechism*.
7. Ludwig Ott, *Fundamentals of Catholic Dogma* (Rockford, Ill.: TAN Books and Publishers, 1974), p. 414.
8. Ibid.
9. *See* O'Brien, *The Faith of Millions*, pp. 235–240.
10. For a full discussion and exegesis of John 6:35–45, see the author's *Drawn by the Father* (Southbridge, Mass.: Crowne Publications, 1991).
11. We do not here enter into the debate over the authorship of Hebrews. Many have seen Paul as its author, and others have suggested many other possibilities. In any case, the writer to the Hebrews often parallels Pauline thought, especially on the person of Christ. However, at other times differences in the use of terminology are evident.
12. Oscar Cullmann, in *The Christology of the New Testament* (London, 1959), p. 99, writes concerning this "once for all-ness" of Christ's sacrifice:

> Christian worship in the light of that "one time" which means "once for all time" is possible only when even the slightest temptation to "reproduce" that central event itself is avoided. Instead, the event must be allowed to remain the divine act of the past time where God the Lord of time placed it—at that exact historical moment in the third decade of our chronology. It is the saving consequences of that atoning act, not the act itself, which become a present event in our worship. The Lord present in worship is the exalted *Kyrios* of the Church and the world, raised to the right hand of God. He is the risen Lord who continues his mediating work on the basis of his unique, completed work of atonement.

13. In fact, we point out that the term "reminder" used in Hebrews 10:3

is the exact same term Paul uses in 1 Corinthians 11:24–25, "do this *in remembrance* of Me" (literally, "unto My remembrance"). As a student of mine rightly pointed out as we discussed this issue, "A sacrifice that is repetitive in nature is a reminder of *sin*, while the Supper, rather than reminding us of our sin, is in remembrance *of Christ*."

14. Should it be argued that Rome is merely offering the same eternal sacrifice, we point out that it was the repeated *offering* of the old sacrifices that demonstrated their insufficiency. This is why the writer to the Hebrews emphasizes that Christ offered His sacrifice *once for all*, and that this offering is not to be made over and over again. Yet Rome *offers*, by her own words, a sacrifice repeatedly in the Mass (see sections 1362–1372 of the *Catholic Catechism* for examples of the use of the term "offer" and "offering"). The repeated *offering* is, according to Hebrews, demonstrative of the *insufficiency* of the sacrifice.

Chapter 12

1. F. X. Shouppe, *Purgatory: Explained by the Lives and Legends of the Saints* (Rockford, Ill.: TAN Books and Publishers, 1986), pp. 136–137.
2. As cited in *The Companion to the Catechism of the Catholic Church: A Compendium of Texts Referred to in the Catechism of the Catholic Church* (San Francisco: Ignatius Press, 1994), p. 406.
3. John Hardon, S. J. *The Catholic Catechism* (New York: Doubleday & Company, Inc., 1975), pp. 273–274.
4. *The Canons and Decrees of the Council of Trent*, trans. H. J. Schroeder, O.P. (Rockford: Ill.: TAN Books and Publishers, 1978), p. 146.
5. Ludwig Ott, *Fundamentals of Catholic Dogma* (Rockford, Ill.: TAN Books and Publishers, 1974), p. 485.
6. Philip Schaff, *History of the Christian Church*, (Grand Rapids: Eerdmans, 1985), VI:767.
7. Paragraphs 1471 through 1479.
8. *Indulgentiarum Doctrina*, 2. Interestingly, the only mention of Jesus Christ in the section entitled "Sins Must Be Expiated" is with reference to the love of God shown to us in Christ, not to His atoning, or expiating, work in behalf of His people.
9. Ibid., p. 3.
10. Ibid., p. 7.
11. Ibid.
12. Ibid., p. 10.
13. Ibid.
14. Ibid., p. 8.
15. Ibid., p. 10.
16. Ibid.

17. Norm number 15.
18. Dr. Schaff rightly noted in his *History of the Christian Church* (Grand Rapids: Eerdmans, 1985), VI:756–757,

> Nowhere, except in the lives of the popes themselves, did the humiliation of the Western Church find more conspicuous exhibition than in the sale of indulgences. The forgiveness of sins was bought and sold for money, and this sacred privilege formed the occasion of the rupture of the Western Christendom. . . . In the thirteenth century, it came to be regarded as a remission of the penalty of sin itself, both here and in purgatory. At a later stage, it was regarded, at least in wide circles, as a release from the guilt of sin as well as from its penalty. The fund of merits at the Church's disposition—*thesaurus meritorum*—as defined by Clement VI., in 1343, is a treasury of spiritual assets, consisting of the infinite merits of the saints, which the Church uses by virtue of the power of the keys. One drop of Christ's blood, so it was argued, was sufficient for the salvation of the world, and yet Christ shed all his blood and Mary was without stain. From the vast surplus accumulation supplied by their merits, the Church had the right to draw in granting remission to sinners from the penalties resulting from the commission of sin.

19. Schaff writes about this (op. cit., p. 758).

> Sixtus' first bull granting indulgences for the dead was issued in 1476 in favor of the church of Saintes. Here was offered to those who paid a certain sum—*certam pecuniam*—for the benefit of the building, the privilege of securing a relaxation of the sufferings of the purgatorial dead, parents for their children, friend for friend. The papal deliverance aroused criticism and in a second bull, issued the following year, the pontiff states that such relaxations were offered by virtue of the fulness of authority vested in the pope from above—*plenitudo potestatis*—to draw upon the fund of merits.
>
> To the abuse, to which this doctrine opened the door, was added the popular belief that letters of indulgence gave exemption both from the culpability and penalty of sin. The expression, "full remission of sins," *plena* or *plenissima remissio peccatorum*, is found again and again in papal bulls from the famous Portiuncula indulgence, granted by Honorius III to the Franciscans, to the last hours of the undisputed sway of the pope in the West. It was the merit of the late Dr. Lea to have called attention to this almost overlooked element of the mediæval indulgence. Catholic authorities of today, as Paulus

and Beringer, without denying the use of the expression, *a poena et culpa*, assert that it was not the intent of any genuine papal message to grant forgiveness from the guilt of sin without contrition of heart.

20. *Indulgentiarum Doctrina*, p. 11.
21. John Calvin, *Institutes of the Christian Religion*, ed. John T. McNeill and trans. Ford Lewis Battles (Philadelphia: Westminster, 1960), III:5:7.
22. The only passage that Roman Catholic theologians can attempt to put into service to defend any of these concepts is found in Paul's letter to the Colossians. We read,

> Now I rejoice in my sufferings for your sake, and in my flesh I do my share on behalf of His body, which is the church, in filling up what is lacking in Christ's afflictions (Colossians 1:24).

J. B. Lightfoot, in his commentary, *Saint Paul's Epistles to the Colossians and to Philemon* (Grand Rapids: Zondervan, 1978), pp. 165–167, demonstrates why this attempted use of this passage fails:

"τῶν θλίψεων τοῦ Χριστοῦ *'of the afflictions of Christ,'* i.e. which Christ endured." This seems to be the only natural interpretation of the words. . . . The theological difficulty, which these and similar explanations are intended to remove, is imaginary and not real. There is a sense in which it is quite legitimate to speak of Christ's afflictions as *incomplete*, a sense in which they may be, and indeed must be, *supplemented*. For the sufferings of Christ may be considered from two different points of view. They are either *satisfactoriæ* or *ædificaatoriæ*. They have their sacrificial efficacy, and they have their ministerial utility. (1) From the former point of view the Passion of Christ was the one full, perfect, and sufficient sacrifice, oblation, and satisfaction for the sins of the whole world. In this sense there could be no ὑστέρημα of Christ's sufferings; for, Christ's sufferings being different *in kind* from those of His servants, the two are incommensurable. But in this sense the Apostle would surely have used some other expression such as τοῦ σταυροῦ (i. 20, Ephesians 2:16, etc.), or τοῦ θανάτου (i. 22, Romans 5:10; Hebrews 2:14, etc.), but hardly τῶν θλίψεων. Indeed θλῖψις, "affliction," is not elsewhere applied in the New Testament in any sense to Christ's sufferings, and certainly would not suggest a sacrificial act. (2) From the latter point of view it is a simple matter of fact that the afflictions of every saint and martyr do supplement the afflictions of Christ. The Church is built up by repeated acts of self-denial in successive individuals and successive generations. They continue the work which Christ began. They bear their part in the sufferings of Christ (2 Corinthians 1:7. . . . Philippians 3:10. . . .); but St. Paul would have been the last to say that they bear their part in the atoning sacrifice of Christ. This being so, St. Paul does not mean to say that his own sufferings filled up all the ὑστερήματα, but only that they *went toward* filling them up. The present tense ἀνταναπληρῶ denotes an inchoate, and not a complete act. These ὑστερήματα will never be fully supplemented, until the struggle of the Church with sin and unbelief is brought to a close.

Thus the idea of expiation or satisfaction is wholly absent from this passage. . . . Romanist commentators . . . have found in this passage an assertion of the merits of the saints, and (as a necessary consequence) of the doctrine of indulgences. They have not observed that, if the idea of vicarious satisfaction comes into the passage at all, the satisfaction of St. Paul is represented here as the same in kind with the satisfaction of Christ, however different it may be in degree. . . . It is sufficient to say that, so far as regards this particular passage, the Roman doctrine can only be imported into it at the cost of a contradiction to the Pauline doctrine."

23. *Indulgentiarum doctrina*, p. 2.

Chapter 13

1. That is, the two views mentioned earlier designated as the "*partim=partim*" view and the "*Totum in Scriptura, totum in Traditione*" view.
2. Without taking the time to discuss the fall, sin, etc., we note in passing that we would not wish to put Mary in the same category as aborted children and those born with mental handicaps.
3. Greek: θεότητος.
4. Greek: ἐγὼ εἰμί.
5. Karl Keating, *Catholicism and Fundamentalism* (San Francisco: Ignatius Press, 1988), p. 269.
6. Greek: κεχαριτωμένη.
7. Greek: χαριτόω.
8. Bauer, Arndt, Gingrich, and Danker, *A Greek-English Lexicon of the New Testament and Other Early Christian Literature*, 2nd ed. (Chicago: The University of Chicago Press, 1979), p. 879.
9. In this case, however, we have a vocative participle, and no main verb in what is in actuality simply a greeting. The fact that the Roman Catholic Church has to attempt to build such a complex theology on the form of a participle in a greeting should say a great deal in and of itself.
10. *See* H. E. Dana and J. R. Mantey, *A Manual Grammar of the Greek New*

Testament (New York: The Macmillan Company, 1955), p. 202.

11. Greek: εὐλογημένη σὺ ἐν γυναιξὶν.

12. Greek: εὐλογέω.

13. John Hardon, *Pocket Catholic Dictionary* (Garden City, New York: Image Books, 1985), p. 222.

14. Greek: λατρεία. Romans 12:1 uses this term, and renders it one's "service of worship."

15. Robert Broderick, *The Catholic Encyclopedia* (Huntington, Ind.: Our Sunday Visitor, 1976), p. 174.

16. Hardon also gives this indication when he writes in reference to the meaning of cult, "A definite term of worship or of religious observance, sometimes rendered 'cultus,' especially when referring to the worship of the saints" (p. 99).

17. Broderick, *Catholic Encyclopedia*, p. 278.

18. Hardon, *Pocket Catholic Dictionary*, p. 448.

19. Some Catholic apologists also attempt to bring in the meaning of the English word "worship" and show that it has secular usages, just as the Greek term προσκυνέω (*proskuneo*, to worship, to bow down to) did in the New Testament. However, it is obvious that what worship means in English is of no importance in determining what worship means in the Bible; that concept, as contained in Scripture, was laid down millennia before the English language developed. Again, the important concept to understand is what the term means in the Bible and not what it means in a translation made thousands of years after the original was written.

20. John Calvin, *Institutes of the Christian Religion*, I:12:2.

21. Hebrew: אבד.

22. ἐδουλεύσατε, from δουλεύω, the verb form of *dulia*.

23. A strengthened form, *deservio*, is also used.

24. Excellent treatments of this topic are currently available in: Elliot Miller and Kenneth Samples, *The Cult of the Virgin* (Grand Rapids: Baker, 1992); James McCarthy, *The Gospel According to Rome* (Eugene, Ore.: Harvest House Publishers, 1995); Norman Geisler and Ralph MacKenzie, *Roman Catholics and Evangelicals: Agreements and Differences* (Grand Rapids: Baker, 1995); Robert Zins, *Romanism* (Huntsville, Ala.: White Horse Publications, 1995), John Armstrong, ed., *Roman Catholicism* (Chicago: Moody Press, 1994), and Timothy Kauffman, *Quite Contrary* (Huntsville, Ala.: White Horse Publications, 1994).

25. From "Devotions in Honor of Our Mother of Perpetual Help," published by The Redemptorists. A very similar prayer appears in St. Alphonsus de Ligouri, *The Glories of Mary*, also a Redemptorist publication (p. 98). The Ligouri edition ends, "O Mary, I hope all from thee; for thou art all-powerful with God." Should the reader wonder how

popular Ligouri's work is, the book has gone through *800 editions!*
26. Ligouri, pp. 195–196.
27. William Webster, writing in *Roman Catholicism* (pp. 292–293) cites Benedict XV's encyclical *De Corredemptione* in these words,

> Thus, she (Mary) suffered and all but died along with her Son suffering and dying; thus, for the salvation of men she abdicated the rights of a mother toward her Son, and insofar as was hers to do, she immolated the Son to placate God's justice, so that she herself may justly be said to have redeemed together with Christ the human race.

28. There are, in fact, many more such references. Particularly clear is the belief that Mary is the "mediatrix of all graces." The following note, found in Ligouri, pp. 175–176, provides this information:

> The doctrine of Mary's dignity as mediatrix of all graces is commonly accepted by theologians today, and recent pontiffs have occasionally alluded to it. We know that Benedict XIV has left these words on record: "Mary is like a celestial river by which the water of all graces and gifts are conveyed to poor mortals." Pius IX. In speaking to the bishops of the whole world made use of the words of St. Bernard: "God wills that every grace should come to us through her." . . . Pius X declares: "She is the dispensatrix of the graces that Jesus Christ has merited for us by His blood and His death." The following are the words of Benedict XV: "It has pleased God to grant us all graces through the intercession of Mary." Again: "All the graces which the Giver of all good deigns to grant to the descendants of Adam, are dispensed to us, in the disposition of a loving Providence, through the hands of the Blessed Virgin." And finally: "The graces of all kinds that we receive from the treasury of the Redemption are dispensed by the hands of the Sorrowful Virgin."

29. Ligouri, p. 103.
30. Ibid., p. 83.
31. Ibid., p. 94.
32. Ibid., p. 124.
33. Ibid., pp. 136–137.
34. Ibid., p. 169.
35. Ibid., p. 180.
36. Ibid., pp. 181–182.
37. Ibid., p. 198.
38. Ibid., p. 273.
39. Ibid., p. 566.
40. Keating, *Catholicism and Fundamentalism*, p. 279.

Chapter 14

1. J. I. Packer in James Buchanan, *The Doctrine of Justification*, (Edinburgh: The Banner of Truth Trust, 1984), p. 7.
2. Charles Colson and Richard Neuhaus, editors, *Evangelicals & Catholics Together: Toward a Common Mission* (Dallas: Word Publishing, 1995), p. 18.
3. Though we are forced to wonder if the document means the Roman Catholic concept of justification, i.e., the state of grace, or the biblical one, having the perfect and enduring righteousness of Christ imputed to one by the Father. And is the grace spoken of what is seen in the impartation of indulgences or the grace that is unmerited and free?

INDEX

General Index

Scripture Index

Comments?

Please address them to:

Alpha and Omega Ministries
P.O. Box 37106
Phoenix, AZ 85069

Or via Internet:

Orthopodeo@aol.com